STRATEGIC MANAGEMENT OF NOT-FOR-PROFIT ORGANIZATIONS

STRATEGIC MANAGEMENT OF NOT-FOR-PROFIT ORGANIZATIONS

From Survival to Success

Israel Unterman
and
Richard H. Davis

PRAEGER

PRAEGER SPECIAL STUDIES • PRAEGER SCIENTIFIC

New York • Philadelphia • Eastbourne, UK
Toronto • Hong Kong • Tokyo • Sydney

Library of Congress Cataloging in Publication Data

Unterman, Israel.
  Strategic management of not-for-profit organizations.

  Includes index.
  1. Corporations, Nonprofit–Management. I. Davis,
Richard H. (Richard Hart), 1942-   . II. Title.
HD62.6.U57   1984   658′.048   83-24641
ISBN 0-03-068776-4 (alk. paper)

Published in 1984 by Praeger Publishers
CBS Educational and Professional Publishing
a Division of CBS Inc.
521 Fifth Avenue, New York, NY 10175 USA

© 1984 by Israel Unterman and Richard H. Davis

  56789 052 98765432

Printed in the United States of America
on acid-free paper

To my loving family:
Ruth, Lee,
Gail, Robert, and Matthew

Israel Unterman

To my wife Jan,
daughters Melissa and Amanda,
and mother Betty:
for their love, patience,
and inspiration

Richard Hart Davis

Acknowledgments
Israel Unterman

As everyone knows, or at least suspects, not-for-profit organizations are even more complex than the creation of the earth. Therefore, this book had more than one beginning. It was first written as a dissertation for my doctorate at the Harvard Business School, where after 25 years of prior business experience I elected to major in the social responsibility of business. My first orals did not go well because examining professors believed I was too emotionally involved with the subject and could not be objective in my research. To establish objectivity, I changed my topic to "The Strategic Planning of Financial Institutions," a less emotional one. Ultimately, however, I am indebted to Harvard University and the *Harvard Business Review* for encouraging our original article and research on NFPs. Special thanks to Harvard's Kenneth R. Andrews, David W. Ewing, and G. Scott Hutchison for their past and present assistance.

A second beginning goes back to the age of 15 when I was elected president of a youth temple with 200 members. All of the classic NFP problems were there: infighting and politics of the board members; tiny annual budgets ("with only $1,000 more all our problems would be solved"); no agreement on mission, etc. After my two-year term as president I resolved never, ever, to again be on the board of a not-for-profit organization.

Despite my resolution, I became an officer, consultant, or researcher of approximately 50 different NFPs. My taste was very eclectic, ranging from the local Little League to the White House; from a local school board to an attempt to change Nicaragua's hospital system; from a Long Island Festival Committee to my current role as part-time consultant at the U.S. Department of State. The funding levels in each organization varied considerably, from the small amount of my college Red Cross to millions raised as the Chairman of the Financial Division of New York's United Jewish Appeal.

Becoming acquainted with Mr. Richard H. Davis marked the third practical beginning of this book. He, too, shared a strong commitment to social improvement. All of his life, he has been active with NFPs, including approximately 15 years at the board level. His experience has also included four years as a full-time executive director of an NFP. With a private business sector background, he experimented with the application of business management techniques for the NFP. In my judgment, the result has been one of the most successful NFPs in the country, the San Diego Economic Development Corporation. His focus there encompassed both initial strategic planning and continuing management direction. Much of his direct experience is interwoven in the other elements of this work. Deserving special thanks are: Debra Ford and Rodney Tompkins for the case on Community Social Services for the Handicapped; Dorothy Anderson and Glenn Allison for the Episcopal Social Services case; Professors Dinoo Vanier and John B. McFall of San Diego State University for their San Diego Symphony Marketing Information Study, and Martin Buncher for the Blood Drive Focus Group Research Project. In a very real and personal sense I also thank Drs. Flocks, Mayman, Needel, Flippen, and Braun who kept me in bearable health so that I could work on the book; Professor C. Rowland Christensen for encouraging the learning experience through case histories; and Professor Max Wortman, former president of the Academy of Management, who encouraged the academic research in the NFP sector. Additional thanks to Professors Andrews and Christensen for permission to use their illustration of the "strategic framework."

Appreciation also to John Brooks, Richard Burt, Christopher Hamilos, Hubert Kaltenbach, Dr. Irwin Jacobs, Bruce Moore, and Rodney Tomkins, who were all trustees of various NFPs and who were the original readers and commentators on the basic concepts explored in the book; Georgia Cohen, Patricia Dyer, Josephine Kicklighter, and George Mobus for their editorial help; and finally, to Ruth Unterman who quietly listened to each and every trial and tribulation throughout the process of writing this book.

Acknowledgments
Richard Hart Davis

Special thanks to my co-author, Dr. Israel Unterman, friend and mentor, both on this project and on our *Harvard Business Review* article on not-for-profits. His perspective and drive have been crucial to our work. Additional special thanks to Praeger's Barbara Leffel, Marilyn Weinstein Ehrlich, and Maruta Mitchell, as well as Elizabeth King, formerly of Praeger and now at Boston University, whose editorial work involved both broad perspectives and detailed assistance. Continued appreciation also to Louis Neiheisel for illustrations and Jane Tripp for manuscript typing—and retyping.

Thanks are also due to the San Diego Economic Development Corporation, which gave me the opportunity to view the nonprofit world from the "inside." Without that experience, I would have had neither the knowledge, inspiration, nor desire to work with Dr. Unterman and our contributors on this project.

Contents

CHAPTER

List of Figures and Tables

TABLES

FIGURES

1

Introduction

Not-for-profits fail in record numbers.

Not-for-profits also contribute more to U.S. life than ever before.

Hundreds of thousands of not-for-profit organizations affect every fabric of our lives. Newspaper headlines and all media chronicle their successes and failures:

- Another record year for United Way
- Government support up $80 billion in 15 years
- Emergency care cut
- Failing symphonies
- Church sells property to fund outreach work
- $35 billion in annual voluntary gifts
- $25 billion cut facing NFPs in eighties
- Tax-exempt may not mean no taxes
- Fund-raising abuses continue

The litany of concerns could be endless—and the success stories in human and financial terms are overwhelming. As our Fund Accounting chapter explains in detail, "not-for-profit" or "nonprofit" groups are defined as "nonbusiness organizations" by the accounting and legal professions and government agencies. As such, they are "all organizations other than profit-oriented business enterprises," including governmental entities.*

---

*To sharpen our focus on the volunteer sector of the "nonprofit" world, we have left government out of this work with the exception of Chapter Eleven,

The basic thrust of this book is that private business techniques will directly help NFP management. Classic are the stories of bridge or railroad builders starting at two ends and failing to meet. Not as visible but just as expensive are the organizational efforts—governmental, private, and not-for-profit—that have failed to serve a unified purpose.

As authors, we have questioned ourselves on the need for this book. Is it worthwhile to accumulate a mountain of information when, for years, the administration and strategic directions of not-for-profits (NFPs) have been ignored? Will the work be meaningful to the reader? While a few years ago the answer might have been unclear, our recent article on the NFP field (Unterman and Davis, "Strategy Gap in Not-for-Profits," *Harvard Business Review*, May–June 1982) evoked overwhelmingly positive responses to our basic observations:

1. NFPs suffer from the lack of well-planned strategic directions and the broader need of strategic management. (A useful definition of strategic management is "a conscious effort by any organization to select critical objectives and goals and then create policies to achieve those goals. These goals should then be clearly stated so that everyone involved knows where the organization is going and how it should get there. Implementation must include the structure of the organization, the authority and responsibilities of people in it, a system of rewards and punishments, a control and information system, and a selection and training system.")

2. The average NFP trustee is not being well used.

3. Most, if not all, private business techniques can be successfully adapted to the NFP world.

Each NFP segment (education, social services, health organizations, etc.) has its own set of nomenclature and literature, but perspective from the vantage point of the trustee cuts across all sectors of the NFP world. Furthermore, it is not unusual for the same trustee to sit on many different boards of different types of NFPs. The same trustee who is an attractive candidate for one institution will be just as attractive to an unrelated NFP seeking similar board levels of public recognition, funding, and/or leadership.

"NFP, Public Agency, and Private Partnerships." For reasons of consistency, we will use only the term "not-for-profit," or NFP, to describe the hospitals, social service groups, schools, churches, performing arts groups, museums, and other NFPs studied.

THE ILLNESS

There are successful NFPs, but a significant part of our research sample (over 100 direct experiences or case histories) seems to have very real longevity problems. At a minimum, they seem to survive from crisis to crisis. For example:

- Symphonies throughout the United States run chronic deficits, with several shutting down operations each year.
- In one case in the performing arts, the board of trustees had three factions which could come to no agreement on strategy over a three-year period. To add fuel to the fire, the executive director (ED) and board of trustees (BOT) could not even agree on the selection of performers. The consequence was a loss of community support, resulting in a fatal deficit and the death of the organization.
- The director of a major social service agency expressed concern to a visiting management consultant:

I was a damned good social worker, so they made me a supervisor . . . then in five years an assistant director and finally the Executive Director. In all that time I was still a good social worker, but knew nothing about management and finance. At my age, how do I learn enough about administration to run a $10 million organization?

The sequel is that three months later, perhaps obviously, with no additional training, the local ED was promoted to the national presidency of the NFP.

- In one poll of leading business people, the overwhelming majority rate NFP staff high on dedication and social consciousness and markedly lacking in business and financial management skills.
- A variety of social work agencies studied have mislaid, not accounted for, or suffered opportunity losses of hundreds of thousands of dollars of funding.

An entire book could be devoted to the failings of NFP administrators, just as we see hundreds of books published regularly on the improvement of business management. Mismanagement in the NFP world is, of course, not done deliberately but through lack of knowledge and training.

THE REMEDY

Although not a daily occurrence, a significant amount of writing has been done about the differences between the NFP world and the profit sector. Apart from differences in mission, accounting practice, and a few other obvious and not-so-obvious operational aspects, the authors believe it a waste of time to belabor the semantics or theoretical differences found in the two sectors. As noted, the basic and prevailing concept behind this book is that the application of private business managerial techniques can directly help NFP management. It is not claimed that this transferability is a permanent and comprehensive panacea for curing all the ills of the NFP sector. However, we strongly believe that the broader adoption of this basic concept can contribute material, positive changes to the working relationships within and ultimate performance of NFPs. In so doing, if we can alleviate the chronic financial pressure facing boards of trustees, volunteers, and other supporters, our writing efforts will have been worthwhile.

SUCCESS SIDE OF THE LEDGER

Certainly, there are success stories which should not be ignored. For example:

A. One health organization was 85 percent dependent, at one time, on federal grants to support its operations. With the hiring of a new executive director, who did not accept the risks of public funding, a strategic shift in funding and operational directions was approved by the board of trustees. In eight years' time, relying upon private sector and local support, the organization tripled its operating budget and cut federal dependency to less than 15 percent. At that point, the ED and BOT rejected/returned all federal funds to the government, rather than maintain any purse strings to Washington.

B. A chamber of commerce decided it needed to revamp its industrial development activities in a dramatic manner. Within four years it was able to triple job generation funding, increase the percentage of private sector support, and contribute to the growth of several thousand jobs per year.

C. One major performing arts company has operated in the black for the past decade. Its board of trustees (BOT) has a simple credo: "We spend only what we have."

D. In several parts of the United States, individual public schools have gone to private business with an "adopt a school" program. At a minimum, a process has been set in motion fostering improved relations and contact between the private and public sectors. Private funding and the contribution of equipment have also increased. Our judgment is that the long-term impact can only be positive.

In summary, however, the overall picture of NFP management performance is more negative than positive. There are thousands of successful NFPs but, throughout the United States' total of 850,000 not-for-profit organizations, there is unnecessary waste, turnover, and failure. Our focus is to ameliorate these problems with two focal points of modern private sector management:

Strategic management—with very careful emphasis on both strategy and management.
The broad array of hard, management expertise available to all professional managers. Here we will point only to examples since it would be difficult to catalog all current "buzzwords," let alone explain them in a meaningful and useful manner.

AUDIENCE

Since most of us have a variety of roles in NFP affairs, we are only partially concerned that we deal with our audience in any order of priority. Our focus on strategic management, however, dictates that boards of trustees must head the list:

● Members of boards of trustees, particularly the business and professional people who devote their time and money to over 850,000 different NFPs.

● Not-for-profit executives and administrators.

● Volunteers working for these same NFPs. Most estimates indicate over one-third of all Americans perform some form of volunteer work.

● Foundation executives who make the hard choices of whom to support and the form of that support.

● Public officials who contribute directly to most NFPs in the United States. Beyond the role of government, these same officials (and NFP employees, for that matter) give their own time and money as private citizens to those very same not-for-profits.

OUTLINE OF CONTENTS

The next chapter, "The Boards of Trustees and Missions," focuses on the most significant aspect—and certainly the first step in setting a strategy—of an NFP. The mission is crucial to the direction of the NFP, and all too often neglected by a BOT as it establishes and maintains board and staff roles.

Chapter Three, "Strategic Planning and Strategic Management," gives an explanation of a variety of strategic approaches. This chapter will distinguish between planning and management. There are case histories describing how policies have been set in a variety of organizations. In many respects, this is the heart of our book and the focus of our concern. If the reader retains only one key message from our work, it is that strategic planning comprises only one-half of an NFP's strategic concerns, and the easier half at that. Knowing or deciding upon what needs to be done is only a prelude to the accomplishment which will follow with the implementation of this plan. The strategic management of the NFP, the implementation and recycling of strategy, must be explicitly studied and monitored on a continuing basis.

Chapter Four, "Organizational Structure and Formal Communications," covers organizational structure from an NFP perspective and points out profit sector parallels. As noted in the preliminary definition of strategic management, structure is considered an integral part of the strategic process. Conscious identification of existing structure and planned changes must be related to overall strategy.

Chapter Five, "Marketing," focuses on the successful use of private sector techniques in NFP activities. In the NFP world, many elements of the marketing "mix" are often unknown or ignored. Therefore, these elements are discussed: the service itself, market research, pricing, delivery, sales, advertising, sales promotion, public relations, and post delivery follow-up/evaluation.

Chapter Six, "Fund Raising," is less theoretical and more specific, with a discussion of fund-raising perspectives and practices. In the business world, boards of directors do not have operational responsibilities. In the NFP world trustees, by definition, should be setting policy and supervising the executive director. Most trustees, however, are also volunteer fund raisers and participants in NFP operations.

Chapter Seven, "Fund Accounting," emphasizes the importance of understanding the difference in accounting practices between the business world and NFPs. A knowledge of fund accounting by trustees is often a necessity in larger, more complex, not-for-profit organizations. At a minimum, a trustee should understand the advantages and pitfalls (along with the "generally accepted" requirements) of NFP fund accounting.

Chapter Eight, "Volunteers," offers an explanation of how to attract and control volunteers at a basic level. Here again, there will be case history examples. As with Chapter Six, this is intended as less philosophical than operational in focus and value.

Chapter Nine, "Rewards and Punishments Systems," reviews reward systems (and, more briefly, punishments) in both the business and the NFP worlds. As with strategic management, our thesis is that most private sector ideas and modes of flexibility are readily adaptable to NFPs. Unfortunately, many NFPs have suffered unnecessary turnover, mediocre performance, and a variety of other ills because of their reluctance to approach responsibilities, such as compensation policy, in a realistic and systematic manner.

Chapter Ten, "The Executive Director," provides examples of different leadership traits relating to the post of executive director. Styles of leadership are discussed and the interrelationship between the executive director and the board members is explored. A board of trustees can go only so far in guiding policy without solving the question of what full-time executive director is the best available to work with the board in achieving the NFP's goals.

Chapter Eleven, "NFP, Public Agency, and Private Sector Partnerships," reviews examples of these partnerships; where they work and how improvements in the partnership can be made. As with volunteerism and fund raising, it is useful to look at recent developments in the NFP world. The government—at all levels—is finding increasingly willing and productive partners in the NFP and business worlds.

Chapter Twelve, "Conclusions," is not a cookbook or "how-to-fix-it" guaranteed solution. Specific cautions and recommendations are provided, however, for questioning and evaluating NFP performance. Although 850,000 different NFPs in the United States may have a million different nuances and operating quirks, successful NFPs have certain similarities in patterns of operations that are worthwhile to recognize. When a board of trustees sets in motion a major policy shift, approves an annual budget, or hires an executive director, that board should know and understand its options and responsibilities.

2

The Boards of Trustees
and Missions

PROFILES

Ed Dyer

Ed Dyer awoke one hour before his usual schedule. He lay in bed thinking of the importance of the hours ahead. As Executive Director of the Multiple Community Services, he was to present a new strategic plan to his board of trustees. At the insistence of his volunteer workers, the new plan called for expanded responsibilities and services to meet the needs of a growing city. In view of the national economic situation, Ed knew that some of the board members would object to any expansion. How many would vote against his proposal, he did not know. He was counting on Bill O'Connor, the chairman, to "direct" the votes in favor of the plan.

Ed recognized why he woke up so early. He had been dreaming, and in his dream he had been four different people:

    a. the employee of the board of trustees;

    b. the employer of his staff and volunteers;

    c. the facilitator of a fund-raising organization;

    d. the provider of the organization's services to a large number of recipients.

Just how insistent he would be with his trustees, even at this late hour, he had not decided.

William O'Connor

William O'Connor was troubled. As president of the largest company in the city, he did not have time to go to his office this morning. Instead, he was meeting with Ed to discuss the agenda of the BOT meeting. Without doubt, Ed would submit a strategic plan which would include an expansion of services. As the Chairman, and one of the founders of Multiple Services, everyone would expect him to take a stand for, or against, the new plan.

Bill felt tired before the day began. Lately, he had been neglecting his own business in favor of his work with the charity. He was concerned that he allowed himself to be at the beck and call of Ed. Bill knew that Ed was a good manager of the organization. Yet, at times, Ed was not pragmatic. Ed did not understand that time was a high-priced resource for any businessman. Bill recognized that his friend and co-trustee, Bob Fleming, would certainly object to any expansion. Bill resolved that this would be the last year he would accept the position of chairman.

Robert Fleming

Robert Fleming admired his face while he was shaving. Despite his fixed smile, he felt grouchy. The weather was perfect for a day of tennis. Yet he had to attend the meeting of Multiple Services. As one of the leading bankers in town, he felt compelled to accept a position on the board of trustees. People always expected bankers to be "do-gooders." Where that tradition first began, no one knew, but today was going to be a chore.

Bob was aware that Ed had cooked up a new strategic plan. Obviously, Ed had no idea what it meant for an organization to stand still and consolidate its resources. But why should that be any bother? Usually, Bob would sit at the meeting of the trustees without saying a word. It was always expedient to vote the way Bill did, and avoid any personal squabble. Bob admitted to himself that he volunteered as a trustee because it was the "proper" thing to do. In any event, he always found it useful to meet his friends and customers at the meetings.

THE MISSION

Bill and Bob are representative of the thousands of executives and professionals who are active in setting the policies of more than 825,000 organizations that are exempted by the Internal Revenue Service from paying taxes. Trustees in many charities join for a variety of reasons, past experiences, strong beliefs, business expediencies, and social mores. Trustees may be asked to act as fund raisers, lobbyists, and managers.

In the course of implementing these responsibilities, a vital board function is often overlooked, the selection and establishment of a planned strategy and the policies for the implementation of such a plan. The prime duty of a board is "to contribute something more than rubber-stamping management's formulation of strategy." Ed, Bill, and Bob each have entirely different motivations for their activities with a particular NFP. However, there is one specific that binds them all, and that is the mission. There are many definitions of a mission. The concept of a mission can be derived from the term in general use by religious organizations, which states that a process or purpose of extending religious teaching is called a *mission.**

Often, the "raison d'être" is intangible, as with religious organizations. At other times, it may be quite tangible, as in the saving of lives in hospitals. A great deal of the time, for many organizations, it is somewhere between the tangible and the intangible, such as the many different social service agencies. The one thing to remember is that it is the mission, and the mission only, that is the binding tie uniting all of the members of the organization whether they be board members, underpaid staff members, or volunteers.

Attitude Towards Mission

The degree of activity of a board of trustees member may be related directly to the individual's attitude toward the mission. The

---

*The dictionary defines a "mission" as a person or group of persons acting as an envoy, or the task or objective of those acting as envoys. Likewise, the sending of an individual or group, by an authority, to perform a specific service such as a religious mission, military mission, etc. Other definitions relate the word "mission" to errands, tasks, assignments, purposes, and ends. All of these definitions seem to be much too sparse in defining the word "mission" as applied to an NFP. Perhaps the French phrase "raison d'être" would be a much better description of the word. The "reason for existence" is the literal translation from the French. It is the core, essence, or soul of many NFP organizations.

degree of variance is considerable—from the crusader who would pay with his life to accomplish a mission to the mature woman who spends two hours a week reading to blind patients in a hospital. This broad variance mirrors itself in the number of hours that trustees devote to their organization. Studies have shown that the range of trustee activity goes from two hours per month to 100 hours per month.

Just as Bill O'Connor, the President, is willing to spend a great deal of his time, his best friend Robert Fleming is unwilling to spend much time at all. In the study of the Episcopalian Social Services, it was found that the average active board member spent about ten to fifteen hours per month on the organization; others spent merely two to four hours monthly, at the board meeting. Invariably, the 100-hour trustee is the chairman or the president of the organization. The devotion to the mission has a tendency to be reinforced by spending this many hours in the organization.

Differences Between Boards of Directors of Profit-Making Organizations and Boards of Trustees

1. Rewards and Punishments

Both trustees and directors are motivated, rewarded, and "punished" by many of the same things. Prestige of selection, the opportunity for greater responsibility, and public recognition are the motivators in both private and NFP boards. Although trustees do not receive direct monetary rewards, they do receive more psychic rewards by performing a recognized public service or mission for the NFP.

2. Range of Activities

In the private sector, the key functions of the directors are the selection of the chief executive officer, a review of financial performance, consideration of social impact or corporate activity, and the development of policies and the implementation of procedures. It should be noted that many of these functions are primarily formulative, or evaluative. Only the latter responsibility inches into the area of operations.

The activities outlined for the business board of directors are only a small part of the functions required of a board of trustees. In practice, trustees are a significant *operational* arm of their NFP organization. It was in this arena that William O'Connor was spending most of his volunteer time. He would have preferred to work on strategic planning with Ed Dyer instead of assisting on operational matters. In nearly all of the NFPs examined, trustees were expected to play an active role in fund raising. (See chapter on Fund Raising.) This role is pervasive in pursuing public, private, corporate, or foundation funds. (It may be noted that one of the authors, in a given NFP, spent 90 percent of his time in fund-raising activities).

Additionally, many organizations, especially the smaller ones, expect each of the trustees to give sizable personal contributions to the organization and donate personal skills where appropriate. Accountants and lawyers are always in short supply. Trustees are also asked to take operational roles in community relations. At times, direct personal involvement in the political environment is required of a trustee, whether it be the Little League petitioning the Parks and Recreation Board or the local arts council asking for rehearsal space.

3. Politicians and Celebrities

It is not unusual to find that the honored guest at a fund-raising dinner is the local political aspirant or sports hero. In recent years, the use of politicians and celebrities at local television marathons and dinners has become commonplace. This interplay between not-for-profit organizations and local political organizations is frequently at the heart of "networking" in an NFP fund-raising system. However, such interchanges create additional activities for the trustee.

Small Organizations

Of course, on a much smaller, local level such as the Girl Scouts and the Little League, the difference between working at an operational level and being a policy-maker nears the edge of a combined duty. Many smaller organizations are first operational; then policies are set on the basis of the operations they are able to perform. Therefore, the board member and the functional person may be one and the same. Board members have been known to "sweep the floor" at times.

What is Overlooked

In the process of beoming operational, so much time and effort is devoted to the mission of the organization that a vital board function is often overlooked, the selection and establishment of a planned

TABLE 2.1   The NFP Trustee versus the Business Board Director

	NFP Trustee	Business Director
Board size	Large	Small
Use of inside directors	Minimal	Significant
Directors' business experience	Highly variable	Substantial
Directors' terms of service	Short	Long
Directors' time given	Highly variable	Consistent
Directors' attendance	50-60%	90%
Range of directors' activities	Wide	Narrow
Results measurements	None or non-standard	Profits
Planning horizon	None (reactive) or short	Long
CEO		
—Tenure	Insecure	Secure
—Administrative experience	Often weak	Strong
—Independent initiative	Highly variable	Moderately high
Rewards		
—Directors	Non-monetary	Monetary and non-monetary
—CEO	Generally modest financial incentives	Broad array, including substantial reliance on bonus
Board selection	Self-selection	CEO often selects

strategy and the policies for the implementation of the plan. In essence, few missions can be accomplished without a viable strategy. The mission is, of course, the essential part of a strategy because it is the major objective of a strategic plan. However, all studies have shown that the prime duty of a board of trustees is to create the strategy and to design systems to control and manage that strategy. (See chapter on Strategic Planning and Strategic Management.)

SELECTION OF A BOARD

The selection of members of the board of trustees should be done with great care.

1. Number of Trustees

Experience has shown that the size of the board of trustees is significant when decisions are to be made. That is, the larger the board, the more difficult it becomes to make strategic decisions. It is most useful to compare boards of directors in the profit sector with boards of trustees in the NFP sector. Conference Board studies* show that the median board size of profit-making organizations is in the 10-15 member range. However, an NFP usually has upwards of 30 members on the board. A number of professional arts groups in other NFP studies have over 100 trustees. Such huge numbers are broken up with nomenclatures such as Officers and Board Trustees, Honorary Trustees, Advisory Trustees, and a host of committees. One music association lists 36 board members, 6 honorary board members, and 31 advisory members. There are also 44 chairpersons of committees. That is by no means the whole story. In addition to the association there is a Council of Guilds with 21 chairmen and advisors, and an association center with 18 board members.

Moreover, administrators such as Ed Dyer prefer a large board in the organization because it satisfies volunteer desires for "involvement." It also provides the nonworker Robert Fleming (the other person who is a frequent espouser of large boards) a public platform, business contacts, and the opportunity to avoid responsibility as his vote gets "lost" among the many others. (And, as long as Robert Fleming is providing funding, or some other significant support, an "involvement" without a policy-setting role may be appropriate in many NFPs. For example, the "honorary board" device is used in NFPs to accomplish token participation.)

2. Importance of Size

Some NFP executives have argued that the authors pay too much attention to the different sizes of BODs and BOTs. Our research has

---

*Jeremy Bacon, "Corporate Directorship Practices," The Conference Board, New York, 1973.

TABLE 2.2   Size of Board Membership, NFPs versus Private Business

	(511) Corporate BODs[1]	(296) NFP BOTs[2]
Assets		
Less than $10 million	6	NA
$10–100 million	9	NA
$1 billion +	15	NA
Median	11	34

[1] Conference Board
[2] Weber and Hartogs, Greater NY Fund Study of Boards, Oceana, New York.

found that in both the profit-making and NFP worlds, there is no way to separate directors/trustees' *personal values* from the "rational economic" decision process. The diversified value systems of 50–100 trustees tend to neutralize each other.

Many trustees do not actively participate in strategic decisions because they find it difficult to infuse *their* values into the strategic process. Secondly, the neutralization of trustees' values tends to reinforce the value system of the executive director, Ed Dyer. Additionally, the Robert Flemings can disassociate themselves from controversial board actions. Therefore, the size of the board of trustees is a significant element in the dynamics of strategic planning.

We strongly recommend that one segment of the board, or a superstructure of the board of trustees (for example, "executive board") be limited to 8–15 members (or fewer). This should be the maximum number of "strategists." However, other sections or subcommittees related to the board can be called upon to monitor finance, control, fund raising or development, public relations, etc.

3. Other Motivations

When selecting trustees, do not overlook the power of economics, power, prestige, and self-esteem as motivators for involvement. (Chapter Seven explores reward systems in greater detail.) Moreover, consider the financial or other types of contributions a trustee might make. Someone who can share computer time, printing services, secretarial or mailing assistance, or corporate executives can be very valuable. Remember that every NFP needs a balance of skills and resources for the board: the lawyer, the accountant, the experienced strategist, the person skilled in organizational development. Perhaps the most important single qualification of potential board members would be involvement in, and dedication to, the mission of the organization.

SUMMARY

To sum up, the NFP organizations' board members tend to enter the stage from three different directions, in a manner similar to Ed Dyer, Bill O'Connor, and Robert Fleming. First, there is the professional director whose prime purpose is to promote the mission of the organization (and to keep his job). (See chapter on Executive Director.) Next enters the volunteer business leader, motivated to become a trustee by a sense of mission plus a strong commitment to fulfill social responsibilities. The third person joining the cast is the volunteer trustee who becomes a trustee because it is the "right" thing to do and/or because connections made on the board may be useful for professional advancement. In countless organizations, each of these three actors plays a major, though at times counterproductive, role.

3

Strategic Planning and Management

This chapter offers an explanation of a variety of strategic approaches. In doing so, it is vital to distinguish between *planning* and *management*. A continuing precept of our work, and the book as a whole, is that there is a significant difference between "strategic planning" and "strategic management."

THE STRATEGIC PROCESS

It is important to define strategy and the process by which it is converted from thought into action. A *strategy* is a changing pattern of a company's business and social purposes, its sense of mission, its goals and objectives, and the implementation policies needed to achieve its selective ends. Strategic formulation, implementation, and control, particularly as they relate to change in the organization, are all parts of this process. The strategic process, the development and implementation of long-range or large-scale plans, invariably results in changes in the structure and function of organizations. These changes alter both human relationships and the utilization of other resources. The key words in this process are *continuous* change.

Although abstract policy may be interesting to discuss, board members are dealing mainly with the problems of people and money. This section deals with the people side of the equation; and the problems of money are addressed in other chapters.

"Strategy" is not a set of decisions made on high and set into holy tablets, such as the one-year or three-year plan *or* a one-year budget. Rather, it is the result of an ongoing process. Contrary to earlier thinking and literature on strategic planning and many of the practices of NFP boards, even today, the current concept of strategy is a very dynamic framework. This view of a *changing* process, rather than a set pattern, may be rejected by many boards because it requires continuous effort to keep the strategy up-to-date.

In reviewing many of the so-called strategies of the NFPs, it has been found that they contain principally objectives and missions. Further, many of these objectives are based upon budgetary considerations rather than upon the mission of the organization. Relatively few organizations have a strategy that explicitly explains the implementation policies necessary to achieve given objectives. This concept of having both the ends and means included in one given strategy has eluded many members of boards of directors. Typically, the board members prefer to set some specific goal such as "X" dollars of fund raising, two dinners per year, "X" number of cocktail parties, growth of staff, public relations campaign, etc. It is unusual to read a strategy (see San Diego Economic Development Corporation case in Appendix) that contains details of how such goals will be accomplished, if, in fact, broad strategic goals are even considered. Unfortunately, many board members refuse to dirty their hands in the task of accomplishing whatever goals have been decided upon. (In larger NFPs such refusal actually is appropriate as long as they have adequate benchmarks to evaluate staff success in achieving goals. This, of course, assumes that adequate resources are provided to the professional implementors.)

This chapter does not differentiate between the words "goals" and "objectives"; a semantic discussion here is largely irrelevant. Some management thinkers arbitrarily specify that "goals" might be specific benchmarks of broader "objectives." From a semantic standpoint, however, the two are interchangeable, along with other synonyms such as "results," "achievements," "targets," "purposes," "intentions," etc. It is enough to say that an NFP board can use the terminology with which it is comfortable—as long as it translates into real strategic thinking and action.

When viewed in a totality ("holistically" is the buzzword) strategy is really the result of a continuing process. The ongoing strategic process may be described best in terms of a cycle (Figure 3.1). It is composed of several distinct phases:

FIGURE 3.1 Continuous and Dynamic Strategic Management Cycle

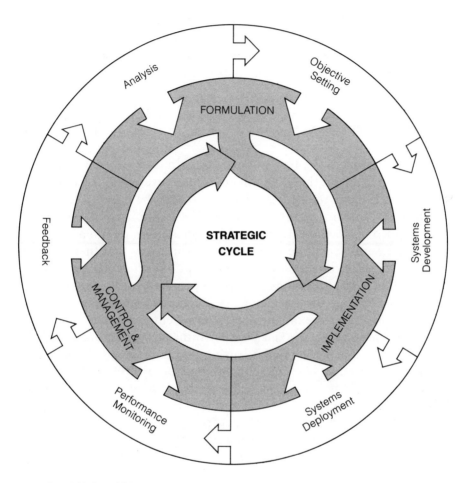

© 1983 Israel Unterman

1. formulation (comprised of analysis and objective setting),
2. implementation (systems development and deployment), and
3. management control (monitoring the effects).

The cycle comes full circle when the data generated from monitoring lead back to analysis. Here the board determines whether or not the objectives are being met. Invariably, the environment has changed in some way since the initial formulation. Thus, with the results of past performance and the current state of the environment, the cycle continues indefinitely. To assume that an annual review is the magic answer to good strategic management ignores the reality of the process of change. A frequent mistake is to assume that annual budgeting and strategic planning are synonymous.

Strategic Formulation

Formulation is the first phase of the strategic process. It begins with an analysis of the environment and an evaluation of potential opportunities and threats. In actuality, it may be impossible to distinguish a "starting" point. A strategy is a multiplicity of elements, each with its own time frame and implementation requirements. All of these essentials will be interlaced in such a way that there will be no definitive starting point. In simple words, the board is always formulating a strategy; it is a nonstop process because the environmental systems are always changing. Individuals conducting the strategic process have to examine the environment and also evaluate the strengths and weaknesses and past performances of the organization. Often, this phase alone creates some anxiety in the minds of board members; and many such members refuse to go through the process of evaluation. This is especially true as they become good friends of the executive director.

Finally, the environmental factors and the company's abilities must be combined with the value systems of whoever is actually running the organization. Depending on the NFP this might be the board members themselves or the executive director or both.

Value Systems

Often the values of boards are not explicitly addressed; the subject is difficult to "neatly package" in the planning process. The value systems of the decision-makers—whoever they may be—have a major effect upon the goals that are selected, and the policies to implement those goals. These systems, in turn, create different kinds of relationships among board members, the executive director, the staff, and the volunteers. Where large NFPs are concerned, the fastest way to make any change is to either change the entire board of directors, or to change the executive director, or both. An example of this is a large, well-known museum which moved dramatically from a single executive director to a dual top management scheme with the business manager separate from the curator. Another is a hospital which changed 80 percent of its board and its general director within a one-year period as it fought million dollar deficits.

The sharing or reduction of responsibilities can often be painful, and is not usually easy even when the artistic or executive director is extremely amenable to the readjustment. In the case of the museum, results have been very positive financially with no loss of quality in exhibits. Stronger organizational control, in fact, has led to long forgotten resources and more easily understandable exhibits. The hospital case is unresolved to date, but the hemorrhaging loss of funds has been largely stopped by a new director and an involved board.

Values can be very personal, and surprisingly diverse even in NFP organizations such as small churches, where one might expect easy consensus. Although one might expect it, this is often not the case. (See Episcopal Community Services case in Appendix.) Values of trustees can vary markedly.

For example, a symphony was in profound trouble, lacking both funds and adequate audience levels. Upon investigation, it was clearly seen that the board was split into three factions. All decisions were usually delayed so that times and places necessary for scheduling concerts were difficult to achieve or impossible to implement. Such lack of unanimity also created strong antipathies between the executive director and the board. In turn, this led to extreme difficulties in implementing even the very few policies that had been agreed upon. After a period of time, when the symphony was in great debt and would have been disbanded, a new board was formed with a new executive director. That combination resulted in the first season in many years that had run in the black.

The symphony revitalization was due to a variety of factors. In this case, the most important single element was the selection of a volunteer president, one who was willing to devote the necessary time of 40 hours +/month and corporate resources to the turn-around effort. (Many NFPs fail in similar revival efforts because of the difficulty in finding a person who has the ability, time, and experience necessary to lead a turn-around.) Other factors contributing to the successful resuscitation included:

1. A "product" worth saving in community opinion—with minimal loss of professional support and quality.

2. A large enough region to provide additional volunteer and financial support not yet "tapped."
3. A gradually improving economy.
4. Generally positive political, community, and media support, despite a history of smaller crises.

The opportunities and risk factors in the environment, and the company's resources and abilities, must be combined with an understanding of the value systems of the decision-makers (environment X resources X value systems).

Environmental Systems

The formulation phase should begin with an evaluation of the many systems in the environment:

1. economic forces, such as competition, foundations and other funding sources;
2. government policies, such as state and federal grants;
3. technological changes, such as new drug or medical therapy;
4. social systems (most likely, the strongest force for NFPs).

The key aspect of environmental factors is that these systems are largely beyond the control of any given organization. This is certainly the case in the short run, such as one month to a year, and may also extend to longer timeframes. As strategists the board members must consider the conditions of their markets and the resources available today and tomorrow. In the business world, the financial strength of a company is usually related to its market performance. In contrast the NFP has two separate markets, its source of funds and the market it serves. Ideally there would be a tie, but the vagaries of government and foundation support often create conflict between the two markets. These are all affected by the social and governmental climate and trends that may be developing in these, and other, environments. From these considerations, the strategist will project potential opportunities or those conditions that may enhance the organization (and enable it to fulfill its mission) and also identify risks and threats (those conditions that may hinder the organization).

FIGURE 3.2 Corporate Strategy

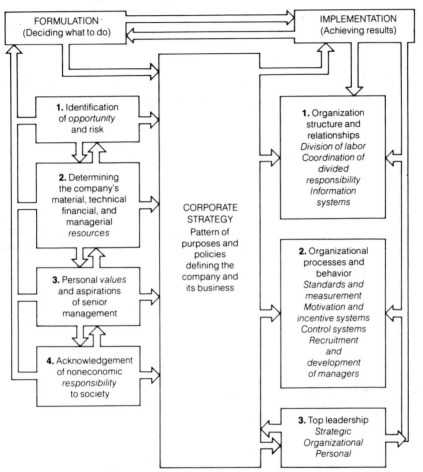

Source: Reproduced from C. Roland Christensen, Kenneth R. Andrews, Joseph L. Bower, Richard G. Hamermesh, and Michael E. Porter, *Business Policy: Text and Cases*, 5th ed. 1982, Richard D. Irwin, p. 99.

Time and Money

The length of time that it takes to go through the dynamic process of strategy, and the amount of money that can be spent in going through the process, vary considerably. In working with a very small NFP, such as a PTA, the time involved in strategizing may take perhaps half a day, or as little as one hour. On the other hand, a major NFP may spend a full month and develop a large budget devoted to planning, including the hiring of outside consultants. Typically, however, many organizations fit into a midpoint between these two examples. Usually there is one weekend retreat involving the board of directors, the executive director, and perhaps some staff members, in which the entire weekend is devoted to strategic planning. However, most board members do not really understand the concept of a dynamic strategy. Usually only budgeting and fund-raising problems are considered. These are just small parts of a successful strategy. Along with the total environment, past performance, structure, management style, future expectations, and a host of other elements must be considered. Many of the so-called "strategic retreats" that look only at financial concerns wind up with very little accomplished, and all the participants feel frustrated. A typical comment after such a retreat is "We enjoyed getting to know each other."

Self-Evaluation

Typically, it is impossible for board members themselves to evaluate their past history and accomplishments. At best, it is a most difficult exercise. The members of the board are so imbued with the importance of the "mission" (whatever it may be, whether secular or spiritual) that it may be difficult for them to evaluate any of the strengths and weaknesses of the organization. As a result, the entire strategic process fails to operate and all the board members involved feel they are wasting their time. To put it another way, it is one thing to devote some time to a strategy and quite another to have the ability and skills to design a strategy. By and large, research has shown that most boards of NFPs do not understand, or at least do not have the skills and perspectives, to build a strategic process. Perhaps this is also true of the business sector.

A Comparative Base

It is important to reemphasize the point of this lack of skills. The reader might compare the management of his or her local church strategy with that of the Economic Development Corporation case in the Appendix.

Strengths and Weaknesses

Evaluation of the environment is followed by an evaluation of the organization's strengths and weaknesses. In reality, it is only possible to define opportunities against a backdrop of the organization's capability to capitalize on them, its strengths. Likewise, it is possible to identify threats only with knowledge of the organization's weaknesses. If the NFP's effectiveness is limited by certain factors, they should be clearly identified. Analysis, therefore, is actually an iterative process. In many situations the implementation process may, in effect, set the objectives of the organization. In many small or just starting NFPs, the mission of the organization may be ill-defined until such time as the board members involved are out practicing the mission, whatever it may be: scientific, educational, religious, or artistic.

For example: One organization began as a housing foundation for the poor. In the initial course of activity by several trustees, it was discovered that the poor could not even afford to live in housing that was given to them as they had no funds for furniture or other household equipment. As a result of this situation, a cooperative manufacturing effort was established to build furniture. This, in turn, led to the outside sale of some of the furniture; the housing foundation thus became a major cooperative both for its own members and for the environment.

In addition to the economic aspects of the environment, and the management strengths within the organization, the degree to which board members' values play a large role in the formulation of strategy cannot be underestimated. Nor can the board strategists ignore the fact that noneconomic factors can have an overriding influence over purely pragmatic decisions. (Just think of the Crusaders in the Middle Ages.)

Egos and Values

In dealing with NFPs, another practical aspect is the value system of board members and the executive director. What must be taken into account is the ego of the various members. Some people are active in NFPs *only* to satisfy their need for public status. This can be either detrimental or a major asset to the organization, depending upon how much ego satisfaction is employed.

In a major museum, the main donor of funds has a vote in the kinds of paintings bought by the museum. Since his taste is based upon an art education, and intuitive good taste, the museum is now recognized as one of the best in the world. On the other hand, the major donor of funds to a dramatic society lacked experience (or "taste") in drama. Furthermore, his wife dictated which plays were performed and, as a result, the organization gained no public recognition or success.

It is not unusual for starting NFPs to be controlled by the major donor of funds. Many of our current organizations, such as the Boston Symphony, would never have been launched without the prevailing egos of such founders as Major Henry Lee Higginson. It would be unwise to underestimate the role of the value system of the decision-maker, or makers, in the formulation of a strategy.

Goals and Objectives

Once the analysis of the environmental factors, and the internal resources, is complete, the board strategists must formulate a set of goals and objectives toward which the organization must move, on the basis of its mission. In essence, a strategy consists of multiple sets or systems of objectives (a strategy is not a set of budgets). The systems are then broken down into elements, or parts. Contrary to the popular notion, any one element taken out of a strategy by itself does not define the strategy of an organization. A human being is not made up of a head alone, or two arms alone. A human being is a set of different systems. The development of these systems constitutes the formulation or thinking phase of the strategic process. Up to this point, nothing has been done by board members except talking, thinking, analyzing, and perhaps, decision-making.

Strategic Implementation

All of the talk and decision-making in the formulation process may come to naught if such decisions cannot be implemented appropriately. Even in cases in which the strategic formulation of objectives is done well, failure can result when management attempts to carry out the plan. In fact, it is the impression of some consultants that the more time spent on analysis the less time is spent in creating implementation policies and procedures. This sometimes is true. Once an NFP has a solid strategy in place, future planning sessions may be more fruitful if it limits the emphasis to two or three critical areas of interest or performance. Formulation of a strategy alone is no guarantee of success.

There has been very little hard research on the mortality of NFPs. We believe, however, that in the birth and death of NFPs, the pattern of their lifespans may be similar to that of the business world where the largest cause, by far, in the discontinuance (90%) of new businesses is the lack of managerial skill.

Implementation

It is reasonable to assume that board members do the best job they can in formulating elements of their strategies. Why then do these elements fail so frequently? The answer is insufficient attention to the other side of the strategic process, *implementation.* In particular, there is little thought given to the aspect of getting the human support system to participate in carrying through whatever plan has been determined. Turning a plan into action is the second, and major, part of the strategic process. People are the only means of turning thoughts into actions.

Implementation involves deciding on the actions needed to carry out the plan. Responsibilities and authority must be delegated to individuals capable and willing to act. Systems of communication and control, rewards and punishments, recruitment and training, and monitoring and feedback must be designed and set in motion.

It is in the strategic implementation of the strategic process that management begins turning its thoughts into actions. The design and deployment of new systems or the overhaul of already existing, but inadequate ones, is required. It is quite easy for board members in large organizations to forget this aspect of the process. There may be many levels of management between the board and the operating levels of the organization. Because of this distance and the nature of the technical details involved in implementing programs, board members begin to believe that it is only necessary to determine the course to follow and to then leave it up to others. Nothing could be further from the truth. Board members must be just as involved in certain elements of the implementation process as they are in the formulation of programs and policies.

The key to the implementation process of any strategy is getting people to fully support the selected objectives and goals. This process is forgotten by the board members of many organizations. Any change in the strategic goals and objectives of the organization *must be sold to and accepted by* those who implement, whether they be staff or volunteers. Without such acceptance, the goals are rarely attained.

The strategic process is sure to fail if the board strategists do not address adequately the human issues of implementation. A failure of the process can be avoided through strategic control, the process of getting people to support the new direction of the organization. Although it is near the end of the cycle of the strategic process, it is just as important as any other phase, for success.

Strategic Management

Strategic management is the management or control of the strategic process for the purpose of instigating change. The strategic process is not something that just happens because of goals set by the board. It must be actively managed. Once the elements of the strategy have been implemented, the process should provide continuing feedback to the board. With such information, the manager can evaluate actual performance along any of the many dimensions of the strategy. Performance evaluation is the basis for judging the effectiveness of any of the objectives of the strategy, the implementation process, and the people.

It is crucial to manage the strategic process in a way that the performance is timely and the feedback information is concise and useful for decision-making. One of the problems contributing to the failure of many NFPs is the lack of adequate information systems, feedback, and evaluation mechanisms. Most board members have no effective way of assessing the organization's performance and adjusting their decisions. Instead of adapting to the realities of the environment, NFPs forge ahead for many years before the message from the "bottom line" is heeded. The bottom line in the environment is usually our social systems. Our society is one of continuous change, and with the communications media, the pace of change has become even more rapid.

The Management Team

The strategic process has a major effect upon the management team because these are the people on whom the success of strategic implementation and control depends.

The management team varies with different types of NFPs. In some organizations, particularly smaller ones, the board members may act as the total management team. For example, a local Little League group or soccer league may rely strictly on volunteers, both to make overall plans and then to implement them.

The larger the size of the organization and the larger the geographic coverage, the greater the segmenting and fragmentation of the management team will be. In many of the larger organizations, the prime role of the board members is solely to set strategic policy. Other than in the fund-raising area, the board of the large NFP is nonoperational. That is, no other participation of the board in NFP operations is expected or, in some cases, desirable or wanted. The operational and functional aspects may be 100 percent in the hands of the executive director who, in turn, forms his or her own management team. Therefore, no generalization can be made regarding the composition of a management team in a NFP. It can vary from the above noted local Little League to a hundred million-dollar research clinic. The capabilities and focus of the management team must be tied to the strategy of the NFP.

The Strategic Cycle

Even though the time frame of the strategic cycle may be a lengthy one, the actual time cycle for strategic management is much shorter. Measurement of progress toward a strategic objective must be made frequently enough to allow the board members to detect and correct poor performance. For example, in the case of the Episcopal Community Services, the need for the various missions was taken for granted yet little attention was paid to a decreasing fund allotment from government agencies. As a result, the organization was $250,000 in debt to the federal government and was being prosecuted by the Internal Revenue Service *without* the knowledge of the board members. This major crisis (environmental change) resulted in a complete turnaround of the implementation process of the goals and objectives formulated by board members.

Criteria of Evaluation

One major phenomenon that is evident in the study of not-for-profit organizations, and members of the board, is the common absence of criteria of performance as they relate to the goals and objectives set by the board. Obviously, in the business world, the prime measures of success are the degree of profitability, the growth of profit, and the share of market obtained. Many NFPs believe these and other criteria are not available to their particular organizations. However, such thinking is not correct and is one reason for the discontinuance of NFPs. Where the total budget of revenue and expenditures is involved, it is not too difficult to change the word profit to *surplus*. Simply put, the equation would read: *Income minus outgo should equal surplus*. This is but one measure that could be used by the board of directors. A more complex device is cost-benefit analysis. (Difficult as it may seem, the medical profession and our system of justice regularly attempt to place a dollar value on many benefits, including that of human life itself.)

Quantification

It is vital to performance evaluation that most criteria be based on some quantitative measure. It is all too common for board members to use their own personal feelings to evaluate the progress of the particular organizations. Therefore, reality sometimes escapes reason.

One suggestion for strategic planning sessions is for each NFP board member to contribute one quantitative measure that has significance to the organization. The following is a list of some measures that have been used, depending on the kind of NFP. (Also see chapter on Volunteers.)

1. Increase in the number of beneficiaries or members
2. Percentage of increase in the number of grants or revenues
3. Decrease in the cost/effectiveness for each individual beneficiary
4. Decrease in the fixed cost of accomplishing the mission
5. The total number of hours spent by volunteers
6. The percentage increase in the number of volunteers
7. The increase (or decrease) of time spent by the board members
8. The ability of the executive director to stay within or decrease the expenditure budget
9. The number of articles in the newspapers, and other public relations material related to the community

It should be noted that each organization has to choose its own set of standards or criteria. As was stated, it is impossible to use only one criterion, as the one selected may not reflect the achievement of a given mission. Furthermore, those criteria which may be important to one organization, such as a church, may or may not be viable for a hospital or a museum. It should be apparent that normal accounting systems do not automatically supply the data described in the above listing. However, many of the criteria can be pruned from the accounting system.

In addition to the quantitative factors, other criteria may be based solely on qualitative factors. In some organizations, the following yardsticks have been used to measure quality:

1. The relationship between the board members and the executive director
2. The personal relationships among board members
3. The relationship of staff to the executive director
4. The quality of the relationship of volunteers to both the executive director and the board members
5. The general attitude of the community toward the mission of the organization
6. The degree of positive impressions the community has of the organization and/or mission
7. The ease of fund raising
8. The ease of attracting board members and volunteers
9. The ease of attracting foundation funds, and other sources of funds

It is obvious that many of the above items are not measurable in mere dollars and cents, but are based on some sort of subjective evaluation and poll-taking. Quality, like the choice of colors, is not a matter of right or wrong but of individual value systems. However, this does not disparage the ability of social scientists to translate subjective feelings into objective quantifiable data. For example, one religious group suddenly found itself having difficulties in attracting volunteers and raising revenue. A simple telephone call to a sample of the volunteers still active revealed a great deal of resentment toward the new assistant executive administrator. She had been a volunteer before her appointment and in the opinion of many of the volunteers, this woman's behavior had changed substantially since she had been appointed a paid member of the staff. She had antagonized a number of volunteers and donors. It became apparent that she did not understand her new role and the board members were compelled to ask for her resignation.

CONCLUSION

The strategic process is a dynamic one, moving from strategic formulation to implementation, then to management and control. In every case, the entire process must be followed up, based upon the actual performance of the organization as it relates to a given objective or goal or the mission as a whole. Board members and the executive director must stay on top of this continuous process as it unfolds. Throughout the year (not just one day a year) the formulation or implementation policies may have to be changed. Or, perhaps based upon the degree of distance from the desired criteria, the entire process may have to be done two or three, even four times a year. *Strategic management can be summed up then as managing the process of change.* The *board must create* an environment where the *ongoing analysis* of both the environmental system and the resources of the NFP are taken into account along with the value systems of the board members and the executive director. It is important to reiterate that people make changes; systems do not. Surprisingly, it is this latter thought that is most often overlooked by board members.

All of the literature and a good part of the research done for NFPs clearly indicate that the prime role of the members of the boards of trustees is to create, guide, and evaluate the process of strategic planning, implementation, and management.

ADDITIONAL INFORMATION AND EXAMPLES

"The Gotham YWCA" prepared by Ellen Greenberg with E. S. Sares, The Institute for NFP Management, Columbia University, New York, 1978.

"Latinos Housing Foundation," Israel Unterman, Harvard Business School Case Services 9-377-791, Boston, 1979.

"Boston Symphony," Intercollegiate Case Clearing House 9375340, Boston, 1975.

4

Organizational Structure and Communications

No one man can see all with his own eyes or do all with his own hands. Whoever is engaged in multiplicity of business must transact much by substitution and leave something to hazard, and he who attempts to do all will waste his life in doing little.

Samuel Johnson in *The Idler*

Two hundred years ago, Sam Johnson outlined the essential management dilemma—and opportunity. To accomplish significant goals, we must work through others, and "leave something to hazard" in the process. Management theories of organization and leadership have undergone significant evolution in the 1900s, with varying degrees of emphasis on efficiency, quality, costs, process, worker satisfaction, span of control, the innate needs of man, etc.

STRUCTURE AND PROCESS

It is difficult to separate form and function. Only at the time of "start-up" is there a clean slate from which a strategic plan can clearly determine the structure of the organization. At the same time the "ideal" management style to achieve strategic goals would be set in motion with trustees, managers, and employees best suited to implement and recycle plans.

The reality in both private business and the not-for-profit sector is that it's an imperfect world undergoing continuing change. As with the board's approach to strategic management in total, it is vital that the board and NFP staff understand what their current structure is, and evaluate whether it is equipped to achieve future goals.

One good example of an "entrepreneurial start-up" approach is a crime victim's assistance group with one paid staff member. After several months of frustration about everything from funding to who should sweep the floors, the group realized it must have a plan for both immediate needs and its transition to larger operations. Although the group may not have consciously realized it, it was embracing a concept of "dynamic strategy" by anticipating several stages of growth.

As part of the strategic management planning process, board and top staff must ask themselves—after defining mission and goals— such key self-analysis questions as:

- Do current structure and policies encourage achievement of those goals?
- Is management style and ability compatible with that structure?
- How flat or hierarchical is the structure itself?
- What gaps and overlap exist in managing key functions?
- Are spans of control appropriate?
- Does the information system used fit the structure for appropriate feedback?

It may properly fit a management team's style to "keep the organization chart filed away," if a flat "hierarchy" and informality are desired virtues, but periodic strategic review requires reexamination of the location of direct lines of responsibility and communication and informal lines of communication. (Periodic staff meetings or newsletters are far preferable to rumor mills.) From a day-to-day standpoint, structure and/or communications must also be questioned if needless duplication or omission occur as an organization seeks to accomplish its goals. The strategic planning time is one logical milepost at which to evaluate management structure, style, and procedures.

Often the reassessment process provides surprises. Trustee perceptions may differ significantly from those of the receptionist at the out-patient office or the den mother or the ticket-seller. In fact, consulting experience shows that trustees are rarely aware of the attitudes of lower level employees and volunteers. Those differences may or may not be appropriate, but there's no excuse for management not knowing the differences. Especially where service delivery suffers through lack of knowledge or motivation, NFP management is failing.

Unless one is caught up in the virtues of process as a higher priority unto itself, there should be unanimous agreement that an efficient organizational structure is one that maximizes the efficiency and minimizes the cost (in human terms, dollars, and other assets) of meeting its objectives. In general, this should mean that there is a minimum of gaps and overlap in the assignment or assumption of duties.

EASIER SAID THAN DONE IN THE NFP WORLD

Whether a business organization be an Egyptian-style bureaucracy with deep layers of authoritarianism or a flat matrix of self-actualized dynamos, or a more likely compromise between the two, the not-for-profit world has several potential disadvantages in developing an effective organization. In the chapter "Strategic Planning and Strategic Management," we note how business employees report to a CEO who, in turn, legally if not always in fact, reports to a board of directors. As a direct comparison, NFP staff report to an executive director (ED) who reports to a board of trustees. The potential difficulties of this difference can include:

a. The volunteer who serves as both a trustee (superior to the ED) and staff worker (subordinate to the ED).

b. The staff with a separate reporting relationship from that of the ED (for example, the artistic director of a symphony, the curator of a museum, or a professional council with diffused leadership might all "report" only to a board of trustees). Examples of programs to solve these paradoxes include museums and performing arts groups that have split the "dual personality" of "artistic direction" and "business management" into "equal" roles of responsibilities, reporting separately to the board. Both have identifiable and separate tasks. It is also possible to do this with church groups.

How to Address a Dual or Parallel Structure

It is not easy to separate the volunteer subordinate from the volunteer trustee, especially when they are one and the same person.

Nor is it easy or totally satisfactory to separate professional staff into two people, both reporting separately and sometimes "equally" to a board of trustees for the functions of "artistic management" or "business management." Nonetheless there are many examples of workable solutions where these duties are clearly spelled out and separated.

In the concern for separating "business" from the basic mission (whether it be religion or "art"), we have seen several successful approaches. One performing arts group, after 50 years of floundering, finally gave its business manager a separate reporting relationship from that of the "general" manager/music director area of responsibility. Another group took the same step when the general manager's effectiveness began to decline as he pushed himself into policy and financial matters beyond his capabilities. Several religious groups studied found the need to create and strengthen the business function. The most successful case (in terms of financial strength with no dissatisfaction on the part of the clergy) saw the business manager role taken totally away from the clergy. The consensus solution, however, can be summed up as follows:

> When two executive directors (for example, an administrator or clergy member, etc.) can work together as partners, rather than superior or subordinate, NFP strength not otherwise achievable can be realized. There must be a set of decisions made as to the responsibilities and tasks of each professional. Future quibbling about authority can only be harmful. At the same time, if one person holds both positions (for example, artistic director and business manager), one or both functions will usually suffer.

Volunteers as Part of the Management Structure

In larger national NFP organizations, a common and partial solution is a parallel hierarchy of volunteers and professional staff. In a local Boy Scout council, a professional scouter will report to the "scout executive" or CEO of the council on a line relationship. That same scout executive will have various staff functions manned by professionals who also report to him. A parallel structure for volunteers reporting to the board of trustees covers most of the same functions, from district "commissioner" to a treasurer and/or head of the finance committee. In larger organizations such as scouting, it is customary for roles and responsibilities to be clearly delineated. This is not to say that only a volunteer will do this job or a professional will do that job, but key duties are assigned. Ideally, the professional achieves most of his and the organization's overall goals through and with volunteers, but the ideal is not always realized. In one of the most effective national sectarian fund-raising organizations, volunteers have a separate hierarchy paralleling that of professional staff members. At the lower levels, the professional reports to both the volunteers and his paid superiors.

Those who claim the NFP world is so different, that profit structures are not appropriate, should remember that the diversity of American business can:

a. flourish in employee-owned (if not always fully controlled) firms such as ESOP* organized ventures;
b. support pure research or advertising creativity in an unstructured environment;
c. use inside subordinates effectively on a board of directors, board of advisors, or consulting group;
d. offer a changing array of "firm" (direct reporting relationships) and informal lines to suit changing objectives.

The above latter point is a key one for NFP trustees and executives to grasp. If it is within the capabilities of the board or executive director to adapt to the organization's structural needs, the NFP structure should follow the form best able to accomplish the long-term mission, goals, and, in turn, the strategic directions of the NFP. There is no such thing as one organizational structure. As with strategy, it should be continually changing.

The Link to Action

Agreement on general directions or programs is not enough; neither is the logical extension of "good strategic management" into a manageable number of specific action plans that can be accomplished.

---

*ESOP—Employee Stock Ownership Plan.

(Good strategic management can be defined as that which achieves its mission with a minimum or optimal cost, in both dollar and human terms.) These plans must detail who will do which steps by what dates.

In their simplest forms, there need only be a listing of the key sequential steps, tracked by both the implementing manager and (unless they are on the "trust me" system) his superior. In the case of the executive director, it is up to him or her and the board chairman to agree on reporting and control content, format, and frequency. As crucial to success as the proper tracking procedure and information system is the update of "next steps"; who is responsible, and what is the next benchmark/date.

Short-Term Versus Long-Term

It may be obvious to many, but countless NFPs and business organizations seem to go through endless reorganizations. We strongly recommend careful deliberation before tinkering with a workable status quo. Change for the sake of change may be useful every few years, but a short-term project can benefit more from a task force or a temporary assignment than from a "permanent" reorganization. Here, however, is a very real difference between the NFP world and business organizations. Where the latter are often accused rightly of mortgaging the future to achieve short-term goals and concrete results, the NFP world still in a directional sense suffers from a lack of pressure to produce achievable success.

An example of change for the sake of change, without careful attention to resulting impact, is an NFP business organization in which the executive director's staff of over 25 was extremely "flat." Twelve people reported to him directly; and he was responsible for all volunteer committees. A large consulting firm analyzed the situation and (as all consultants do) recommended a radical change.

The above is an extreme example of the "Unterman Amoeba Principle," which is basically that *for every reorganization effort to solve a problem, a new problem will result.* Unless thought is carefully given to such proposals, there will be a fifty-fifty chance that the new problem will be worse than the old one.

If under the microscope the organizational amoeba is pricked with a pin to solve problem a, the amoeba will readjust, but in so doing problem or situation b will be created. It may be easier to solve than problem a, but rarely will all problems be resolved completely.

FIGURE 4.1 Unterman Amoeba Principle

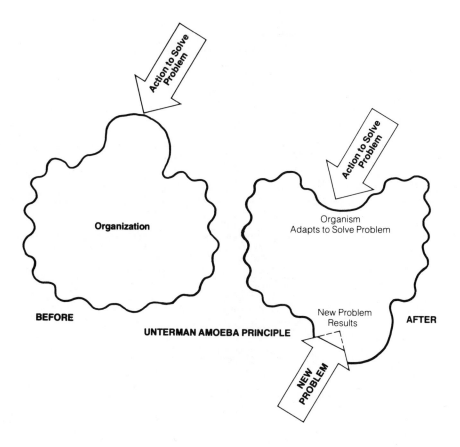

In the case of the NFP organization which moved from flat to vertical, the executive director's time pressures were only slightly reduced. He still felt an obligation to attend most volunteer committee meetings; and now his three key subordinates increased their meeting frequency. And, for a variety of necessary and unnecessary reasons, they were outnumbered by volunteers who forced a lot of meetings for the sake of meeting (as opposed to doing).

The message for a board of trustees is to be very careful in implementing a new structure.

FIGURE 4.2 Tightening Span of Control Change from Flat to More Vertical Pyramid Structure

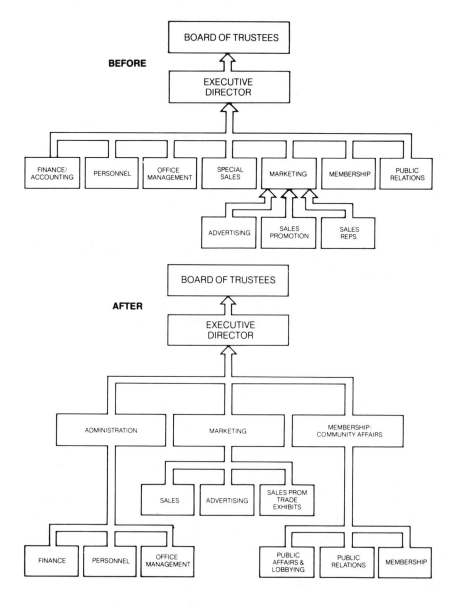

Vertical Hierarchy versus Flat Organization

In keeping with out belief in minimizing gaps and overlap, we recommend the "flattest" possible structure that can successfully achieve an NFP's goals.

FIGURE 4.3 Board and Staff Parallel Flat Structure in a Chamber of Commerce

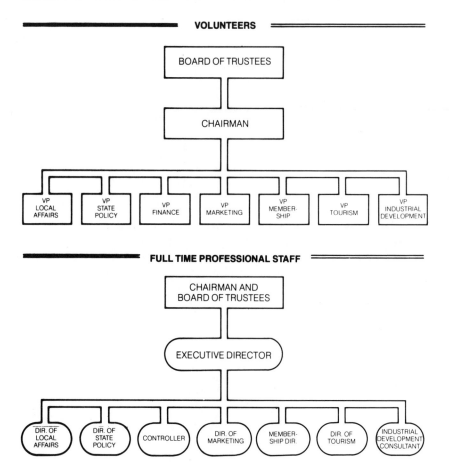

FIGURE 4.4 Example of Highly Vertical Structure

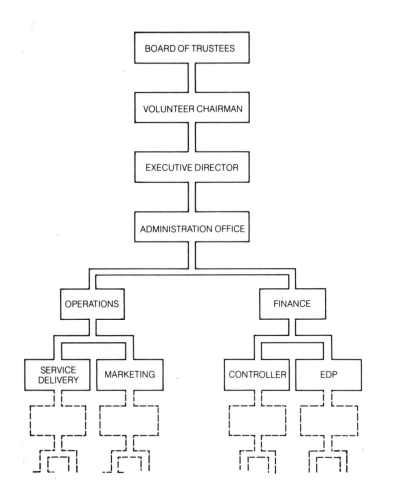

FIGURE 4.5 Example of Flat Management Structure

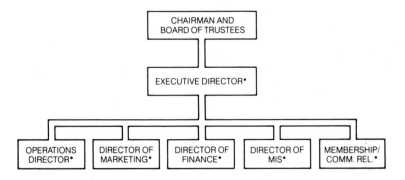

MANAGEMENT BY OBJECTIVES (MBO)

Management by objectives has come and partially gone, or at least has gone by the time it reaches the abuse stage. For a few decades "management by objectives" has been used to set goals and guidelines for both individuals and larger work units (or organizations as a whole). In some aspects it need not differ greatly from elements of strategic management. MBO was originally devised to serve personnel management and budget needs. Unfortunately, it was considered by some to also take the place of all strategic planning and management. If certain specific or general results are desired by a board, or an NFP department or individual, those results should be kept in mind as performance is directed and measured.

In MBO practice, an individual employee is required to draw up a list of his objectives for a period of time, often a year, which is tied to the organization's fiscal year, calendar year, etc. The employee then reviews the objectives with a superior. They must agree upon a final set of goals and the means of measuring results. At the end of the year or whatever time period is set, actual results are compared to the objectives that were previously specified.

Several problems have developed, especially in organizations which have rigidly employed MBO and enforce severe penalties for failure to meet objectives. One example of these difficulties is the setting of minimal objectives, thereby increasing to a high level the probability of "achievement." Even more basic is the problem of setting objectives that aren't tied to the organization's overall goals. In effect, "separate tables" or agenda are established for each manager; and all too often they don't relate well to the NFP's overall mission. This is especially true in a large NFP or in an NFP covering a large geographic area. The lack of team effort or concern, compounded by regular turnover in the board chairman position, can make a rigid MBO approach all the more dangerous. In the NFP world, where quantification of service delivery and quality of service can be difficult, MBO is difficult to use well.

Some public agencies and NFPs have experimented with "Zero Base Budgeting." This is a system in which the organization must create an annual budget as though none existed before. In effect, departments must make a new case for their existence every year. In practice this becomes unworkable, with budget preparation time crowding out mission performance. In addition all the problems of MBO (below average goals, etc.) are also present.

As with many other management approaches (some of which amount to only buzzwords and gimmicks), management by objectives can be a useful tool when it ties individual performance, as far as is appropriate, to the strategic directions of the organization. It should focus on priorities; it should tolerate failure; it should be flexible; and it should reemphasize the mission of the entire team or organization. However, a long "laundry list" of largely unobtainable wishes is almost as useless as two or three "sure thing" goals. After more than twenty years of MBO successes and failure, "moderation," "flexibility," and "perspective" should guide its future use.

The key issue is to relate each set of "MBO" objectives to the construction of the total organization and its overall mission. Where it can't be done, MBO should be discarded.

Example of Managing an NFP Project

Translating general goals and overall plans into concrete results requires hard work and the specific details of timing, actions, and responsibilities. Religious groups often face the need to provide "bricks and mortar" to back up the growth and success of their spiritual mission. One trustee group very carefully and successfully separated the fund raising effort from that of construction management, but carefully integrated them with compatible timelines (that were also useful in both motivating and noting the benchmarks of progress). Here in greatly simplified form is the plan used in this case:

	Week Number						
	1	8	16	24	32	36	90
Fund Raising Committee/ Chairman	Organize/ plan/ assign duties	Start fund raising	Receive initial pledges	"Second wave"	Evaluate short fall	Secure remaining financing	Work out bank loan repayment/ continue fundraising
Construction Committee/ Chairman	Organize/ plan / assign duties	Provide cost estimate	Hire architect	Secure preliminary city approval	Hire contractor	Begin construction	Dedication/ move in

VOLUNTEER/PROFESSIONAL CONTROL AND INVOLVEMENT

In the NFP world it is both more important and more difficult to coordinate work and achieve results because of volunteer/professional interaction than it is in the business world. It is also difficult for a financially strapped NFP to accept the need to invest hard dollars in modernization, when softer costs of volunteer labor or omission can be accepted in the short term.

The Need for Control

If concern existed that lack of control were allowing unacceptable NFP performance, the authors would be the first to insist on tight communications and control. Fortunately, improved technology can make organizational communications easier. The tools of information systems and others such as word processing, electronic mail, central data bases, remote dictation, and perhaps even home terminals preclude most excuses for bad communications. The electronic office may not be right or affordable for everyone, but when used word processors are selling for less every year, there are few excuses for not having a periodic status report updated.

The need to rethink one's limits was made clear by a continually bankrupt performing arts group. Confronted by a million dollar deficit, professional staff would not risk expanding its fund-raising activity because start-up costs would lessen the chance that payroll could be met from existing funds. One trustee finally broke out of the seeming box by initiating a well-executed personalized letter from an important public official not connected to the NFP. Most recipients didn't realize that the resulting very personal request for support was one of 2,000. Using resources outside of the NFP, well over $100,000 was raised, enough to help the NFP survive the immediate crisis and provide seed money for future fund raising. (See chapter on NFP/Business Partnerships.)

It is important to distinguish between fiscal control (see chapter on Fund Accounting) and operational control. While fiscal control of the board translates into responsibility for the source and use of funds, operational control is the more general need for management to arrange and implement:

- Establishing a basic system of control
- Measuring NFP input and results
- Structuring responsibilities within the system
- Evaluating new and ongoing programs

In the NFPs studied, in fact, better communications and regular control devices have helped flatten management hierarchies. Informal staff interaction may be all the more crucial in the modern office of the future, but a reasonable control system can give managers and trustees the confidence to allow greater freedom of action at lower levels. (And, as noted in the chapter on Rewards and Punishments Systems, we encourage carrying rewards to lower levels for meeting goals and reaching further.)

The Concept of Goal Setting in the Communication Process

If goal setting as previously discussed has value in translating board and executive strategic plans into specific management action, it is at the stage when key criteria and programs are put in writing and when control, information systems, and feedback cycles are operating.

Useful control devices can range from extremely informal contacts to highly structured approaches. A random sharing of a cup of coffee or an elaborate quarterly review against annually set goals and benchmarks can both be effective. Among the successful styles noted were:

a. Monthly director's report to board of trustees on several fixed criteria in a consistent format. (Accounting data, often misunderstood in themselves, are still not enough; operational data should bear the same consistency if at all possible.)

b. Monthly or weekly informal meetings (breakfast, lunch, or whatever) between the chairman of the board and the executive director.

c. Periodic informal meetings (often a lunch) between the director and one or more trustees (a reinforcement of the point that a small number of trustees is preferred). Often this meeting is reserved only for intense lobbying or crisis times, but it can be a more regular (if only annual) event.

d. Informal lunches or receptions with trustees, staff, and community groups (donors, public officials, etc.).

e. Annual reports tied to strategic plans. Depending on membership or funding needs, these may or may not serve several additional purposes.

f. Where word processing is "in-house," regular and heavy updating of influential people, members, staff, etc., on NFP activities.

g. Monthly, *brief* written staff reports to ED on both long-term major projects and short-term tasks. The format is usually along the lines of:

Project	Status	Next Steps	Responsibility of	Due Date

h. Weekly written (often by hand) update or simple listing of "Top 5" (or 3, or 7, or whatever) work priorities for the week.

i. Informal sampling of NFP services by trustees at least twice a year. Talking to beneficiaries of the mission can often give the trustee a more personal and accurate assessment of accomplishments than any formal reports.

j. At lower levels, where subordinates are not performing up to expectations, the common time management device of reviewing daily priorities is most useful. And, of course, the superior should periodically, if not daily, check previous results.

k. Weekly staff meetings, at all levels, with agendas usually set in advance, but allowing time and atmosphere for general discussion.

l. Some forms of in-house recognition for staff and volunteers are more than part of a reward system. They, in themselves, are also control devices in (what should be) a very positive sense.

In summary, it should be apparent that good communications are vital to a well-functioning NFP. Structural barriers should be consciously addressed, at least at annual planning sessions, and programs to facilitate the processes that lead to meaningful results should be established.

Implementing changes in organizational structure is not just drawing a set of charts and lines. Most people think of lines of authority and command without identifying the real importance of organizational structure. Very simply, that is the relationship of each human being in an NFP to other human beings in the same organization. How well volunteer or paid staff relate to each other will directly affect the accomplishments of the organization. An innovative, changing NFP will not allow excessive staff; and communication of good (and bad) ideas up and down the organization will be continually encouraged.

Ultimately the success of the NFP will not be determined by structure, but by achievements through and for people.

5

Marketing

To many volunteers and professional NFP executives, "marketing" is considered to be the same as "selling," or is not considered at all. In Chapter Ten we discuss the key attributes an executive director should have, and one of these is the ability, and better yet the desire, to be an effective salesperson. It is difficult enough to sell tangible goods or products. The ability to sell the often intangible services or support of a not-for-profit organization can be all the more difficult. A second rate marketing program is often one of the basic problems of many service organizations.

In today's business world, a strong selling effort, even if it is the "right product" for the "right audience" at the "right time," usually is not enough to succeed. Since World War II the concept of the *marketing mix* has evolved. Although business professors might argue about whether there are six or eight or whatever elements in "the" marketing mix, the important lesson for an NFP is that marketing and the right mix for each NFP must be considered as an integral part of the organization's overall strategy. Before a strategic plan is translated to individual action and spending plans for an NFP, the full mix must be considered.

THE MARKETING MIX

1. *The product or service itself.* Does it follow from the mission and plans of the NFP? How does it relate to the environment,

competition—public or private, or other parts of the basic strategic plan? Just as important to the validity of that mission is the question of a current or future market for that service or group of services.

2. *Market research*. Often an NFP won't know what service it truly is providing—or could or should provide. Research can be as simple as a director seeking advice from peers or as elaborate as million dollar studies.

3. *Pricing*. What does the beneficiary pay—if anything? Pricing can be zero, positive, or negative. Simply "giving away" a service may be wrong for a variety of reasons.

4. *Delivery/access*. How does the "consumer" (client, audience, visitor, or patient) take advantage of the service? Via telephone, via TV or radio or other media? Downtown or satellite location? Home delivery?

5. *Sales*. Sales is the giving of a product or service in return for money or other considerations. With some services or products the sales part of the marketing mix may be very important. Or, only a modest sales effort may be necessary as opposed to other elements of the mix.

> *Marketing is not synonymous with sales. Sales is one element of marketing, and its relative importance varies dramatically from one NFP to another.*

6. *Advertising*. In a business sense, advertising is the act of making something known via paid media (print, broadcast, etc.). The amount of money (in percent or absolute terms) spent on advertising can vary significantly from NFP to NFP, and certainly from one NFP to another even in the same field.

7. *Sales promotion*. Sales promotion very literally promotes or enhances the selling effort and the total marketing mix. The brochure or other "collateral materials" used to describe an NFP's programs, the incentives used to gain new members, or the bumper sticker or lapel pin all are examples of sales promotion.

8. *Public relations*. PR is the business of inducing public understanding and goodwill. Often overlooked or underestimated, professionally run (for hard dollars or by skilled volunteers) public relations can be more cost effective than most elements of the mix. Where advertising would be paid (or donated) media space or time,

public relations would be reflected in editorial news reports and articles.

9. *Post delivery follow-up and marketing evaluation.* Not purely an "element" of the mix, "after action" analysis is the key to determining what specific "next steps" are appropriate. Although formal market research is an obvious tool, quantitative and qualitative analyses should track the performance of all elements of the mix on a regular basis.

The Product

In the business world the overall marketing program or product also includes parts such as "name" and "packaging." The best way to get a grasp of what "business" or service an NFP is truly in, is by describing the service (or more likely, services) an NFP provides. It's useful for this to be done on paper for continued scrutiny, and discovery of seemingly obvious keys to improvement.

The questions to be asked and answered include:

The Product Itself

- What is a brief overview of the service?
- Among existing services, which offer the most potential?
- What additional features to existing services can be offered? How can they be revitalized? Renamed? Re-"packaged"?
- What is the maturity level or lifecycle status of the service, for example—introduction, growth, saturation, decline?
- What services should be eliminated—because of cost effectiveness, and/or competition, or changing mission?

The Market Environment

- What is the current and potential market? To whom does or should the service appeal?
- Nationally (or internationally) or locally, what is going on in this area? What about competition? Direct? Indirect? (The Boy Scouts and Boys Clubs might be competing directly, while the existence of teenage girls might be indirect competition.)
- If competition is increasing, should the NFP attempt to maintain a monopoly; or is cooperation with competitors possible?

- Will a new or changed service pay for itself? Lose money? Earn money?

New Services

- What gaps or market openings are there?
- Has there been any market research into client needs, clues for new or different related services?
- Is there any systematic generation of new ideas from board members, staff, service recipients?
- Are there any special markets not being served, or not being served adequately? (For example, young, elderly, military, handicapped, gifted, etc.)

Not every planning meeting or marketing plan will cover all the above questions. Some of them overlap; and one invariably leads to another. Appendix Three includes the strategic plan of the San Diego Economic Development Corporation. Major elements of that plan include marketing evaluations of: situation analysis; strengths and weaknesses; service recipients and their needs (developed in this case from three secondary sources and only one original piece of research).

Appendix Four is the raw research format of a symphony questionnaire. Faced with a severe and continuing financial crisis, the San Diego Symphony in the early 1980s was living from paycheck to paycheck. Board restructuring and contract renegotiation were well underway before the study was completed (on a voluntary basis by San Diego State University), so the study was not of immediate survival value. When it came to restructuring the new year's program, however, the NFP was ultimately in a position to better evaluate consumer preferences relating to concert series and ticket sales trends. In turn, both the product itself (elimination of a money losing summer series, second year move to a summer "pops" format) and the selling of the product gained in cost effectiveness. Sometimes art for art's sake is admirable and affordable; but when an NFP is on the brink of failure, every cost-effective dollar must be counted.

Dramatic service changes are often brought about by NFPs in trouble, when it's apparent the "gentle hand on the tiller" is not enough to move the NFP back to an adequate (or surviving) course of action. The growth of profit-making medical care facilities in the past decade offers some of the most striking examples of product change, both in cosmetic and more substantial terms. More local governments are leaving the hospital business; state and federal Medicare requirements continue to change; emergency care is changing dramatically and/or being eliminated; and a host of other "product" questions are continually being decided.

What Product Today?
What Product Tomorrow?

Once the difficult task of product (or service or lobbying focus, etc.) definition is decided, it's easier to reshape the product. For example, the regional hospital in a rural county may continue to have a mission of comprehensive care in as broad a range of services as possible. In contrast, hospitals in cities with many alternative facilities have cut certain services such as emergency care as much as is feasible.

Here again, the product or service being offered today may not be possible tomorrow, even if the current mission argues for it. A hospital providing adequate cardiology care in 1980 may not have the resources to be competitive in 1990, especially as other areas of care require cost-effective improvement. One local clinic might provide nothing more than first aid, while another could decide that preventive medicine, an outreach program of education, and political activism are all appropriate areas of service.

In the theatrical arts, the continuation of prior years' scheduling with a new array of performances or performers is a basic product decision that should be made explicitly rather than implicitly. Consumer demand, labor negotiations, competition, commuting habits, weather, and a host of other factors may encourage a product shift— or creation or elimination of a product. Where one performing arts group decides to expand its number of shows, others might add more series of the same performances to attract more people. (Or others might raise or lower prices or change locations as a result of this increased competition. Both are elements of pricing and service delivery questions.)

Birth control or abortion as a service might have been publicly unmentionable (or at least not allowed in advertising) 20 years ago. Today a planned parenthood group or church might consider it to be its mission to directly address the products, services, and ideas related to the subject. Fighting a toxic waste dump, supporting a tax initiative, or counseling the terminally ill are also examples of ideas and services that have, in effect, been products leading to the creation of NFPs. Once established, the NFP must decide the substance and form of its product.

Naming a Product

NFP names are not spontaneously generated. Either they evolve from attempts to provide generic descriptions, or they are consciously named in their infancy (or regenerated old age, for that matter).

The ideal name doesn't necessarily smack of show business or Madison Avenue. Professional marketers, in fact, usually opt for names that are easy to remember, simple to pronounce, convey positive connotations, and are consonant with the type of service being provided.

Where competition is a concern, trademarks and service marks are useful protectors of an NFP's proprietary interests. On a national level NFPs such as the Boy Scouts, Girl Scouts, Red Cross, and "Y" organizations are especially (and appropriately) protective of their unique programs and the names used to describe them.

Euphemisms can be useful in shortening or positively influencing descriptions of NFP services. "Light Opera," "Shakespeare Festival," and "summer pops" have evolved into two-word descriptions of performing arts directions that might otherwise require a sentence to discuss (or advertise). A "life flight" helicopter may be easier to support than an "emergency" airplane. "Right to life" or "pro-choice" are easier to sell than two-paragraph concepts.

Name generation and selection can usually be fun and also useful when approached from a professional marketing viewpoint. The chairman of the board's wife may be the worst "sample of one"; an employee panel may or may not be better than the board; and solid quantitative[1] research is the best approach when cost justified. (If $100,000 in advertising is going to publicize the name, $500 of research might easily be justified. A one-time promotional event costing $2,000 might be better serviced by the judgment of the board chairman's wife.)

Market Research

The chairman's wife (or husband) consideration is both humorous and serious in business and NFP sectors. A fresh, uneducated opinion is sometimes useful to provoke thought but not to influence decisions unless solid, well thought out market research is providing that opinion. In the consumer marketing arena, market research has proven its worth continually, and is a "line item" budget consideration which doesn't have to justify its existence in concept. (That's not to say individual research projects or department allocations aren't scrutinized carefully for cost justification. Assessing the probabilities and value of additional information is an important research exercise in itself.)

Types of Market Research

Not all research has to be expensive or exotic. For many NFPs the reading of trade journals and other secondary sources, careful tracking of service delivery, and an occasional survey of client or member attitudes is all that is affordable. For a large national NFP a $100,000 research study or half million dollar consulting project might be cost effective. Examples of the range of routine to very special research sources are:

Publications
Trade association memberships/related services
Subscriptions
Seminars/schooling
Attitude and image testing
Service usage/tracking
Testing of marketing elements (for example, advertising copy or
    media, name, pricing, etc.)
Market surveys/studies
Sales forecasting
Test marketing

An example of the use of a comprehensive market study (and a private/public partnership) is the San Diego Economic Development Corporation (EDC) case, for which Appendix Three includes a sample of its strategic plan. The San Diego EDC was the subject of a market study commissioned by the San Diego City Council and administered by the Greater San Diego Chamber of Commerce. Using a professional marketing research supplier, the study performed both quantitative and qualitative (in-depth interviews) studies of ways to improve San Diego's industrial base and generate jobs. The study led to a reorganization of San Diego's EDC and subsequent additional market research using both primary and secondary sources. For example, one of the major study interests was "factors in site selection decision making." In addition to the original study data, the reorganized EDC found three other secondary sources to correlate with the directional (not statistically significant within any high probability ranges) findings. One source used was *Fortune* magazine, which had conducted a similar survey in the expectation that it might assist media purchasers.

In future months EDC took advantage of trade seminars, advertising readership studies (supplied by print media), and sales tracking versus specific quantitative goals. The overall impact of this research and revised organizational/marketing plans was the successful turnaround and achievement of San Diego's job generation goals (6,000+ per year).

Qualitative Research

Qualitative focus groups are commonly used as part of profit sector research programs, but seldom in the nonprofit world. Part of the reason is cost; two focus groups of ten people each by a professional moderator can easily cost $2,000 per group. The results of such a study, which investigated "advertising and promotional opportunities for a local American Association of Blood Banks branch," are shown in the Appendix. The study is entitled "An Analysis of the Range of Donor/Nondonor Attitudes and Experiences Relating to Giving Blood."

The study is an excellent example of solid qualitative research in that it provides appropriate background data, clearly outlines the purpose and objectives of the research, explains the methodology and timing of the study, and presents findings within the limits of the research.

As noted in the study, the group discussion technique is

utilized to generate the qualitative information needed in this exploratory phase. The technique consists of accumulating a small sample of the target population and interviewing them simultaneously. The discussion session is directed by a moderator knowledgeable in the subject area, who uses a loosely structured outline to evoke relevant commentary. Statements are usually probed and interaction of ideas and opinions encouraged. Depending on the situation, a moderator may act as an unbiased mediator, or take a position, to draw out respondent reactions. And at times, the moderator may play "Devil's Advocate," taking a viewpoint opposed to the entire group so as to force a defense of their position.

The basic concept of the group discussion session is to comprehensively explore the various ideas or behavioral patterns which may exist relative to any given subject. Almost without exception there is *no* attempt to quantify these feelings or actions, since the group discussion samples do not reliably represent the general population being examined. Also, there are inherent bias factors in the group context, such as the influence of the moderator and the magnification of specific topics. Thus, the approach was consistent with the research purpose, which was to develop hypotheses rather than firm conclusions.

In the blood bank study two group sessions were utilized as the base of information. The first group consisted of loyal donors, defined as those who had donated blood within the past year and would be likely to do so again in the coming year. The second group consisted of nondonors, recruited from the general population at random and qualified as not having donated blood within any reasonable period of time (5–10 years or more), and not having any immediate intention of doing so in the future.

Both groups of 10 to 12 respondents included a mixture of males and females, married and single, 18–65 years of age. Sessions were held at the blood bank facilities. The donor session was conducted within three weeks of the nondonor session. Because of anticipated lack of involvement, nondonor participants were promised a $10 incentive to attend at the time of recruitment. In fact, it might have been wiser to have used this incentive among donors as well, given that substantial over-recruitment was necessary to obtain a sufficient number of participants arriving at the specified focus group session. It has been established that such an incentive does not significantly affect group responses to questions.

The major emphasis of the study was to develop ideas of how to attract new donors and to maintain the contributions of current donors. To do so the discussion group moderator sought information such as "feelings about the blood bank as an institution," "advertising and word-of-mouth communications," "the reward of giving to the donor," "level of knowledge among donors," reasons for not being a donor, comparisons with the Red Cross, perceptions of alternative marketing strategies, and charitable activities of nondonors.

In retrospect conclusions from this study such as "efforts to promote repeat donations must be quite different from those aimed at inducing initial donations" may appear to be self-evident. To the professional marketer, however, "samples" of one are not as valid as those of 10 or 20, especially when those 20 persons represent a special focus of NFP interest.

Quantitative Studies

Quantitative research involves data accumulation and usually applies a reliable form of analysis to the findings. It may be preliminary or "pilot" in nature, or it may be a final study to provide data with a high level of confidence in its significance. At some point the size, nature, and method of sampling must be decided, within budget levels appropriate to the NFP and the value of the data to be learned.

The NFP has an advantage in that it is often easier to secure business support services at little or no cost. Market research is no exception, and Appendix Four is an example of a quantitative study undertaken at virtually no cost. The study was conducted on a volunteer basis by San Diego State University's College of Business for the San Diego Symphony. Suffering from declining membership support and attendance, the symphony was facing the prospect of closing because of a million dollar deficit. In trying to solve several problems simultaneously, the board leadership decided to look for long-term solutions while it addressed short-term crises.

The survey conducted by San Diego State focused on awareness, image, level of involvement in cultural activities, and reasons for those attitudes. Although it is difficult to accurately predict "purchase intention," the study also examined perceptions of pricing sensitivity. Correlations with basic demographic data and other "cross tabs" provided the NFP with meaningful profiles of its supporters, and indications of how support might be improved. The symphony has struggled back from the depths of near bankruptcy, and a reliable market research study was one modest element in that resurgence.

Where it isn't feasible to field a separate piece of research, it may be possible to convince a professional supplier or private sector user to "tag on" a few extra questions to the end of another survey. At worst, it may be possible to share research costs of a survey with other private or NFP groups.

In · some cases, the results of hard quantitative work can be impressive. A performing arts group or a zoo should know when attendance is strong and why. Before data interpretation can begin, the raw information must be assembled in a meaningful way. "Packing the house" with complimentary tickets for the sake of appearances is different from "standing room only" due to a sell-out. Total attendance records are useful; revenue and expense ("profit and loss") statements, however, are crucial.

Pricing

Pricing can only be a "pure science" when all variables are controlled and can be repeated. In the performing arts this might be more difficult because of the importance of schedule, weather, content, and a host of variables not easily controlled. On the other hand, relatively low cost, repetitive services might be more easily tested. As with other areas of NFPs' marketing mix, market research may be a useful tool in improving NFP pricing strategy if it can be determined that:

- a certain number and type of client will be added or lost due to a pricing shift (upward or downward)
- the pricing shift (or new service introduction) will have an impact on existing services
- pricing will have an effect on timing and frequency of "purchase" (or use of services, etc.)

It's vital to consider the implications of pricing shifts before they are tested and/or fully implemented. Demand curves (that is, the relationship between price and demand) for a particular product may not develop along a smooth, projectable pattern. A clinic may actually increase demand by raising fees from zero to $2 per visit if the patient believes "you get what you pay for" (or it may lose its highest priority patients). A successful advertising or promotion campaign may move the whole demand curve upward despite heavy price increases "across the board."

"One free concert with four" may be perceived as more valuable than "20 percent off"; and a ticket series is usually preferable to selling tickets to regular performances on a one-by-one basis. Price reductions for timely response can improve immediate cash flow and increase the likelihood of a sell-out performance. Success will generate further success, which is why pre-season early subscription sales can be so important to the total year's program. If tickets are "always available," the motivation (for example, from fear of later inability to do so) to buy a series or a season's worth at an early date is lessened.

Equity in Pricing

What is "fair" in pricing NFP services? It's often the norm that ticket sales in the performing arts cover only half an NFP's expenses. Some NFP hospitals earn enough to reinvest in continually improving equipment while others lose money to the point they close down, are absorbed into another hospital group, or are acquired by a profit making firm. A neighborhood clinic may decide its mission is to provide service at no fee, while another may suggest a fee schedule subject to the patient's ability or desire to pay.

Where the private businessman who cannot sustain profitable operations will declare bankruptcy or move his resources elsewhere, the NFP has two challenges: 1) to receive/earn enough income to sustain its operations; 2) decide what pricing of services is compatible with its mission.

We have talked of "optimizing" pricing from a bottom-line income standpoint, whether one pricing schedule is more income effective than another. Once this thinking is completed, and perhaps tested, an NFP board must then evaluate the impact of that pricing on the NFP's overall mission. Although raising the fees or limiting the hours of an emergency room may be a good business decision, it may not fit the particular NFP's mission. If not cost effective, the clear-cut (but not always obvious or easily accepted) conclusion is that uncovered costs must be recouped elsewhere. The elsewhere might be from income-generating services (which may or may not trouble the IRS[2]), private sector partnerships, grants, fund-raising drives, income from endowment (which must have been previously raised), etc.

From a strategic management standpoint it's important to isolate the service pricing question from that of mission until one has measured the impact of pricing shifts. The symphony which "papers" a hall to increase the audience may do so carefully in a fashion compatible with its mission, contributing to the appearance of success of the group and bringing music to more people. That in turn may lead to increased sales. If carelessly handled, however, that seeming benevolence may dissuade other subscribers who believe all should pay their "fair" share. The Scout registration or camp fee may be inflexible, but that doesn't preclude a volunteer from offering special funds on behalf of the disadvantaged child. These and many other pricing decisions quickly blend with both overall strategic concerns and more narrow elements of the marketing mix. Five tickets for the price of four is a pricing decision, but it immediately leads to promotion, advertising, and public relations programs to take advantage of the approach. The need to raise money for a poor child to participate in a youth program may encourage widespread (or quiet and selected) fund-raising activity.

As with all elements of a business plan, the only continuing advice is to test, test, test. Even when finances are strong, an NFP must question itself to see what it could do with an increased budget, for example, build endowment for a rainy day, expand services, charge less to certain recipients, raise benefits to staff for lower turnover, etc. It's always a good budget exercise to question what an NFP would do with 10 percent or 20 percent or $100,000 or $200,000 less. (And in turn, the item that would be cut first might deserve a lesser percentage of whatever total budget is established.) The alternative exercise of building a "wish list" can be just as difficult, but it may lead to a funding program to meet those wishes.

> *NFP pricing is not a zero sum game,*
> *especially in the long term.*

To meet tomorrow's payroll, one plus one probably equals two. Given time to maneuver, however, an NFP can work to improve the effectiveness of its income generation, spending, or both.

Delivery/Access

Where? When? How? In both the private and public sectors a basic service is established for a specific reason, but service delivery is often ignored. "Meals on Wheels" feeding programs, ambulance services, and mobile health clinics are obvious examples of methods of service delivery being vital, if not the total reason-to-be, for the NFP involved.

Many NFPs start in one location offering one or more basic services. From a successful base, however, modes of expansion are virtually limitless. Physical expansion at one central site, creation of satellite facilities, duplication of all services elsewhere are all major facility decisions often requiring months or years of study and implementation. It's prohibitively expensive—to say nothing of embarrassing, frivolous, and plain bad management—to build a new facility and have it be unused. When in doubt, this is an area where paid, outside advice is well worth the cost. Fortune 500 corporations with large real estate staffs use outside assistance, and a local NFP can't pretend to have that expertise within its organization. At a minimum, local architects and contractors (with no potential conflicts of interest) are useful sources of ideas. Factors such as the NFP mission, current and future projected demographics of members and service users, traffic patterns, land and building costs, proximity to support services and public transportation, and as many as 100 other variables could be involved in a site location decision. At a minimum 10 or 15 key criteria must be established to assist the timing and location of facility expansion.

As in all areas of the marketing mix, creative thinking can't hurt at the idea generation stage. For example, $1 per year government leases, land swaps, gifts from developers, selling of air rights, sale in exchange for space in new buildings are all successful modes of facility expansion which could improve service delivery.

Short of building a new structure (or remodeling an old one), there are a host of ways to expand or improve service delivery. Flow-charting existing service procedure, seeking or recording client complaints, encouraging staff or volunteer suggestions can all lead to worthwhile ideas. A great concept may never succeed if careful analysis of service flow is not managed properly. For example, competent medical care may be diminished in value if the patient is unduly delayed in registering for treatment. Walk-in service, mobile delivery, telephone response, and media (radio, TV, newspapers, etc.) delivery are all modes of providing increased service. Expanding or cutting hours, changing staffing levels or expertise, providing parking or shuttle service all can also affect service. The performing arts or Scout group which goes to individual schools, the youth group which embarks on a special program, the symphony which plays at several locations are all examples of changing service delivery. A questioning attitude and the willingness to test reasonable alternatives are the best ways to improve the ultimate NFP payoff—the beneficiary actually using the service.

Sales

Sales is not a dirty word
Sales is not a dirty word
Sales is not a dirty word

Some organizations in the NFP world are more than willing to sell their services or ideas, often when religious belief or politics are the object and mission. For some businesses and some NFP services, sales and word-of-mouth advertising are the only marketing tools used.

Given a belief in one's NFP service, selling might seem easy to the novice. It is not. One of the best known NFP selling programs is, in most respects, a fund-raising venture, Girl Scout cookie sales. Along with God and motherhood, one might take Girl Scout cookies for granted. The Girl Scouts don't, and instead help rebuild year after year a team of volunteers which strengthens itself in the process of raising money. Most Scouters benefit from the experience of knocking on doors, making a sale that benefits both Scouting and themselves with resulting psychic and tangible rewards. The Girl Scouts train professionals, volunteers, and members at all levels. Although sales training doesn't usually go as far as role playing, however, suggestions on dress and scripts are made.

Satisfied customers, patients, service recipients, or members are the most likely to be repeat "business." As personal one-to-one contacts this means that NFP professionals and volunteers who perform well are doing a most valuable marketing job for future sales.

In private business sales hiring and training, use of customer service manuals, selling by phone from prepared scripts, sales forecasting, motivation techniques, time budgeting, and a variety of other elements are standard. Only in large NFPs or fund-raising organizations are these elements widely used. All deserve attention by all NFP personnel, from the ticket booth staffers for the symphony or a hospital receptionist to a Chamber of Commerce membership chairman.

In the private business world, a key axiom for success is that the organization must be close to the customer. In the consumer marketing world a product manager or advertising agency account executive has no sales responsibility, but that person is still expected to have had sales training and regularly scheduled field trips to stay abreast of "what's really going on." The CEO who works behind a counter or spends time as a typical customer is more likely to have a solid "feel" for the service his organization is providing. Periodic market research is one vital way of measuring performance. Personal selling, or patient contact, or telephone answering are equally crucial to measuring "sales" and total NFP performance.

Sales performance may relate directly to the delivery of the service if a mobile preventive medicine program is touring a neighborhood. Or, it may be years before today's selling effort results in the client benefiting from the service (for example, use of crime prevention programs, first aid, etc.).

The sales area is not a simple one; and most NFPs must ask themselves:

- How do we gear our sales effort to fit our overall objectives?
- How many sales people do we need—or what percentage of staff time should be spent on sales?
- How do we motivate our selling effort?
- Do we tie sales results (for example, membership, tickets, etc.) to compensation?
- What formal training is appropriate?

In today's business world marketing is not synonymous with sales. Sales is one element of marketing; and its relative importance varies dramatically from one NFP to another.

Advertising

The amount of money spent on advertising will vary significantly among NFPs, and certainly even from one NFP to another in the same field. Where paid or donated media may be vital to one opera association, another may rely largely on other marketing tools. (The old joke is that half of all advertising is wasted; but you never know which half. Careful goal-setting, marketing planning, "pre"-research and follow-up tracking can all build efficiency into programs.) Within advertising, advertising copy and media (direct mail, telephone, TV, radio, magazines, newspapers, outdoor, etc.) should all be well integrated into total NFP and marketing plans.

Whether advertising is paid for or donated, an NFP must ask itself:

What is the advertising strategy of the NFP?

Who is the audience?

What message is the NFP trying to communicate?

What will that advertising accomplish?

What volunteer or paid support is necessary to reevaluate and implement advertising strategy?

Can spending be related to objectives? Will "free" media be hurt if "hard" dollars are spent in other media? (For example, will a TV station turn down a public service commercial for a performing arts group if the latter is required to pay for newspaper coverage?)

The problem of planning and budgeting for NFP advertising is the same problem facing the small businessman who has never advertised before. It takes a certain leap of faith, especially if results may be initially difficult to evaluate. Where a retailer who tests a specific ad and medium can have a good indication of response in the following day's sale, the church listing its services, or the theatre group announcing performance hours may not be readily able to track the response. There is no magic solution to this dilemma, but NFP approaches include:

1. Using no paid media, relying on free space or time (and even free production in some cases).
2. Walking the tightrope of soliciting some free media support (for example, broadcast) while paying for selected print or direct marketing (mail and telephone) with a more specific and "affordable" focus.
3. Soliciting sponsors to pay for specific advertising programs or elements.
4. Strictly arm's length private sector purchase of advertising services.

There should be no doubt in an NFP's strategic thinking that advertising can't work or pay for itself. The question for the individual NFP is how it might be appropriate for the NFP's specific needs. Some estimates put U.S. federal advertising spending and public relations at the $200 million level. Advertisers such as the military service and U.S. Postal Service have found that paid media can be a proper, major part of their marketing mixes. Testing and years of experience were necessary, however, to move from near total reliance on voluntary support to paid support. Only in the past few years have hospitals and other NFP health care programs moved significantly and successfully into strong advertising projects.

As in the private sector, it's always good advice to use professional assistance and to seek compelling, unique creative solutions (New York's 1969 "Give a Damn" campaign or the more recent Boy Scout reminder of famous Scouts). But sound strategy and hard work must suffice for most times when the "great idea" is not to be found. Ideas as basic as telephone chains or advertising sponsors are simple and effective. One performing arts group, facing a severe financial problem, solicited free advertising space. A major newspaper refused to break its policy of only selling such space, but instead of rejecting the appeal convinced its owner's foundation to provide the necessary funds for the NFP to buy the ads. Oftentimes special events will find sponsors to buy ads, either as a "pure" public service or for a small mention within the ad (or accompanying publicity, etc.).

Advertising is not necessarily an appropriate element of the marketing mix for every NFP, but it increasingly is showing its ability to "pay for itself" with most NFPs. Where it hasn't been used before (for example, by a hospital, church, etc.), its future use shouldn't be rejected out of hand. Instead, the NFP must ask itself these questions:

1. Given overall marketing strategy, what is the appropriate (or possible) role of advertising?
2. Do all elements of the marketing mix fit with each other?
3. What is the final advertising strategy? Why is it better than alternatives? What should be tested?
4. What is the final plan? Why?
5. What is the media plan? Why? How were spending levels determined? (For example, pure judgment, as a percent of revenues, in line with "competitive spending," as part of a business plan yielding an estimated payback, etc.)
6. What research will track advertising?
   a. awareness
   b. service (or "product") use, attendance, membership, etc.
   c. public perceptions of the NFP as a whole or the particular service being advertised

In summary, advertising must pay its way; and it usually can. First, however, the NFP must carefully determine what role it can and should play in the NFP's activities. When in doubt, affordable tests can be created and tracked for concrete results rather than less tangible board or staff guessing.

Sales Promotion

"Sales promotion" is not advertising; and it's not sales. But it should be totally integrated with both. Semantic hair splitting might also define some sales promotion activity as "public relations" or "publicity." Wherever the line items fall in a plan or budget, the key thing is that they be carefully considered and implemented. It may seem tedious to consider objectives, strategy, and tactics for every element of the marketing mix, but careful and hard advance work will preclude wasted dollars.

Elements of sales promotion can include the following:

"Collateral" materials such as brochures, pamphlets, programs, posters, etc.

Promotional or advertising specialty devices such as buttons, pens, pins, membership recognition gifts, etc.

Discounts, rebates, sweepstakes, coupons, and other "trial" stimulating devices

Incentives for generating sales, for example, prizes, special incentive compensation, special recognition, etc.

"Trade" exhibits and special demonstration programs

When a performing arts group decides to push subscription sales and offers "one free concert with four," this can be defined as a promotion or a pricing decision. From a private sector standpoint there might be a preference for the former definition if single ticket sales are significant. Here again, the important thing is that the promotion impact of such a marketing tactic be considered and fully exploited.

What's right for one NFP is not right for another. While the sponsors of a charity rummage sale might want as many garish bumper stickers as possible, a United Way campaign may prefer the simple thank-you and reminder of a more subtle lapel pin. A chamber of commerce membership drive may rely on very tangible incentives where a church would lean toward inner satisfaction or low key recognition.

The most successful promotions usually tie in with and are mutually supportive with total NFP programs, advertising, membership drives, employee performance improvement, etc. The same gold pin or plaque used to reward certain levels of membership or charity support might deserve advertising mention or inclusion in a staff incentive program. Giving to an NFP can be a powerful reward in itself to an anonymous donor. But for every anonymous gift, most NFPs find 9 or 99 donors who appreciate and are motivated by recognition and promotional devices.

Public Relations

Often overlooked or underestimated, professionally run (for hard dollars or by skilled volunteers) public relations is more cost effective than advertising for many NFPs. A well thought out PR program of editorial coverage is as valuable as 1000 lines of newspaper ad space that cost $2000. Most multi-million dollar advertisers would gladly trade a page of advertising for a page of positive, third party, credible (and reprintable) reporting about the NFP's activities.

As noted in the planning of advertising, the use of paid media may preclude a TV station or newspaper from giving public service announcements to the same NFP. Although public service announcements can't be neatly targeted to an NFP's prime audience, the "price is right" if it doesn't require too much staff time or production cost.

The ultimate beginning and end solution for many NFPs' PR and communication needs is to have professional support, whether from a full-time staff member, board volunteers and/or outside counsel. Although the professional is the right person to develop a specific plan, implementation will formally or informally involve every aspect of NFP activity. Although public relations activity is mainly and ideally focused on achieving positive results, minimizing or precluding bad PR can often be a greater concern for troubled NFPs in emergency situations. The museum or symphony which spends a few thousand dollars to announce a new event is wasting its money if ten times as much broadcast or print space is carrying news about the same NFP's financial distress, board strife, or dissatisfied patrons.

While determining external public relations (and internal communications) objectives, an NFP must define its various audiences or constituencies. The $10,000 donor or local politician voting on public

support will require a different approach than the occasional sub-
scriber or service beneficiary. Ideally, also, the message for one target
group is not different from that communicated to another. Where an
occasional press release or newsletter may be satisfactory at a base
level, a concerted schedule of personal letters, meetings, briefings,
etc. will be required for key constituents.

As with other elements of the marketing mix, the public relations
mix will force tradeoffs. A $2000 per month retainer for outside sup-
port may or may not be appropriate if that's all the money the NFP
currently has for marketing. (It's definitely not appropriate unless
that support can be quickly leveraged into higher income and budget
levels.)

The ultimate product of solid public relations—positive awareness,
attitudes, membership, attendance, etc.—cannot always be tracked
immediately. As with advertising, however, interim benchmarks can
be used. The quantity of column inches of publicity generated is not
as clear a goal as long-term attendance improvement, but the amount
of "positive ink" generated today may be the more tangible evidence
that a PR program is working. The NFP that takes its positive press
and merchandises it (via reprints to donors, for use in press kits, for
letters to subscribers, etc.) is, in turn, ahead of the NFP that is not
integrating all elements of its promotional programs.

Post Delivery Evaluation

A continuing theme of solid strategic management and this book
is that sound control devices are crucial. Unless an NFP knows what
marketing elements are working and why, an improved program will
be strictly a matter of chance. Experienced judgment in evaluating a
plan or advertising copy should be better than rolling dice, but performance benchmarks and solid data will often prove preliminary
judgment to be wrong.

THE MARKETING PLANNING PROCESS

A good marketing plan directly follows from the NFP's overall
strategy; and often, the board or staff member with marketing expertise is integrating (implicitly or explicitly) his values and ideas into
the initial strategy. As with strategic management as a whole, marketing management is a never-ending cycle of change. Continuing

research and performance tracking are crucial to staying abreast of external factors (even the spiritual parts of the NFP world have competition) and working to improve marketing efficiency.

As with overall plans, however, all analysis and goal-setting without specific action plans are a waste of time. General programs must be considered; budgets must be set; realistic timetables, benchmarks, and individual assignments must be established; and the work must then be done. Because an advertising program, PR campaign, or a specific program didn't work last year doesn't mean that next year's plans shouldn't contain those elements. Different tools are used for different goals and types of programs. They should be consciously considered and explicitly rejected or tested. Unconscious rejection of a marketing element always increases the odds that the ultimate program is not the best one possible. Highway signs and advertising were seldom used 20 years ago to announce hospital emergency room locations or services. Unless someone hadn't rethought ways to advertise or "sell" this service, countless visitors or newcomers to an area could not take advantage of such a critical service as readily as they now might in an emergency.

> *In the initial stages of developing*
> *a concrete, results-oriented marketing*
> *plan, broad analysis and creative*
> *thinking are vital.*

Only one of ten new ideas might be worth testing in the real world, but unless all ten are encouraged at the preliminary discussion stage, the one good one may never surface. Outdoor concerts, "911" emergency numbers, six tickets for the price of five, mobile blood pressure test, libraries, or a host of other cost-effective programs would never have started without one individual or group deciding they were worth a test.

Plan "By the Numbers"

Creative, intuitive brainstorming is one way to improve marketing effectiveness. Equally important in the long run, and more important in the short term, for those days and years when you don't have "the great idea," is the disciplined, results-oriented examination of all marketing mix elements one at a time. Just as great intuition can lead to great advertising copy, solid deductive reasoning can determine what needs should be met, what communication objectives should in turn be achieved, what marketing tools will achieve them, and what likely costs will be incurred in the marketing program to achieve them.

One step at a time all elements should be weighed for an NFP program; and ultimately hard budget decisions must be made.

The following are examples of how different NFPs have used the varying elements of the mix to improve their programs. Overlap often occurs. The same theme used in advertising, if proven effective, usually should be the same theme used in sales promotion or membership drives. And the same brochure used to solicit new members may double nicely as part of an annual report to public or private members.

Successful and creative marketing solutions cover a wide array. Examples include:

- The annual Girl Scout Cookie sales drive is a classic success, and with fine-tuned improvements is repeated year after year.
- The 1984 Los Angeles Olympic Organizing Committee set high goals and, in turn, found the way to raise hundreds of millions of dollars of private support instead of the tens of millions raised in money-losing prior years.
- Salvation Army Christmas solicitations and Veteran's Day poppy sales were new ideas when they first started, and continue to be both successful fund raisers and visible reminders of the NFPs themselves.
- Celebrities such as Jerry Lewis and Danny Kaye have successfully shown that the right spokesman can be even a stronger force in the NFP world than in private business.
- The annual UNICEF Halloween collection is a modern variation of the Jewish *pshka*. Little coin boxes for both child and adult appeals can be markedly successful, and warrant annual repetition.
- The League of Women Voters regularly works to get out the vote, inform the electorate, and raise money, all at the same time.

Successes can be just as strong and warrant regular or annual repetition at the local level:

- The mobile X-ray or blood pressure testing program can raise awareness and funds at the same time it is providing a crucial service.
- The annual parade may provide a Little League its annual funding, and maintain community visibility.
- The rummage sale, book sale, bake sale, or car wash can provide annual community exposure and raise significant money at the same time. (One Junior League has moved its annual rummage sale net from the low "teens" to almost $100,000 per year through high goals, solid organization, total commitment, and plain hard work.)
- Street shows or summer festivals of performing arts groups are similar to mobile health clinics in that they can provide a service and raise money at the same time.
- Cable TV was not a significant force 20 years ago. Today it's approaching 50 percent penetration in a few markets, and is successfully used for a wide array of NFPs with enough initiative to ask for time and/or studio assistance.
- Groups have more impact in "selling" a public service message than an individual NFP.

Cooperation with the private sector is a chapter unto itself, and the marketing arena is especially suited to joint ventures. If environmental groups can profit from and successfully continue art work projects with forest products companies, there is no reason a local NFP can't work well with a local publisher, bank, or department store to sell subscriptions or credit cards, as long as the NFP manages adequate service, delivery, or fair compensation for lending its name and support.

In summary, the marketing of NFP services to a public involves an "aggregate of functions" that are broken into the marketing mix. Creativity and intuitive problem solving are vital and difficult elements to weave into most fabrics of an organization; they don't replace a disciplined review of what is already known and working. A pedestrian program that is well executed is better than a great idea that is never implemented. The well-implemented great idea, however, must be the ultimate marketing goal—as the means to achieving an NFP's overall mission.

NOTES

1. Quantitative research is that data which can be measured and expressed in quantity or amount, with statistically meaningful precision. $X/patient days, X percent of symphony subscribers willing to pay $X more for a performance, X percent aware of a service, X percent using a service are all examples of quantitative research. See pages 58–60 for discussion of "nonprojectable" qualitative research, which detail the special example of discussion groups in exploratory research work.

2. For example, an exempt zoo must pay the tax on unrelated business income for gift-shop sales of low-cost mementos, but not of stuffed animals, wildlife stamps, and other items which have educational purposes.

6

Fund Raising

Patricia O'Neill

THE ROLE OF THE BOARD OF DIRECTORS

As a board member of a not-for-profit institution, the basic responsibilities undertaken include:

a. Reviewing the institution's budgets and program plans
b. Evaluating the organization's effectiveness in the community
c. Establishing and setting policies and goals for the institution and its professional staff
d. Assuming the role of fiscal steward of the organization
e. Representing the community's need to the organization, as well as representing the organization and its financial needs to the community it serves

Fund raising is a joint board and management process that must· engage the united efforts of the executive director, the president and board of directors, the development committee (a fund-raising subcommittee of the board), and the development officer in order to be both productive and effective.

Effective fund raising can be achieved only when the institution has a recognized and publicly known image in the community. If donors in your community state they have never heard of your organization, the likelihood of securing a gift is remote. The first stage in any effective fund-raising campaign is a public relations effort in the community to make the organization and its mission known. Other elements of the marketing mix will be put to use when they are cost effective. For large capital projects and special events, this may involve the use of outside professional fund raisers and consultants. For most NFPs, however, existing volunteer trustees and professional staff are the logical, cost-effective fund raisers on a day-to-day basis.

THE ROLE OF THE EXECUTIVE DIRECTOR

It is important to recognize that in an NFP the executive director. who is both hired and nurtured by the board, is often the creator and recognized leader in the community for the institutional mission of the organization. His or her belief in the importance of the institution's goals, growth and needs should inspire and capture the imagination of the president and board of directors, corporations, foundations, and individuals within the community. (See chapter on Mission.) The public relations department should utilize the executive director as the spokesperson for the institution. In many not-for-profit organizations, the name of the executive director is known, but the name of the president is not. One of the functions of the executive director is to present the fund-raising goals of the organization to the president and board of directors for their evaluation, review, and suggestions. If not already in existence, the president will appoint one of the directors to chair the development committee, which should include both board members and active volunteers who are capable and dynamic leaders in the community.

THE DEVELOPMENT COMMITTEE

A well-balanced development committee should include:

Presidents of corporations
Foundation representatives
Wealthy patrons who have a history of giving to the organization

Representation from the various services in the community that can aid the institution; for example, the president of an advertising firm, the president of a graphic design house, the owner of a major printing firm, etc.

Community leaders in each of the strongest geographical and economic areas in the community should also be represented on this committee. In this way, the committee can coordinate peer solicitation efforts as broadly as possible.

The development committee defines and identifies the long-range fund-raising needs of the institution in collaboration with the executive director and the development officer. The committee, with the help of the entire board and staff, implements approaches and strategies that accomplish the desired goals.

THE DEVELOPMENT OFFICER

The development officer, working with the executive director, is responsible for preparing a fund-raising plan with proposed sources of funding projected. With input from the development committee and the board of directors, the development officer validates the objectives that were decided upon and turns to the trustees, executive director, and committee members to ask them to become the sales force for the fund-raising task ahead.

THE COMMON FEAR

The most common fear expressed by board and committee members is that they will be expected to ask their friends or strangers for money. There are several areas each trustee should explore before soliciting gifts. If proper preparatory steps are thoroughly undertaken, the trustee is initially startled to learn that not only has he or she successfully asked for and received a gift, but also feels great pride in the accomplishment.

a. The first step a member of the board must take is to gain knowledge of the institution. The trustee must be knowledgeable about the institution's history, purpose, needs, and goals. The trustee should explore with the professional staff every possible way of communicating these purposes and goals to the community.

b. The second step involves the trustee's personal commitment to the institution. Is the trustee giving both his or her creative leadership energies and financial support? The first question asked by corporate and foundation officers is, "How committed is the board financially to the organization?" It is almost impossible to ask members of the community to listen to your case statement if the board members of the institution do not deem the organization worthy of their personal support. A trustee does not fulfill his leadership position if he or she cannot devote creative and intellectual energy to the institution.

c. The third step is the area in which the trustee is exceedingly valuable to the organization. This is the prospective donor identification phase. In a well-run NFP, the board should be balanced with representation from all sectors of the community as well as representatives from the community's power structure. Each trustee should give the development officer a list of all professional, school, and social affiliations. If married, the trustee should include a similar list for a spouse. With this information, the development officer is able to begin a board network chart that enables the organization to call on the proper trustee for research and to contact potential donors. The research phase is essential to identifying the value of the prospect to the organization and to clarify the potential donor's ability to give to the organization.

d. The fourth step, after the proper trustee is identified to make the contact, is to meet with the potential donor and acquaint the person with the organization, its accomplishments and needs. This is the cultivation phase. It is also an opportunity to learn the most important thing about the donor, his or her motivation. It is pointless to make an impassioned plea for the merits of an endowment fund when the donor has given the bulk of his charitable contributions to education projects. One of the most common mistakes made by enthusiastic staff and board members is to care only for the organization they serve, not for what interests the donor. *If the donor's goals are not realized, his gift will not continue.* The most important contribution the trustee can make to the encounter with a donor is *to listen* to the donor's needs. A donor's needs may require publicity on the part of the organization, being honored at social events or, in some cases, anonymity. The critical factor from the donors' standpoint is what they want their gift to achieve for the institution and for themselves. The proper recognition of a gift often has a "ripple effect"; one donation inspires another.

e. The fifth phase occurs in the old-fashioned area of following through with promised materials. If the potential donor has been told that background information will be sent within two or three days, it is critical that the time period be honored. The donor is now interested in knowing specifics about the organization and the momentum of the relationship is accelerating to the final step in the fund-raising process.

"Asking for the Order"

Peer to Peer. Gift solicitation and acknowledgement is the outcome of the trustee's effort if each of the prior steps has been observed. The old adage that "peers give to peers" is still a truism; however, the statement should be paraphrased this way: "Peers give to peers when asked." The trustee must ask each potential donor approached to give the organization a gift of money, services, or expertise. Once donors give to the organization, they like to be thanked by letters from the president and pertinent members of the board whose area of concern their gift benefits. If these common courtesies are extended, the board of directors will effectively transform a one-time gift into an annual gift, make the donor feel a part of the organization, and enable the trustee to take pride in his accomplishment. The institution should also give recognition to its fund raisers. When a trustee or committee member secures a gift for the institution, acknowledgement by the president and the board for these efforts is appreciated. Inexpensive gifts, jewelry, and plaques are also helpful as donor and trustee recognitions. (See chapter on Rewards and Punishment.)

Corporate Foundations

While serving on a board, the trustee will often encounter a world that is unfamiliar—the field of corporate and foundation support. The points of view of corporate and private foundations differ markedly. Major corporations often have a foundation which gives grants to community service organizations. The officer in charge of these contributions is normally designated as the charitable contributions director.

The first interest of a corporation is in the charitable organization's board structure. How many community leaders serve on the board, how effective are they in the community, and in what other community organizations are the board members involved? It is often in the self-interest of the corporation to support health care, public services, and cultural organizations in the community in which they are based, or where they have a large number of employees. Corporate officers, particularly if new to the community, are interested in having their vice presidents serve on local boards. This achieves two goals. It makes the corporation more visible to members of the community while "repaying" the community in which they are based.

COMPLEMENTARY USE OF MARKETING ELEMENTS

All of the steps outlined in our chapter on marketing can be of use when applied to fund raising.

In addition to foundation budgets, corporations also encourage creative marketing and public relations events with cultural organizations that may be funded from their advertising budgets. This type of corporate support from an advertising budget can be illustrated by an example recently undertaken by the San Diego Opera Association. The American premiere production in English of *Henry VIII* by Camille Saint-Saens, featuring world-renowned baritone Sherrill Milnes in the title role, was underwritten by a corporate sponsorship by British Caledonian Airways. After the initial grant request was presented to British Caledonian Airways, and they expressed an interest, a dialogue between the development trustee and staff of the opera association and the marketing people of British Caledonian ensued. This creative collaboration resulted in not only a corporate gift, but the involvement of the corporation on several levels:

a. It offered airline tickets to London that could be used with other prizes for a raffle held in conjunction with the production.

b. The development officer secured six other prizes to make the raffle attractive.

c. Additional revenues of $3,700 were produced for the Opera Association through this drawing.

d. British Caledonian Airways talked to the directors of Madame Tussaud's Wax Museum in London and persuaded them to fly the wax figure of Henry VIII, which heretofore had not left the museum, to San Diego for display in the lobby of the theater during the performances.

e. It also shipped replicas of the English crown jewels for display, as well. These replicas were insured for $1 million. These displays created great interest in the community, which helped bolster ticket sales for the production. The San Diego Opera was $15,000 over budget in single ticket sales at the end of the *Henry VIII* performances.

f. British Caledonian also volunteered to offer a Royal British Opera tour to the patrons of the San Diego Opera, with a donation to the opera of $250 from each participant on the trip. This provided yet another way to generate money for the association.

g. At the final dress rehearsal of the opera production, an English high tea reception was sponored by British Caledonian and attended by prominent donors of the opera association as well as British Caledonian executives. The major opera donors were presented with a wax cameo brooch of Madame Tussaud.

h. The creative interchange between the San Diego Opera Association and British Caledonian Airways resulted in an increased gift to the opera and visibility and recognition in the community for the corporate sponsor.

British Caledonian executives were so pleased with the outcome of this collaboration that they are considering another corporate sponsorship of an opera in the next year. This is an example of a creative use of a promotion budget. A bit of creative thinking, a lot of hard work, and willingness to "ask for the order" snowballed into a successful program with many separate but complementary components.

At a meeting in Seattle, Mr. Don Jones, manager of the Public Affairs department of Chevron, U.S.A., complained to a gathering of development officers and board members that often corporations, having given their gift to a charitable organization, are not thanked or, if they are, their recognition in a newsletter or program is in 8-point type. He went on to state that *"Corporations are run by people and people like to be recognized."* If you are turned down by a corporation on your first approach, do not be discouraged. The relationship between the corporation and the organizations it sponsors is often one that takes a few years to develop. Corporate foundations are impressed by fiscal responsibility, not only by need. Mr. Jones cited an example of an unusual approach to the Chevron U.S.A. Foundation that netted a successful collaboration. Three gentlemen came to his office to request the donation of six steel oil drums. His interest piqued, Mr. Jones asked why they wanted them. The men were part of a steel band. In further conversations, it turned out that they lacked costumes and a place to perform. The delightful conclusion of this story is that Chevron supplied not only the steel drums, costumes, and rehearsal hall, but one of their proudest moments was realized when the steel band performed with the San Francisco Symphony.

Private Foundations

Private foundations have a very different point of view. They are not interested just in the board structure and the fiscal picture of the organization requesting their funding, but are intensely concerned that the organization is fulfilling a need in an area that no one else can provide as well. Foundation officers are very interested in the management of the organization and the artistic or social vision that the organization projects. The relationship between an organization and a private foundation can best be described as a long-term courtship. A board member may be very helpful in arranging an appointment for the executive director and president to approach the foundation. Most trustees of private foundations respect their program officers' opinions, so on only rare occasions will they meet with the executive director and/or president of the organization. This function is fulfilled by the program officer.

Foundations are rarely interested in underwriting deficits, but are highly attracted to projects that break new ground, or fulfill a need the community is unable to supply for itself. Projects that have a final goal of making the requesting organization self-reliant and independent are especially attractive to foundations.

Foundation boards and officers usually like to become involved with the institutions they fund. They like to be kept apprised of new developments in their area of funding; and they also like to receive news affecting the entire institution. Foundations also appreciate hearing from interested board members with updates on the strategic planning in which the board is engaged.

Both corporations and foundations have a common desire to help worthwhile organizations become stronger and self-sufficient. They view community support as the avenue which is most vital to the continued well-being of the organization. All trustees should utilize the time period given to them by grants from corporations and foundations to increase their efforts in broadening community outreach and financial support from within their own community.

CONCLUSION

Grants from foundations and corporations and government gifts are affected by the current economy, *but caring individuals represent 90 percent of all unearned income to charitable organizations.* These individuals are your friends and neighbors and it is they, in the long run, who will make the overall difference in whether your institution is fiscally healthy.

7

Fund Accounting

James Ledwith

INTRODUCTION

The purpose of this chapter is to create an awareness among
trustees and others of the usefulness of the financial information
generated by not-for-profit organizations.

The term "nonbusiness organization" has been adopted by the
Financial Accounting Standards Board (FASB) in its Statement of
Financial Accounting Concepts No. 4, *Objectives of Financial Reporting by Nonbusiness Organizations*, as descriptive of all organizations
other than profit-oriented business enterprises. It includes not-for-
profit organizations such as hospitals, schools, research foundations,
libraries, and fund-raising organizations, as well as governmental and
quasi-governmental entities such as municipalities and county school
districts. The discussion of fund accounting in this chapter is limited
to not-for-profit organizations. As such, this term will be used throughout this chapter. Because of the growing acceptance of the term
"nonbusiness organizations," however, the reader should be aware of
its broader meaning.

A thorough understanding of the not-for-profit organization,
including its financial condition, is important to trustees in fulfilling,
even minimally, their fiduciary responsibilities. In a broader sense,
better accounting control can assist the total management reporting
and control function as well as strategic management.

This chapter will highlight and explain the significant differences
between financial reporting by business enterprises and financial
reporting by NFPs.

Public awareness of the financial aspects of NFPs, coupled with the increasingly competitive market for donations from both the public and private sectors, make it imperative that an NFP issue meaningful, relevant financial information. In order to do this, an NFP must make sure it has the appropriate level of financial expertise both within its management ranks and on its board. The small community-related NFP may be able to function satisfactorily with periodic volunteer support from its CPA firm. Larger not-for-profit organizations should enhance the usefulness of such volunteer efforts by having a financial person in their management ranks or, if size or budget constraints prohibit such a "luxury," by having the records reviewed and/or maintained by an outside party such as a CPA firm. Larger not-for-profit organizations should have an adequate in-house financial management capability, again enhanced by volunteer service and the expertise of the external auditor. In any case, to enhance the credibility of the annual financial statements and provide some comfort to the trustees in carrying out their fiduciary responsibilities, the annual financial statements of the not-for-profit organization should be audited. (See Appendix, Episcopal Community Services.)

In addition, such public disclosure of financial information about the activities of not-for-profit organizations, coupled with the increased public awareness of the responsibilities of trustees, make it imperative that trustees be able to read, understand, and interpret the financial reports of their organizations. This chapter should aid the trustee in gaining that understanding.

Recognizing that some trustees are more well versed in financial accounting and reporting matters than others, the chapter is divided into two parts. The first part presents an overview of the objectives of financial reporting by not-for-profit organizations and contrasts the financial statements of a business enterprise with those of a not-for-profit organization. The second part presents a more detailed analysis of a set of annual financial statements of a hypothetical voluntary health and welfare organization.

OBJECTIVES OF FINANCIAL REPORTING BY NOT-FOR-PROFIT ORGANIZATIONS

The development of generally accepted accounting principles for not-for-profit organizations is discussed in the Appendix to this chapter. Generally, the accounting standards and practices relating to recognition and measurement issues are the same for not-for-profit organizations as they are for business enterprises. However, due to the different purpose, operations, and methods of financing the related organizations, the objectives of financial reporting and, therefore, the resultant formats used to present financial information are different. The objectives of financial reporting by not-for-profit organizations are set forth in the FASB's Statement of Financial Accounting Concepts No. 4:

Objectives of Financial Reporting by Nonbusiness Organizations

Provide information that is useful in making rational decisions about the allocation of resources of an organization.

Provide information to help present and potential resource providers and other users in assessing the service that a not-for-profit organization provides and its ability to continue to provide those services.

Provide information that is useful in assessing how managers of a not-for-profit organization have discharged their stewardship responsibilities and about the other aspects of their performance.

Provide information about the economic resources, obligations, and net resources of an organization, and the effects of transactions, events, and circumstances that change resources and interests in those resources.

Provide information about the performance of an organization during a period.

Provide information about how an organization obtains and spends cash or other liquid resources.

Include explanations and interpretations to help users understand financial information provided.

To accomplish these objectives not-for-profit organizations generally produce a financial report that includes financial statements summarizing financial position, results of operations, and changes in financial position similar to those produced by a business enterprise.

EXHIBIT I Comparison of Primary Financial Statements

Manufacturing Concern	Voluntary Health and Welfare Organization
Financial Position	
A balance sheet presents assets and liabilities generally listed in order of liquidity.	A balance sheet presents assets and liabilities on a fund accounting basis whereby separate accountability is established for the funds of not-for-profit organizations that are restricted for a specific purpose. Within each fund group, the assets and liabilities are generally listed in order of liquidity.
Emphasizes working capital as an important measure of the capabilities of an entity to meet current obligations and finance on-going operations.	Generally does not contain an emphasis on working capital; however, the closer the not-for-profit organization is to a profit-oriented entity, the more likely working capital data will be stressed.
Inventory and accounts receivable are usually the most significant current assets; there is generally a proportionately large percentage of assets invested in fixed assets.	Investments are the most important asset; the amount tied up in fixed assets is generally less because not-for-profit organizations, other than educational institutions or hospitals, are not capital intensive.
Since manufacturing concerns are capital intensive, there is generally long-term debt used to finance fixed asset acquisitions. In addition, the relationship between long-term debt and stockholders' equity is generally important. Investors use the debt/equity ratio as a barometer of the borrowing capacity of an organization.	Many voluntary health and welfare organizations have no long-term debt; others may have minimum debt generally associated with fixed assets. There is no measure of borrowing capacity comparable to the debt/equity ratio used for profit-oriented organizations.
The net ownership position is represented by stockholders' equity that presents the capital stock outstanding and the accumulation of earnings since inception.	There is no ownership interest. Fund balances representing the net results of all activities since inception are presented.

Results of Operations

An income statement, as its name implies, presents the accumulation of operating transactions of the entity during the period. Since the enterprise is profit-oriented, this statement stresses the bottom line, net income.

A statement of support, revenues, and expenses in an accumulation of the transactions of the entity showing sources and the purpose for these funds; the net results of those transactions are of lesser importance because the organization was not formed to make a profit.

Primary income statement terms include sales, cost of sales, selling expenses, general and administrative expenses, and income taxes.

Primary statement of support, revenues, and expense terms includes contributions, investment income, salaries and wages (not-for-profit organizations are generally personal service rather than capital intensive), and fund-raising expenses.

Changes in Financial Position

A statement of changes in financial position is presented in a format that stresses the results of operations (profits), the funds generated from those profitable operations, and where those generated funds were used in the conduct of the business.

The statement of support, revenues, and expenses, and the statement of changes in fund balances provide information as to what funds have been received, how the use of those funds has been restricted by the donor, and how those funds have actually been used.

Changes in Ownership Interest

A statement of stockholders' equity documents additional investments by owners as well as payments to owners, usually in the form of dividends.

A statement of changes in fund balances, when coupled with the portions of a statement of revenues, support, and expenses related to restricted funds, presents additional donations and other forms of support restricted by the donors as well as transfers between funds. Such transfers take place as certain restricted funds are used. There are no payments or distributions to owners.

Financial Reporting

Financial reports issued by business enterprises generally contain four primary financial statements:

Balance sheet—a statement which provides a snapshot of the financial position of an enterprise at a point in time. The financial position consists of the assets owned, liabilities owed, and the net ownership interest in the organization. It is important to note that the balance sheet is set down at a particular point in time; in theory, each transaction that an entity enters into could change the balance sheet.

Income statement—a statement which shows the accumulation of operating transactions during a particular period and the net results of the business activities entered into for a profit during that period.

Statement of changes in financial position—a statement which shows the sources of an entity's funds and the uses of those funds. Like the income statement, this statement represents the accumulation of a series of individual transactions over a period of time.

Statement of stockholders' equity—a statement which reconciles the ownership interests at the beginning of a period to the ownership interests at the end of a period.

Financial reporting by the not-for-profit organization has a counterpart to each of these statements. However, they are different in detail and format due to the difference in objectives and sources of financing of the underlying entities. The not-for-profit entity considered in this chapter is a voluntary health and welfare organization (a tax-exempt organization formed for the purpose of performing voluntary services for various segments of society, supported by the public and operated on a not-for-profit basis). Exhibit I contrasts the primary financial statements of a typical manufacturing (profit-motivated) concern with those of a voluntary health and welfare organization, a typical not-for-profit organization.

Summary

As Exhibit I demonstrates, there are many similarities between the financial statements presented by a business enterprise and those presented by a not-for-profit organization. They both present financial position, results of operations, and changes in financial position. Then to insure the achievement of an articulated set of financial statements, business enterprises present a statement of stockholders' equity and not-for-profit organizations present a statement of changes in fund balances.

The differences rest in the different underlying purposes for the existence of these entities, their different methods of operation, and different sources of capital and financing. The format used for the financial statements of a business enterprise is geared toward presenting a viable, profitable organization while the format used for the financial statements of a not-for-profit organization is geared to fulfilling the objectives of financial reporting by not-for-profit organizations as stated by the FASB.

FINANCIAL STATEMENTS OF A HYPOTHETICAL NFP

Given the overview just presented, this section of the chapter presents a more detailed review of the financial statements of a hypothetical voluntary health and welfare association. Exhibit II presents the balance sheets; Exhibit III presents the statement of support, revenue, and expenses and changes in fund balances; Exhibit IV presents the statement of functional expenses. The narrative that follows should be read in conjunction with these exhibits.

Balance Sheet

A balance sheet of a voluntary health and welfare association in a format recommended by the AICPA Audit Guide, *Audits of Voluntary Health and Welfare Organizations* (the Guide), is shown in Exhibit II. The development of the Guide and its inherent authority are discussed at the end of this chapter. These balance sheets are snapshots of the resources of the association as of a point in time, and have been prepared on a fund-accounting basis. This separate accountability for the various funds of a not-for-profit organization is the significant difference between the balance sheet of a business enterprise and the balance sheet of a not-for-profit entity. These balance sheets fairly present the total resources available to carry out the programs of the association, and at the same time, document the fact that the management of the association does not have complete

EXHIBIT II Voluntary Health and Welfare Association Balance Sheets (December 31, 1982 and 1981)

CURRENT FUNDS

Unrestricted

Assets	1982	1981	Liabilities and Fund Balances	1982	1981
Cash	$ 841,000	$ 636,000	Accounts payable	$ 376,000	$ 289,000
Investments	3,642,000	3,187,000	Accrued expenses	146,000	119,000
Pledges receivable	500,000	600,000			
Accrued interest	84,000	69,000	Total liabilities	522,000	408,000
Prepaid expenses	101,000	117,000			
			Fund balances:		
			Designated by the trustees for:		
			Purchases of new equipment	500,000	180,000
			Research purposes	1,800,000	1,600,000
			Undesignated	2,346,000	2,421,000
			Total fund balance	4,646,000	4,201,000
TOTAL	$5,168,000	$4,609,000	TOTAL	$5,168,000	$4,609,000

Restricted

Cash	$ 18,000	Fund balances	$ 205,000	$ 189,000
Investments	87,000			
Grants receivable	100,000			
TOTAL	$ 205,000	TOTAL	$ 205,000	$ 189,000

LAND, BUILDING, AND EQUIPMENT FUND

Cash	$ 1,000	Mortgage payable	$ 817,000	$ 846,000
Investments	64,000	Fund balances:		
Pledges receivable	26,000	Expended	697,000	522,000
Land, buildings, and equipment, at		Unexpended—restricted	91,000	59,000
cost less accumulated depreciation				
of $1,413,000 and $1,286,000	1,514,000	Total fund balance	788,000	581,000
TOTAL	$1,605,000	TOTAL	$1,605,000	$1,427,000

ENDOWMENT FUNDS

Cash	$ 6,000	Fund balance	$3,864,000	$3,118,000
Investments	3,112,000			
TOTAL	$3,864,000	TOTAL	$3,864,000	$3,118,000

EXHIBIT III Voluntary Health and Welfare Association, Statement of Support, Revenue, and Expenses and Changes in Fund Balances (Year Ended December 31, 1982 with Comparative Totals for 1981)

| | 1982 | | | | TOTAL ALL FUNDS | |
| | CURRENT FUNDS | | LAND, BUILDING, AND EQUIPMENT FUND | ENDOWMENT FUND | | |
	Unrestricted	Restricted			1982	1981
PUBLIC SUPPORT AND REVENUE:						
Public support:						
Contributions	$4,121,000	$186,000	$152,000	$ 119,000	$4,578,000	$3,621,000
Special craft sale	107,000				107,000	88,000
Bequests		4,000		500,000	504,000	
Received from national organization	3,000,000				3,000,000	3,000,000
Total public support	7,228,000	190,000	152,000	619,000	8,189,000	6,709,000
Revenue:						
Investment income	782,000	8,000	3,000		793,000	684,000
Realized gain on investment transactions	438,000			127,000	565,000	1,208,000
Total revenue	1,220,000	8,000	3,000	127,000	1,358,000	1,892,000
Total support and revenue	8,448,000	198,000	155,000	746,000	9,547,000	8,601,000
EXPENSES:						
Program services:						
Research	4,211,000	167,000	101,000		4,479,000	3,954,000
Public awareness	1,008,000	5,000	8,000		1,021,000	864,000

Professional training	651,000	5,000	12,000		668,000	761,000
Community services	218,000	5,000	4,000		227,000	487,000
Total program services	6,088,000	182,000	125,000		6,395,000	6,066,000
Supporting services:						
Management and general	1,250,000		65,000		1,315,000	1,201,000
Fund raising	421,000		2,000		423,000	386,000
Total supporting services	1,671,000		67,000		1,738,000	1,587,000
Total expenses	7,759,000	182,000	192,000		8,133,000	7,653,000
EXCESS (DEFICIENCY) OF PUBLIC SUPPORT AND REVENUE OVER EXPENSES	689,000	16,000	(37,000)	746,000	$1,414,000	$ 948,000
OTHER CHANGES IN FUND BALANCES: Property and equipment acquisitions from unrestricted funds	(244,000)		244,000			
FUND BALANCES, BEGINNING OF YEAR	4,201,000	189,000	581,000	3,118,000		
FUND BALANCES, END OF YEAR	$4,646,000	$205,000	$788,000	$3,864,000		

EXHIBIT IV Voluntary Health and Welfare Association, Statement of Functional Expenses (Year Ended December 31, 1982 with Comparative Totals for 1981)

				1982
	Program Services			
	Research	Public Awareness	Professional Training	Community Services
Salaries	$3,651,000	$ 657,000	$362,000	$117,000
Professional fees	162,000		118,000	
Supplies	87,000	41,000	7,000	62,000
Telephone and telegraph	41,000	18,000	6,000	29,000
Postage and shipping	12,000	68,000	18,000	
Rent	260,000	75,000	51,000	15,000
Meetings	104,000	12,000		
Printing and publications	61,000	142,000	94,000	
Total expenses before depreciation	4,378,000	1,013,000	656,000	223,000
Depreciation of buildings and equipment	101,000	8,000	12,000	4,000
Total expenses	$4,479,000	$1,021,000	$668,000	$227,000

discretion as to the use of these resources. Voluntary health and welfare organizations are supported by contributions from the public. However, contributors often place restrictions on how their contributions can be used. Fund accounting recognizes such restrictions by establishing a separate fund to record the sources and uses of such restricted monies. Each fund has its own separate self-balancing set of accounts.

Legal Liability

From the trustees' viewpoint, it is imperative that the restrictions placed on a gift or contribution not be violated. A violation, such as using funds restricted for the purchase of a fixed asset to fund a loss from operations, could subject the management and trustees to liability for misuse of those funds. As a result, understanding the nature of the restrictions placed on the use of monies by donors and gaining

| | Supporting Services | | | Total Expenses | |
Total	Management and General	Fund Raising	Total	1982	1981
$4,787,000	$ 711,000	$ 33,000	$ 744,000	$5,531,000	$5,381,000
280,000	200,000	25,000	225,000	505,000	456,000
197,000	14,000	121,000	135,000	332,000	321,000
94,000	101,000	57,000	158,000	252,000	312,000
98,000	42,000	101,000	143,000	241,000	201,000
401,000	187,000		187,000	588,000	452,000
116,000	48,000		48,000	164,000	101,000
297,000	12,000	84,000	96,000	393,000	309,000
6,270,000	1,315,000	421,000	1,736,000	8,006,000	7,533,000
125,000		2,000	2,000	127,000	120,000
$6,395,000	$1,315,000	$423,000	$1,738,000	$8,133,000	$7,653,000

assurances that restricted monies are being used only for their restricted purposes is an important responsibility of management and each trustee. The balance sheets in this fund-accounting format will assist trustees in ascertaining compliance with donor restrictions.

The most common categories of funds are shown in the balance sheet in Exhibit II. *Unrestricted funds* are just that, resources of the association that are not restricted and may be used for any purpose deemed appropriate to carry on the operations of the association. *Current restricted funds* are funds restricted by donors or grantors for use for a specific purpose that would otherwise be considered part of operations. An example of such a fund would be a gift made to a research organization restricted for the payment of a researcher's salary. Generally, payment of a researcher's salary in a research organization would be part of normal operations. However, since the donor has so restricted the use of the gift, it is incumbent on the organization to make sure those funds are used for that purpose.

Land, building, and equipment funds accumulate an entity's net investment in fixed assets. In addition, accountability for gifts or grants restricted by the donor or grantor for expenditures for additional fixed assets is maintained in that fund.

Endowment funds represent the principal of gifts or bequests, where the donor has stated that income earned on the principal may be spent (perhaps for a specific purpose or perhaps for general operations) but that the principal must remain intact for a set period of time or permanently. In some cases, the income available to the association may include gains from sale of investments; in other cases, such gains may be returned to the principal of the fund that is not available for current use. If the endowment is a permanent endowment and the purpose for which the endowment was established becomes irrelevant to the operations of the association, it is possible, through court action, to have the wishes of the original donor changed to meet a more current need. Trustees must be sure that such a change is court approved; any other use contrary to the wishes of the donor could subject trustees and management to criticism for misuse of funds.

Note that the balance sheets in Exhibit II do not present a number labeled "total assets." Exhibit II shows that the Voluntary Health and Welfare Association has $10,842,000 in total assets; yet, because of the restrictions placed on the use or availability of many of those assets, the number representing the total is not presented. The omission of this number avoids any implication that all of the assets shown in the balance sheet are equally available to the association.

On the other hand, some users of financial information may find it a meaningful disclosure to know that the association has $10 million in assets available to accomplish its overall purpose. As a result, in some instances you will see a total and in others it will be omitted, depending on the nature of the document in which such financial information is included, and the perceived needs of the users of this document. If a total is given it must be understood that there may have been restrictions placed on some of those assets and that they are not all equally available for use at the discretion of the management of the organization.

The balance sheets presented in Exhibit II have been prepared to conform with the recommendations of the Guide. As discussed in the final section of this chapter, there are other accounting pronouncements relating to other types of not-for-profit organizations. The balance sheets proposed by other authoritative accounting pronouncements may not be as detailed as those shown in Exhibit II. For example, not-for-profit organizations covered by AICPA Statement of Position 78–10, *Accounting Principles and Reporting Practices for Certain Non-Profit Organizations* (SOP 78–10) are sometimes not supported by gifts that are restricted; as a result, there is no need for the separate fund accountability for donor-restricted funds. Therefore, the balance sheet for the self-supporting not-for-profit entity covered by SOP 78–10 (that is, able to support itself through normal operations) is surprisingly similar to the balance sheet of a business enterprise. Generally, assets and liabilities are divided between current and noncurrent because the ability of the entity to continue may well depend on its liquidity and ability to meet obligations as they become due. Such an organization cannot look to the public for more support. As a not-for-profit organization becomes more like a business enterprise, the financial statements more closely resemble those of a profit-oriented entity. The difference, of course, is in the equity section of the balance sheet; stockholders' equity is still replaced by fund balance.

Statements of Operations and Changes in Financial Position

Various formats are prescribed in the not-for-profit area for a statement comparable to the income statement in the financial reports of business enterprises. Generally, for a not-for-profit entity to call such a statement an income statement would be misleading because not-for-profit organizations *are not in existence to make income*. As a result, the name and format of a comparable statement for not-for-profit organizations varies with the nature and purpose of the organization.

For voluntary health and welfare organizations, two statements are used to fill this gap. The first is called the Statement of Support, Revenues and Expenses, and Changes in Fund Balances, and the second is called the Statement of Functional Expenses. As with the balance sheet, the statement of support, revenues and expenses, and changes in fund balances differentiates between activities with restricted funds and activities with unrestricted funds. Exhibit III presents a Statement of Support, Revenues and Expenses, and Changes in Fund Balances for the Voluntary Health and Welfare Association. That statement is divided into the same fund classifications as the balance sheet, making it easy to see what was done with restricted funds and to provide the reader with information useful in ascertaining that the association is fulfilling the mandate of using restricted funds for restricted purposes.

In fact, this statement actually takes the place of three statements issued by a business enterprise. The income statement of a business enterprise is comparable to the unrestricted column of the statement of support, revenues and expenses, and changes in fund balance down to the caption labeled as the excess of support and revenues over expenses. The information generally presented on the statement of changes in financial position of a business enterprise is also included in this statement, and the statement of stockholders' equity is encompassed in the sections of the statement that disclose restricted fund activity and changes in fund balances.

A reading of Exhibit III will highlight the following facts concerning the operations of Voluntary Health and Welfare Association. In total, during 1982 the association received $1,414,000 more than it spent. (The term *received* is used in its accrual accounting sense, meaning total cash actually received, plus amounts that were receivable at year end, minus amounts included in receipts that were recorded as receivables as of the beginning of the year. A similar meaning applies to *spent*.) However, of that amount, $746,000 is not available to the association because it represents the addition to the endowment fund during the year; additionally, of that amount, $127,000 represents gains realized on certain investment transactions. Such an amount in the endowment funds column indicates that certain endowment funds contain restrictions on the use of gains on securities transactions that differ from restrictions associated with income earned on investments (that is, gains on the sale of the securities must be returned to the principal of the endowment fund).

With respect to continuing unrestricted operations, this statement shows that the association took in $689,000 more than was required for expenses. Included in income was $782,000 of investment income. This amount relates to the investments of the association classified on the balance sheet as either assets of unrestricted funds or endowment funds. With respect to other revenues, the unrestricted column indicates that $4,121,000 came from contributions, $3 million from a national affiliated organization, and $107,000 from a special event, a craft sale. These monies, when combined with the investment income, total $8,448,000.

That public support and revenue was spent primarily on program services, that is, on programs related to the underlying purpose for the existence of this not-for-profit organization. These programs were divided into four categories: research programs, public awareness programs, professional training programs, and community service programs. The amount shown as costs for these four program services includes their direct costs, as well as the allocation of an appropriate amount of certain costs common to all programs. The allocation of costs becomes very important to certain not-for-profit organizations which receive grants to support their activities, where the grant provides for reimbursement of costs incurred or reimbursement of actual overhead. Management has some discretion regarding the methods used to allocate common costs to specific programs. Generally, however, any method used should represent management's best estimate of the costs incurred that are justifiably related to the program to which such costs are allocated.

In addition to the expenditures on program services, $1,671,000 was spent on supporting services, that is, those expenses which the organization must incur in order to be able to provide the program services. Generally, such supporting services relate to the two categories shown in Exhibit III, management and general expenses, and fund-raising expenses.

In addition to the unrestricted activities, Exhibit III also shows that the organization received $186,000 from contributions and $4,000 as a bequest that was restricted for specific operating purposes. These amounts were added to the fund balance entitled "restricted current funds"; during the year, $182,000 was spent from these restricted funds on items that normally would have been included as operating expenses of the programs supported. Since these amounts were provided by donations that were restricted, the expenditures are shown under the restricted column.

This statement also has a column for activity in the land, building, and equipment fund. During 1982, Voluntary Health and Welfare Association received $152,000 in contributions and $3,000 from investment income associated with the investments classified with the land, building, and equipment fund on the balance sheet. The expenses of the land, building, and equipment fund are primarily depreciation on the building and equipment, and the interest related to the mortgage payable associated with the land and building. As discussed earlier, these expenses are appropriately allocated to either a program service or a supporting service and shown as expenses in the land, building, and equipment column.

The activity summarized at the bottom of Exhibit III documents the other changes that took place in fund balances which did not result from receipts and disbursements. The most common type of activity shown in this section is a transfer between funds. In this case, the management of Voluntary Health and Welfare Association has decided to use some unrestricted funds for the purchase of property and equipment. As a result, in Exhibit III we see listed a transfer of $244,000 from the unrestricted fund balance to the land, building, and equipment fund balance, indicating that unrestricted funds were utilized for the purchase of fixed assets.

Exhibit IV presents the Statement of Functional Expenses for Voluntary Health and Welfare Association. It is to be used to analyze expenditures. For instance, this statement shows that of the total of $8,133,000 in expenses for 1982, $5,531,000 was spent on salaries. Of the $5,531,000 spent on salaries, $4,787,000, or 86 percent, was spent on programs for which the association is in existence, and only 14 percent was spent on either fund raising or administrative activities. As can be seen, Exhibit IV presents a wealth of information that can be useful to the trustee or reader of the financial statements in analyzing whether the association is spending its monies on its priorities. Additionally, this statement provides a way to compare total expenses by function with the prior year's expenses by function. In this case we can see that salaries increased by only $150,000, or 2.7 percent. Such an increase may be the result of a combination of a reduction in the work force and an increase in the salaries of those remaining. Such information may be useful to the trustee in evaluating the direction taken by the association in response to trustee decisions, or to evaluate the overall effectiveness of management.

It should be noted that the statement of functional expenses is not prepared in a fund-accounting format; rather it is prepared on an overall basis that permits the analysis of all costs incurred by the association for a particular program or service, even if such expenses were appropriately paid for from restricted funds.

In contrast to these statements recommended by the Guide, SOP 78-10 presents a variety of formats that may be used by the other types of not-for-profit organizations to present results of operations and changes in financial position. The choice of format depends on the entity's purpose and how it is organized and financed. The closer the entity is to a business-type entity, the closer the financial statements will be to those prepared by a business enterprise. Conversely, the closer the entity is to a voluntary health and welfare organization, the closer the statements recommended by SOP 78–10 will be to those prescribed by the Guide.

In all cases, the format of the financial statements and the information presented in those financial statements are meant to meet the objectives of financial reporting by not-for-profit organizations as stated by the Financial Accounting Standards Board in Concept Statement No. 4.

CONCLUSION

After reading this chapter and going through the material contained herein, readers of financial statements of not-for-profit organizations should have a better understanding of why the financial statements of the not-for-profit organization are somewhat different from the financial statements of a business enterprise. These differences relate primarily to the restrictions placed on certain funds available to a not-for-profit entity and to the differing purposes for which a not-for-profit entity is in existence. Not-for-profit entities are not in existence to generate income; they are in existence to provide services to the public and to respond to the needs of the public. Financial statements are meant to assist the readers of financial information and others interested in not-for-profit entities in making rational decisions about the allocation of their resources, performance of management, and service efforts and accomplishments of the organization. Financial statements are just one in a series of tools available to trustees and other interested parties in coming to conclusions on such matters.

APPENDIX: Development of Generally Accepted Accounting Principles for Not-for-Profit Organizations

In the past, the financial statements of not-for-profit organizations were difficult to interpret, in part, because of a lack of comparability in methods of financial reporting by similar organizations. The financial statements issued by the local museum were very different from the financial statements issued by the local chapter of a national fund-raising organization. However, in many instances the same people belonged to the boards of both organizations. That situation did not exist in the financial reporting by business enterprises.

Any board member examining the annual reports of two commercial enterprises would be able to make a reasonably intelligent comparison of their financial positions and results of operations because the balance sheets and income statements of the two entities were in comparable formats. The reason for this comparability is the use of a common measuring unit of performance, profit. Given that common goal, it is easy to compute such yardsticks as return on investment, return on assets, return on sales, or any number of ratios geared to present a meaningful measure of profitability. Comparing such amounts for two business enterprises is, at least, a starting place for more in-depth analyses and future action.

Underlying the comparable financial reporting for business enterprises is a body of conventions, rules, and procedures that combine to make up generally accepted accounting principles (GAAP). The evolution of GAAP for commercial enterprises has progressed at a much faster pace than for not-for-profit organizations. Financial reporting by not-for-profit organizations has evolved more through practice than by mandate. In fact, development of authoritative accounting literature applicable solely to not-for-profit organizations is a relatively recent phenomenon.

Before looking at some specific examples of authoritative accounting pronouncements for nonbusiness organizations, it is important to understand the source of this authority. *Generally accepted accounting principles* (GAAP) is a technical term which encompasses those conventions, rules, and procedures that make up accepted accounting and financial reporting practices at a particular point in time. Rule 203 of the Code of Professional Ethics of the American Institute of Certified Public Accountants (AICPA) requires that a certified public accountant (CPA) "not express an opinion that financial statements are presented in conformity with generally accepted accounting principles if such statements contain any departure from an accounting principle promulgated by the body designated by Council [of the AICPA] to establish such principles."

The impact of this ruling is that the Council of the AICPA has the authority to designate the rule-making body (bodies) whose pronouncements will be considered enforceable as generally accepted accounting principles. Since 1973, the Financial Accounting Standards Board (FASB), an independent rule-making body, has been designated by Council as the only body promulgating generally accepted accounting principles. Statements and interpretations issued by the FASB are GAAP.

In addition to the pronouncements of the FASB, the body of conventions, rules, and procedures that combine to make up GAAP include the Opinions of the Accounting Principles Board of the AICPA and the Accounting Research Bulletins issued by the Committee on Accounting Procedure of the AICPA. These organizations had the Council's designation as promulgators of GAAP before the FASB was organized.

A review of a listing of the titles of all Accounting Research Bulletins, Opinions of the Accounting Principles Board, and Statements and Interpretations of the FASB (a listing of more than 150 documents in all) reveals that most documents issued to date discuss accounting issues aimed at the measurement of amounts to be recognized in financial statements as a result of specific transactions or events. It is very important to note that there are no differences in the accounting principles governing measurement for business enterprises and those for not-for-profit organizations.

In addition to general measurement standards, a number of standards have been aimed at the reporting requirements for specific industries such as oil and gas producers, insurance companies, real estate companies, movie producers and others in the entertainment industry, and mortgage banking. No authoritative pronouncements have been issued that specifically address the financial reporting practices of not-for-profit organizations.

This lack of standards aimed specifically at the financial reporting practices of not-for-profit organizations, combined with the lack of a clear-cut objective of financial reporting for not-for-profit entities, has led to a variety of reporting practices by these organizations. Each such financial report attempts to fairly present the financial position and results of operations of an individual entity and, accordingly, each format is biased by the individual concerns, objectives, and interests of those who prepare such financial reports, usually the management of the not-for-profit organization.

During the 1970s, in an attempt to bring some harmony to financial reporting by not-for-profit organizations, a new series of documents was issued by the Accounting Standards Executive Committee (AcSEC) of the AICPA. While these documents were not issued by the body sanctioned by the Council, they do present the conclusions of at least a majority of the members of the senior technical body of the AICPA authorized to speak for the institute in the areas of financial accounting and reporting. As such, these documents have been very influential in the development of more uniform reporting by not-for-profit organizations. In fact, these documents have now been sanctioned as representing "preferable" accounting methods by the FASB for purposes of justifying a change in accounting. This means that once an entity adopts the accounting and reporting requirements of one of these pronouncements, it cannot change to a different method of accounting because such a change would be from an accounting principle or reporting practice deemed preferable to one that then must be less preferable.

The documents issued by AcSEC in this series that directly relate to not-for-profit organizations include the following:

Audit Guides:
    Hospital Audit Guide (1972)
    Audits of Voluntary Health and Welfare Organizations (1974)
Statements of Position (SOPs):
    SOP 74–8—Financial Accounting and Reporting by Colleges and Universities (1974)
    SOP 78–1—Accounting by Hospitals for Certain Marketable Equity Securities (1978)

SOP 78-7 —Financial Accounting and Reporting by Hospitals Operated by a Governmental Unit (1978)

SOP 78-10—Accounting Principles and Reporting Practices for Certain Non-Profit Organizations (1978)

Currently, the FASB is working on a project that will eventually result in one or more FASB statements on financial accounting and reporting by not-for-profit organizations. As a basis for such statements, the FASB has issued Statement of Financial Accounting Concepts No. 4, *Objectives of Financial Reporting by Nonbusiness Organizations*. A statement of financial accounting concepts is intended to set forth objectives and fundamentals that will be the basis for future accounting standards, but statements of financial accounting concepts alone do not establish generally accepted accounting principles.

8

Focusing the Board on the Needs of Volunteers

Judy Rauner

The members of the board of a nonprofit organization are them-selves volunteers who reach and influence all other volunteers, down to the last person who just stopped in the door and asked: "Is there anything I can do to help?"

The need for volunteer workers in America is enormous. More and more projects are being initiated, and the projects are becoming larger and more complex. People in greater numbers are offering their services, to a level at which over a third of all adults and teenagers in the United States are volunteers. All of this must be organized and directed, which is the ultimate responsibility of governing boards of trustees. Increasingly, board members are required to learn and apply the skills and methods of business organizations. However complex their role may be as board members, they must remain aware of the grass-roots volunteer.

Few people would argue about the total value of the work done by volunteers. Their work can be seen everywhere: in schools, churches and synagogues, hospitals; among the young and the old; at cultural events and civic projects. They are visible and they work quietly behind the scenes. A close look at any organization will identify volunteers in every type of work: policy-making, management, direct service, fund raising, and support. The volunteer board has the final responsibility for both charting the direction and ultimate survival of the organization. As noted, some management or administrative roles are filled by volunteers who are responsible or share the responsibil-ity for planning, organizing, staffing, directing, and controlling the program activities. Direct service volunteers meet the needs of the clients or members of the organization. Volunteers actively raise funds through a variety of methods. Still other volunteers help keep the organization functioning by such support activities as office work and maintenance.

In many NFPs, especially the larger ones, there will be a paid staff of regular employees who work as managers, provide direct service, raise funds, and fulfill the support function of the organization. The paid staff may have the primary responsibility for meeting the goals of the organization or they may be responsible for giving support to the volunteers. How much is done by the paid staff and how much by the volunteers depends upon the size of the paid staff, the magnitude and complexity of the programs, and the organization's own desires.

It is apparent that there could be conflicts between a full-time paid staff person and a part-time unpaid volunteer since either, depending on the circumstances, could do at least some of the work of the other. As programs expand, the need for personnel expands. In the current economy, nonprofit organizations often cannot easily add paid staff; and the need for volunteers continues to grow. It is one of the important functions of the board to establish policies that clarify roles and responsibilities of the paid staff and the volunteers.

The board has a far larger concern for the volunteer than just fitting him or her into the organization. The volunteer can be the very basis of the organization. Many nonprofit organizations not only need volunteers, but could not exist without them. If they are to fill their many diverse roles, they must be supported and their needs as individuals must be met in a way that keeps them in the organization, keeps them involved. John, a retired executive seeking community activity and some variety in his life, isn't going to stay involved if asked to stuff envelopes by himself. Beth is a college student who wants to explore her interest in psychology as a possible career direction. Her volunteer commitment at a juvenile residential treatment and referral center would not meet her needs or the needs of the agency if she didn't receive training and support.

THE BOARD MUST LEAD THE WAY

Just how effective the board is in meeting volunteer needs depends upon its awareness of how volunteers give their time, what they

FIGURE 8.1 Use of Volunteers in Management

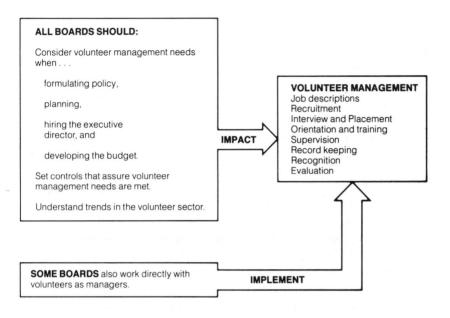

receive from the organization, and how their involvement is influenced by trends in the United States today. The board formulates policy and makes plans that affect volunteers, hires the executive director who should be responsive to volunteer needs, and passes a budget that includes adequate funding for volunteer support. Some boards also actively implement the organization plans. This means directly working with other volunteers as supervisors or managers. A board member might chair a fund-raising campaign and supervise other volunteers who contact businesses and corporations for major gifts. A long-range planning committee might include several organization members who aren't on the board. The board member who chairs the committee assumes a management role.

Figure 8.1 presents a summary of the board's responsibility to volunteers. All of these points will be discussed in the following sections.

Policy decisions set the tone of the organization's commitment, or lack of commitment, to volunteers. No matter how many volunteers are active in the organization, the board should ask whether volunteer involvement is planned and implemented according to policies made by the board. Although the board is ultimately responsible for making policy, it doesn't work in a vacuum. Often the executive director identifies situations that warrant board policy and brings the information to the board for its action. Part of the policy-making process is to assemble materials needed for informed decision-making. The limits and scope of the policy must be defined and input gathered from staff, clients, and members. All written policies should be current and reflect the purpose of the organization and the intention of the board.

The board must be involved in formulating long-term plans for the total organization, generally for periods as long as three to five years. Implicit in strategic management is the board's responsibility to see that the organization's personnel energy and funds will accomplish the organization's purpose. Other short-term planning is done by those paid staff and volunteers working directly with a specific department or program. The effective management of volunteers in an organization isn't likely to happen without this specific planning. The board may or may not plan the overall volunteer management directly, but would establish personnel and funding precedent in long-range plans and budgets. A review of volunteer management plans is a board responsibility. People from all groups who will be affected by the volunteer management plan and who will be implementing it should be given an opportunity to be involved in assessing needs, actual planning, or reviewing the plan. When people share their ideas and actually participate in the NFP planning process, they also share ownership and enthusiasm for the final plan. The following table shows how people in an organization might contribute to a planning process for volunteer involvement.

	Needs assessment	Planning	Review of plan
Board			X
Administration/management	X	X	X
Supervisors	X	X	X
Volunteers	X	X	X
Members/clients	X		

The board works directly with the executive director who is then the administrator for the rest of the staff. The executive director's approach to volunteer management influences how others in the organization interact with volunteers. There is sometimes staff resistance to having volunteers, partly because of fear that volunteers might replace paid staff. In "Community Service Center for the Disabled" (see case study in Appendix), a staff member stated another common block to effective volunteer management when she expressed a desire to "keep the volunteer program informal . . . not too much like a business." The executive is responsible for providing management education for volunteer staff.

The budget approved by the board must determine how much funding is available for volunteer management. Depending upon the size of the staff and number of volunteers, there may be a position specifically designated as "coordinator of volunteers." Even if there aren't many volunteers, some paid staff members will spend part of their time with volunteer management. Other costs that are generated by the volunteer program may include: office space for the person or persons responsible for management of the volunteer program, personal amenities (small but important items include places provided for volunteers to secure their belongings and have coffee), cost of training the volunteers and the staff working with them, and other office operating expenses. The printing and mailing of recruitment brochures, newsletters, and other information pieces are expenses that can be expected. Recognition of volunteers takes many forms: for example, an end-of-the-year or holiday event, a letter of recognition that acknowledges specific accomplishments, participation in community-wide recognition events. (See chapter on Rewards and Punishment for a detailed review.) All of these volunteer management budget items are an investment in people, the unpaid personnel.

The board can very conscientiously make policy and plan for volunteer management in the organization. Controls must be established by the board to insure that volunteer needs are met. The person or persons who manage the volunteer involvement will be accountable (whether volunteer or staff themselves) to the executive director. In turn, the executive director should report to the board, quarterly or at some regular interval, specific records on:

1. the number of volunteers
2. the number of hours given by volunteers

3. the length of commitment made by volunteers
4. the number of staff in relation to the number of volunteers
5. the qualitative and quantitative effect of volunteer involvement, such as the numbers served, changes influenced, etc.

Media coverage and in-house publications that provide information about volunteers should be sent to the board members. The board must know what communication lines are available to volunteers. Is the volunteer coordinator or supervisor accessible to the volunteer when the volunteer has a concern or needs information? Do volunteers who assume leadership roles have adequate support? Is an exit interview held when a volunteer leaves a position and are records kept of why the volunteer left? Finally, what communication is established between the board and the organization volunteers? One way to open communication and gather information about volunteer attitudes and knowledge is to ask, through a questionnaire or through interviews. For example:

Volunteers! Do you know:

Who our board members are?
What responsibility the board has?
How the board relates to the staff?
How to communicate with board members?

Please give your suggestions on how the board might be in contact with volunteers in our organization and how the board might respond to volunteers' needs.

Trends that Affect Volunteer Involvements

Volunteering today is receiving increasing support from public and private leaders, but it can't be taken for granted. Some general trends in the United States exist that affect volunteers and their organizations. The board must be aware of these trends and respond to them, if volunteers are to be effectively recruited and retained.

Trends	Effects
1. More volunteers from diverse backgrounds	Wider variety of volunteer needs to meet
2. Competition for volunteers	Organizations must market need for volunteers and be continually responsive to volunteers
3. Government funding decreases	More competition for funding sought by nonprofits, from other sources, including local government, foundations, etc., along with traditional private sources
4. Business involvement expanding	Creative response to some of society's needs
5. Effective management expected by volunteers	More visible and accepted need for professional management skills
6. High visibility of volunteers in media	Effect on volunteer recruitment can be positive or negative

Trend 1: More Volunteers

There are more volunteers today from professional and nonprofessional backgrounds, from all age and ethnic groups. A common trait of these diversified people is that they are conscious of their rights and how they want their talents to be utilized.

In a 1981 Gallup study commissioned by the "Independent Sector," a national coalition of over 350 voluntary organizations, private foundations, and corporations states that 52 percent of American adults and 53 percent of teenagers volunteered between March 1980 and March 1981. People have more discretionary time available. Employers are encouraging their employees to donate volunteer services (see Trend 4). People are retiring earlier and living longer, so retirees have more time to give. Young people see volunteer work as career exploration, work experience, and a positive way to express their idealism. Groups seeking change organize volunteer projects in sections of the population where formalized volunteering isn't a tradition, such as action groups in low-income neighborhoods.

Volunteers have two different sets of expectations, those influencing their decision to begin commitment and those involving a decision to continue. A belief in the purpose or mission of the organization influenced 45 percent of the volunteers, according to the 1981 Gallup study. Today's volunteers also expect personal needs to be met:

> career exploration
> work experience
> class credit
> outlet for creativity and talents
> leadership opportunity
> recognition
> socialization
> personal growth

It is important to distinguish between a person's ability to do something and his or her willingness to do it. Some volunteers may prefer to be placed in a position that doesn't utilize their professional expertise or skill. An accountant may want a change from work with numbers and choose a volunteer position that provides a chance to relate informally to a young person through a Big Brother or Big Sister program. A teacher may prefer a break from students and enjoy working with other adults on a fund-raising event. (A harsh reality is also the reverse—the aspiring volunteer who is not capable of handling a responsibility he or she seeks.)

With more volunteers being involved and consequently more volunteer needs to meet, the board must establish ways to see that volunteers understand what they want to receive from their experience, and organization personnel are responsive to those needs. Effective communication among board, paid personnel, and volunteers is imperative. The board needs to know:

1. that a volunteer coordinator or supervisor is accessible when a volunteer needs information or has a concern;
2. that volunteers who assume leadership roles receive training and support so that they are prepared to meet volunteer needs;
3. that an exit interview is held when volunteers leave their position or change positions and that records are kept of why they leave; and

4. that appropriate communication is established between the board and the organization's volunteers.

Trend 2: Competition for Volunteers

Volunteer needs are diverse and so are the opportunities for having an interesting volunteer experience. The competition for volunteers exists because organizations and agencies who traditionally have used volunteers are expanding the ways in which people are involved. Until the early 1970s, volunteers in schools primarily helped with special projects and were seldom seen in the classroom. Now a majority of classrooms have volunteers who tutor students or work with small groups under the teacher's supervision.

Organizations who in the past did not traditionally use volunteers are recognizing the benefits of volunteer service and competing for those people willing to donate their time. All levels of government have formal volunteer programs that include advisory board membership, student internships, and community service opportunities. Former Governor Robert Ray of Iowa received national recognition for initiating the state's innovative "Community Betterment Program" which involved 460 concurrent projects with an impact equivalent estimated to be $175 million. Program staff assisted community groups to assess their community needs, plan and implement such things as park improvement, refurbishing a public building, and other projects that improved community image and services.

New groups have emerged that provide volunteer opportunities and add to the competition for volunteers. Self-help groups, for example, must have someone who assumes leadership. Those who share a medical problem gather together for mutual support, such as "Make Today Count," for those with life-threatening illnesses. Arrangements have to be made for a meeting place, newsletters have to be edited and mailed; all this is done by volunteers.

These examples of organizations that expand use of volunteers or are using volunteers for the first time, plus new programs that are volunteer-based have an underlying mutual concern. The current economy influences the fact that funds are limited and the need for services expanded. Volunteers are part of the answer to the question, "How can we meet our organization goals?" Since there is competition for volunteers, it's logical that a marketing plan be developed to attract volunteers.

People who are connected to the organization, including the board of trustees, must stay informed about current volunteer involvement. The director of volunteers, or a person designated as responsible for overall volunteer management, keeps records that show what volunteers are needed, where volunteers are currently working, and how volunteers are brought into the organization. These records provide valuable data for determining who potential volunteers are and what might attract them.

A marketing effort can involve recruitment by all the people in the organization. The most effective marketing is often done by satisfied volunteers and others in the organization who are excited about the volunteer activity.

Remember that a dissatisfied volunteer negatively affects the efforts to market the organization's need for volunteers. When people decide to volunteer, they don't want their time underutilized. If a volunteer feels time is wasted or if other time pressures make volunteering less important in his or her order of priorities, a person may decide to terminate volunteering. Some turnover is to be expected. When a volunteer completes the time commitment he or she agreed upon, it's not an issue of "quitting."

To investigate whether volunteer turnover is positive or negative, check:

Number of individuals who complete the agreed upon volunteer commitment	____	(positive)
Number who make an additional commitment in the same position in a different position	____ ____	(positive)
Number who don't complete commitment	____	(possible
Number of these who were dissatisfied	____	negative)

It also may be helpful to determine:

Average length of time commitment asked of volunteers	____
Average length of time served	____

(If less time is served than originally asked, are the time commitments too long? Do volunteers leave because they are dissatisfied?)

*Trend 3: Government Funding Decreases and Legislation Impacts
Nonprofit Organizations*

Many new organizations have been heavily subsidized by government funding during the past two decades. Current cutbacks in government budgets affect many of the human service organizations and public agencies. Private foundations typically report 25 percent to 50 percent increases in requests for funds. Seventy percent of such organizations asking for help had in the past received federal funds. An Urban Institute study estimated that between 1981 and 1984, federal budget cuts to volunteer organizations and in areas where philanthropic organizations generally participate will have totaled over $125 billion.

Government legislation also has an impact on volunteers with tax benefit guidelines such as gas mileage allowances and contribution deductions. Listed below are some tax deductions. Recently proposed volunteer benefit legislation includes a deduction for dependent care and a tax credit for volunteer service. Whether these changes occur or other legislation is passed, the board should stay alert to and notify staff and volunteers of any available tax advantages.

Legislation affecting volunteers:

Tax-deductible	*Nondeductible*
Donations—money or property	Volunteer time or service
Out-of-pocket costs incurred while volunteering (postage, telephone costs, transportation—9¢ a mile)	Dependent care expenses
	Meals—unless away overnight
Reasonable meals and lodging when away from home	
Special uniforms	

Trend 4: Business Involvement Expanding

Businesses continue to become more actively involved in community programs. In addition to financial help, they are urging their employees to become volunteers. In the 1982 report of the "President's Task Force of Private Sector Initiatives," it was recommended that business double both its cash contributions and commitment to volunteer programs before 1986. Many companies, however, either reply that it should not be expected that they make up the loss of government funds or that their ultimate after-tax profits suffer from such volunteer support.

Historically, corporate involvement in direct volunteer activity began after corporate funding programs became common. In the early 1950s some corporate foundations were established to give contributions. Corporate philosophy emerged stating that companies benefit from communities and thus have a responsibility to give back to the community. Now many companies establish foundations and involve employees in the decisions about who will receive funds. Hundreds of larger corporations have a matching gifts policy, in which any donation made by an employee is matched by the company.

An example of creative public/private sector partnership is the Adopt-A-School program. The CEO of a business meets with a school principal to discuss the school's needs; then a planning process is initiated that fits the school's needs and the resources the business can offer. This can involve on-the-job training where employees work in a one-to-one relationship with a student trainee. In communities that have high unemployment this project offers students job experience and preparation for the workforce. Another Adopt-A-School partnership involved a high school and a computer company, in which both computers and personnel time for training students were donated.

The Levi Strauss Community Involvement Teams (CIT) are examples of active employee participation in the communities where they live. Employees throughout the company, sewing machine operators to accountants, are encouraged to improve the quality of the community's life. First, the CIT identifies community needs and formulates a plan to meet a specific need. Through the Community Affairs Department, a planning and implementation team is established for the specific project. This team recruits volunteers, raises funds from the employees and the community, and supervises the project. One ambitious project was a two-year renovation of an agency center, with work crews doing the remodeling.

Businesses also donate equipment, postage, and technology. Contributed management expertise is offered to nonprofit organizations through "loaned executive" programs. Xerox Corporation has, for example, given as much as one year's time to executives choosing to work in a recognized nonprofit organization.

Employees and the businesses benefit from their volunteer involvement. The business usually receives positive public relations benefits and may benefit in terms of potential customers, potential employees, and tax benefits. The employees who volunteer can experience great personal enrichment, add new skills, and gain autonomy through job expansion that the paid position doesn't always offer.

Trend 5: Effective Management Expected by Volunteers

There is a growing expectation today that volunteer-based programs be effectively managed. People can quickly learn which organizations are well managed, often through satisfied volunteers. It takes time and energy to meet volunteer needs.

The management of volunteer programs is a growing professional field; and many organizations now hire staff specifically for this role. A paid staff member is in a strong position to represent volunteer needs to other paid personnel and to the general community, because he or she is more likely to understand the volunteer involvement in relation to the total organization operation. When a volunteer fills the primary volunteer management role, however, there may not be continuity when that person leaves. Also, a volunteer isn't likely to be available as consistently as is a paid staff person.

National and local organizations support professional volunteer management through training events, advocacy, resource information, and development of special community awareness projects. For over 20 years the Association for Volunteer Administration has promoted the profession, providing for the education and development of members. Local chapters of DOVIA, Directors of Volunteers in Agencies, also offer information exchange and growth opportunities for volunteer coordinators or directors. Community colleges, university departments of continuing education, and privately sponsored seminars provide additional opportunities for management training. Many communities have Volunteer Bureaus/Voluntary Action Centers that offer information and referral, training, and consultation services to the nonprofit organizations in their community.

Other national level resources that offer technical assistance include the Independent Sector, the National Committee for Responsive Philanthropy, and The National Executive Service Corps. Volunteer: The National Center for Citizen Involvement is a national organization dedicated to stimulating and strengthening voluntary action and volunteer involvement.

Trend 6: High Visibility of Volunteer in the Media

Volunteer activities make the news. Human interest stories highlight individual volunteers and innovative programs. However, the media don't hesitate to report controversy either (see the Episcopal Community Services case).

The board must see that public relations efforts are ongoing, and that volunteer involvement is included in the information published within the organization and the community media. There should be strategic and marketing planning that assesses what public relations efforts are currently underway and their effects. A plan developed for future image-building can often be based on what the organization wants to accomplish with volunteer involvement.

Media coverage also makes it possible for board members to stay aware of what is happening in nonprofit organizations locally and nationally.

Are these societal trends identifiable in your community?

____ More volunteers from diverse backgrounds

____ Competition for volunteers

____ Decreased government funding

____ Expanding community involvement by private sector

____ Expectation of well-managed volunteer program

____ High visibility in the media

VOLUNTEER MANAGEMENT— PLANNING FOR EFFECTIVENESS

The board's responsibility for a volunteer management plan and its implementation begins with an assessment of what is currently happening. A written survey or informal interviews covering all the management components will help determine: 1) what's working well, 2) what needs to be initiated or improved, and 3) what is not needed at this time or is not as important as other management action steps.

It is important to plan management programs that can realistically be implemented by the staff (paid and volunteer) and within the budget that is available. A valueing component can be added to the survey to determine what areas of management that currently are not being accomplished are most important for the volunteers. The greatest visible change is made by accomplishing these first.

The following survey can be used one of two ways. The initial question could be answered by most paid staff and volunteers invited to give their input. The quantitative questions following that initial question may not be information that those completing the survey have. The amount of input that can be gathered may be expanded by using both the complete and the abbreviated survey.

Volunteer Management Survey

1. Is there a planning process for volunteer management?
    Are board members, paid staff, volunteers, and members/clients asked to participate in needs assessment and planning (number asked to participate, number who participate)?
    Does the volunteer management program have a specific budget (amounts requested and allocated for current and projected years)? If not, do other budget line items cover this?
2. Do job descriptions reflect what is needed by volunteer involvement?
    Do all positions have written job descriptions that are developed with input from those supervising and filling the position?
    Are all job descriptions reviewed annually and updated if needed? (Who is responsible for update? Date reported and to whom?)
3. Are there the needed numbers and types of volunteers recruited?
    What is the cost of recruitment effort (brochures printed, staff time for development, etc.)?
    How many volunteers were recruited and by what methods? (Tabulate recruitment cost per volunteer; determine which recruitment efforts are most cost effective.)
4. Are orientations held for volunteers and staff where adequate initial information is presented?
    How many new volunteers attend orientation and how many do not?
    After the evaluation of orientation sessions is reviewed, what percentages found the orientation helpful/not helpful?

5. Are volunteers placed in positions that meet their needs and the needs of the program?

Of the ____ volunteer placements requested, ____ were filled and ____ were not filled.

What percentage of volunteers completed their initial time commitment?

6. Is preservice and inservice training received by the volunteers?

How often is training offered and what numbers attend?

From summaries of training evaluations, what percentage of those participating are satisfied, not satisfied?

7. Are the supervisors given preparation and time to supervise effectively?

What is the average amount of supervisor training time attended by staff who work with volunteers?

What percentage of staff time is allocated to supervision of volunteers?

8. Are relevant records kept and is feedback given to those involved with the volunteers?

What are the dates that records are summarized?

Which people in the organization have reports presented summarizing volunteer involvement? Who has reports available to them?

9. Is there opportunity to evaluate the volunteer involvement throughout the year?

What methods of evaluation are used and when are these methods used?

Are results of evaluations used in future planning?

10. Do the volunteers feel that what they contribute is recognized and appreciated?

What recognition activities are used and when?

What is the budget for recognition, how many volunteers are recognized, and what is the average cost of recognition?

After completing the survey: 1) review each section and determine whether the management is effective, needs to be initiated or improved; 2) of those needing to be initiated or improved, decide what you perceive as their order of priority.

Management task	Effective	Needs improvement/ initiation	Order of priority
Planning			
Job descriptions			
Recruitment			
Orientation			
Placement			
Training			
Supervision			
Recordkeeping			
Evaluation			
Recognition			

Job descriptions—Potential volunteers want information about a job before they commit their time and talents. They need to know what is expected of them before deciding whether a job is possible or of interest to them. The basic information for a complete volunteer job description includes: what the job title is; how the job is important to the program goals; what the benefits, requirements, and time commitments are. The job description should be written in simple language.

Recruitment—An important tactic is first to plan on retaining volunteers, then recruitment. Numbers brought into an organization have little significance if there are equally large numbers leaving. Recruitment takes place as an ongoing, dynamic process, accomplished by everyone involved in the program. The reasons why volunteers are being recruited must be clear and be communicated to potential volunteers. Invitations to become involved should be issued in as many different places and ways as is practical within time and funding limitations. Both media and personal invitations can be useful.

A sample recruitment plan—marketing the organization's need for volunteers—is shown below.*

*See Marketing chapter for other suggestions of "Marketing Mix" elements.

Ongoing projects:

Brochures that tell how and why to volunteer and whom to contact	Distributed throughout the organization, libraries, schools, and colleges
Monthly update of volunteer position openings	Available to board members and current volunteers
Organization newletter— column about volunteer activities	Mailed to members, volunteers, and clients

Community media:
   Monthly "Volunteer Opportunities" column

   X articles submitted each year—human interest or "success" stories

Special projects:

Annual recognition dinner—speaker on "Volunteering Today— You Make a Difference"

Develop a slide presentation of the organization's volunteers for use with orientation and the speaker's bureau

Orientation—Any person considering a volunteer commitment deserves to know some basic things about the organization and the volunteer program through an orientation. A short, well-presented orientation can be reinforced by written information, but the personal presentation encourages two-way communication. Questions can be answered; information can be clarified. Some of the content of an orientation would include:

a. the purpose of the program and of the volunteer involvement,
b. how the program is organized,
c. who the people in the organization are and how they work together,
d. organization policies and goals,
e. volunteer expectations and benefits,

f. specific job descriptions, and

g. a tour of facilities

Interview and placement—The results of effective placement are significant. Program goals can be better met when volunteers are working in positions they desire and are capable of handling well. Volunteer satisfaction increases and problems are prevented when placement is carefully accomplished through an interview process. During an interview, information is exchanged that clarifies both volunteer expectations and program needs. Once an agreement is made on an initial placement, a trial period and understanding of how renegotiation will take place is reached. A written agreement offers an advantage in that it clarifies the terms (time, money, duties, etc.) that are understood and agreed upon.

Training—Training prepares volunteers to provide greater benefit or service and also to experience job satisfaction. Preservice training offers basic knowledge and skills needed before starting a job. These include task responsibilities and limitations, general information on how to perform tasks, and location of items required for the job. Once a person is functioning in a position, inservice training can offer opportunity for more specific understanding of tasks and how interrelationships occur. All training, behavioral or technical, should be designed to meet the ability and skill level of the volunteers. Management training for supervisors enables those people who work with volunteers to increase their supervisory skills which support the volunteers.

Supervision—Almost every volunteer needs some support and guidance from supervisors. Supervisors include project chairpersons and people who have volunteers working in their particular department, committee, or area of responsibility. The skills used in working with volunteers are the same used in supervising paid personnel: organization, communication, delegation, training, negotiation, team development, etc. Examples of these include:

a. *Organization* involves having work ready for the volunteer, being able to accomplish his or her own task, coordinating and guiding the work of others, and using time effectively.

b. *Communication skills* enable mutual understanding among coworkers, listening to verbal and nonverbal communication, and sharing of information.

c. *Delegation* is the "activating" of or achieving goals through others, and being able to share responsibility.

d. *Negotiation* involves problem solving and working toward agreement.

e. *Team development* utilizes skills in group planning and evaluation, effectively developing and maintaining work relationships. Interpersonal interaction is vitally important when working with volunteers; a dissatisfied volunteer can choose not to remain on the job.

Recordkeeping and control—Records of how volunteer involvement is managed and the effects of volunteer work performed should be integrated in a system that works. Careful consideration of what records are really necessary limits what could become time-consuming paperwork. Basic information about the volunteers and their work records prepares the organization to document the value of individual volunteers and the total volunteer program. The programs where volunteers work also need to be documented, so energy isn't wasted by people working without the benefit of others' experience. This is particularly important when volunteer turnover limits the continuity of personnel. If a volunteer has good records when starting a job, it is easier to update records. There is an incentive to look for a replacement if records are intact and an interest in continuty is promoted. Recognition of volunteers is also dependent upon having records that include hours worked, training attended, and effectiveness of performance.

Recordkeeping Overview:

Information needed	*Type of form*
Initial volunteer enrollment	
—name, address, phone	—enrollment form
—skills and interests	—placement interview report
—time available	
—job preference	
Work records	
—hours worked	—volunteer sign-in sheet
—training attended	—training record
—type of work	—placement records
—performance evaluation	—supervisor's evaluation

Effect of volunteer involvement

—numbers served	—program records
—changes influenced	—program records
—total number of hours	—sign-in sheets

Management records

- —volunteer program management plan
- —copies of public relations materials, forms
- —job descriptions
- —training content and evaluations
- —recognition records

Recognition—The reasons why a person volunteers are often linked with what recognition is meaningful to that person (see Rewards and Punishment chapter).

If a volunteer wants:	*Appropriate recognition is:*
Work experience or class credit	A letter of recommendation
Outlet for creativity or leadership	Opportunity to train other volunteers or be in charge of a project
Social interaction	Assignment to group projects; an area provided for a volunteer lounge; a holiday party; a recognition dinner
Personal growth	Training options; good supervision; opportunity for achievement

Public acknowledgment of time and talent given is always appreciated. Formal end-of-the-year recognition serves to remind staff, clients, program participants, and volunteers how important the volunteer involvement is. However, the effective management of a volunteer-based program is what volunteers most appreciate. It is recognized that the contributions made by volunteers should be without hassle and they be made aware of how their efforts contribute to organization goals.

Evaluation—As in overall strategic management, it is a crucial component of the volunteer planning cycle to determine effectiveness and control quality, both of the program and of the volunteer. Evaluation helps determine how effective the program management is and also how the individual volunteer contributes. Most people involved in the volunteer program should be invited to contribute to the evaluation throughout the year. Ideas can be both formally requested and informally heard. Simple forms, interviews, and observation all can be combined for systematic evaluation.

In summary, the individual volunteer is often the central and key person in nonprofit organizations of all kinds. However, if the board of an organization takes a careless attitude and assumes that the volunteer will always be there when needed, then that board and that organization can be "headed for trouble." Effective boards that direct outstanding organizations must constantly focus on the needs of the volunteer. The board must not only function internally in the ways that have been suggested, but must also reach out to the volunteer with a well-formulated plan and a continuing program that satisfies both the needs of the organization and the needs of the individual.

ADDITIONAL INFORMATION AND EXAMPLES

The Effective Management of Volunteer Programs, Marlene Wilson, Volunteer Management Associates, Boulder, 1976.

Gaining Momentum for Board Action, Arty Trost and Judy Rauner, Marlborough Publications, San Diego, 1983.

Helping People Volunteer, Judy Rauner, Marlborough Publications, San Diego, 1980.

The Volunteer Community, Eva Schindler-Rainman and Ronald Lippitt, University Associates, San Diego, 1975.

9

Rewards and Punishments Systems

In the private sector, financial compensation is one of the cornerstones of reward systems, whether for a board of directors, a chief executive officer, or other employees. In NFPs only the executive director and paid staff generally receive direct financial rewards. Trustees and volunteers should also be rewarded, but without the pay that by definition separates the "volunteers" from "staff."

BUSINESS ORGANIZATION VERSUS
NFP FINANCIAL COMPENSATION

Financial compensation can serve two major purposes for business and NFPs.

1. Compensate the employee at a fair and equitable level for the "relative worth" of the job. Although marketplace realities can greatly affect "base pay" levels, salary ranges can usually be readily developed for most jobs. This base salary is, in effect, a fixed cost, because only separation or a rare reduction will lower it.

2. Periodic added compensation (often an annual bonus or regular commission) can be tied to performance rewards.

One school of management thought argues that performance evaluations should not be tied directly to discussion of compensation. In contrast, some believe it artificial to separate the two, and that most employees and managers do not separate the questions of performance and compensation.

Business organizations can and do offer an array of taxable and nontaxable benefits from base pay and bonus/commission to stock options, savings plans, health plans, deferred compensation, added vacations, etc. With the exception of profit sector devices such as stock options and earnings-related pay, in theory an NFP can reward its employees in virtually any way business organizations can. Only in the last few years, and usually only in larger NFPs or business-oriented trade associations, has the NFP world broadened its thinking in using the full array of available compensation techniques.

In many volunteer-based NFPs, a corollary of "man does not live by bread alone" is that the paid staff is expected to forego all but existence-level wages. "Psychic benefits" are supposedly abundantly supplied. In certain fields adequate performance can be maintained with this approach, but we argue that over the long term an NFP "gets what it pays for."

We strongly recommend a systematic, broad-based approach to compensation, looking at all major alternatives. At a minimum, fringes that save the employee taxes and are "simply" part of an employee's total package should be high on the priority list. Whether the compensation is an automobile for an executive director or basic health coverage or pension for all employees, the logic of using before-tax dollars is difficult to refute. It is ironic that in some of the church and service groups studied, where human welfare is a very high priority, nonclergy and lower "ranking" staff often suffer from lack of insurance coverage and pension benefits considered a permanent fixture in business and government sectors.

CEO Versus ED Compensation

Apart from monetary compensation, NFP trustees and private directors are motivated, rewarded, and "punished" by many of the same things: (a) prestige of selection, (b) the opportunity for greater responsibility, (c) re-election, and (d) public recognition. Where trustees lack direct monetary rewards, they have an advantage in "psychic" rewards (and tax deductions) from performing a recognized public service or mission.

Moving down to the CEO or executive director (ED) level, boards of directors and trustees have operated very differently. These differences have tended to reinforce results-oriented management in business organizations, and may be ignored by the NFP. It is here that executive directors feel they have been unappreciated, especially when they compare their incomes and even security with those in the business world.

Tenure and the Golden Parachute

Just as directors serve longer than trustees, the CEO of a business firm is given more tangible guarantees and incentives (beyond compensation levels) which encourage independent action. Although a number of business firms do not provide "tenure" or severance protection (the "golden parachute" is not just for firms vulnerable to public takeover), these firms tend to be the ones promoting a CEO from within after many years of service. The CEO hired from the outside often has protection with multi-year commitments. Many local NFPs, in contrast, hire an ED with minimal or no assurance of employment longevity. Where the ED is promoted from within the organization, it is not unusual that he or she be professionally educated but lacking in administrative experience. (Think of the last dean or president of your college.) Where an ED's employment is annually renewed or at the "pleasure of the board," there are two common results. Either the ED will offend enough trustees over time that he or she must change jobs every few years, or the ED will exercise minimal leadership and no initiative. Deferring totally to the whims of the trustees, "survival instincts" keep the ED in the job but may reduce the director's ability to recommend policy changes or innovations.

If the ED does attain tenure, there is also a danger in the NFP as in the profit sector that trustees will serve only as a rubberstamp to the director. If performance is not measured periodically by trustees in a meaningful way, the NFP can suffer from the opposite of an insecure ED. An extremely confident and secure ED may run the organization with no real influence or control by the board of trustees.

While it is often difficult to hire professional managers for the NFP, it can be even more difficult to discharge them. Commonplace is the NFP manager who has been "on the way out" for several years. Forcing a separation or firing is not an easy task for the BOT. In an NFP it is often "easier" for a trustee chairman to serve his one- or two-year term without investing the time and commitment necessary to properly justify discharging an ED. The trustee would not relish the hassle that may occur. The ED can usually outwait and outlast a "controversial" chairman. If performance standards are not clear, it may be impossible for the volunteer annual chairman to muster enough reasons, time, or energy to push separation.

Since part of the difficulty facing the NFP is the lack of tangible goals and benchmarks, this deficiency can relate directly to another ED reward rarely used by the NFP. The bonus incentive common to private industry is an exception in the NFP. In one chamber of commerce studied, the ED was hired from the private sector. He insisted upon an annual bonus, which was tied to specific performance goals. He then carried the bonus program in profit-sector style to other salaried employees. The bonus was both a tangible reward and a symbol of total organization focus on achieving the NFP goals. At the end of each calendar year the board (as a whole the first two years, via a compensation committee in later years) established two numbers, the executive director's bonus and a bonus pool for the remainder of the staff. The latter was allocated at the ED's discretion. In both cases, the ED made his own recommendations (and although not obligated, provided a schedule for all staff bonuses) prior to the compensation decision. Given a strong ED and board, combined with a solid working relationship, the ED's recommendations were rarely overruled.

Although many boards of trustees have been reluctant to employ bonuses or business "perks," the important lesson for the NFP using them is that they can be a valuable tool for rewarding and motivating performance. Within the bounds of reasonable control and IRS regulations, a flexible approach to compensation can maximize staff satisfaction with compensation at an agreed upon, fixed cost to the NFP. Examples of potential compensation items include:

Base pay
Guaranteed bonus
Bonus tied to specific criteria/performance (based on weightings agreed to in advance)
Deferred compensation
Additional vacation
"Portable" pension
Pension tied to set years of service/age

Part-time compensation or consulting service (useful for specialized
financial or marketing management support, not usually to
replace ED)

Augmented health coverage (for example, 100 percent expenses,
annual physical exams, adequate dental plan, etc.)

Automobile plus expenses

Club memberships

Dues and subscriptions

Family benefits (education, travel of spouse, child care, etc.)

Sabbaticals (every 7, 20, or whatever number of years)

Establishing Appropriate Incentives

In creating an incentive-based system for NFP management, it is
vital that there be:

1. Clear standards of measurable group and individual performance. As noted in discussions of management by objectives (MBO),
benchmarks should be reasonable and mutually set.

2. A reward system tied to individual performance, with weight-
ing objectives for both quantitative and qualitative goals established
in advance. Whatever is more important—membership, expenses,
service delivery, or attendance—as an annual goal for the NFP, then it
should be a more important goal for the executive director. If external factors are difficult to anticipate or weigh, qualitative judgment
should take precedence.

This is more difficult in practice than in concept. Wide swings in
performance, external factors, the importance of group interaction/
results and subjective judgment areas all affect the value of an incentive system. Where a "flat salary" approach or, at the other end of
the spectrum, a Japanese-style percentage bonus for all truly is effective, it could be an exception worth keeping. On judgment from an
American value standpoint, however, we strongly encourage individual
assessment and resulting compensation for most NFPs. Team spirit is
vital to organizational success; and, at lower levels similar job descriptions may argue for or require similar compensation levels. For the
ED and other key staff members, the annual salary review is the least
frequent occasion on which an organization should examine results.

VOLUNTEERISM REWARDS

Not-for-profits have an additional dimension of both strength
and weakness—the volunteer. Some estimates indicate as many as

50 percent of all Americans are engaged in volunteer activities (see chapter on Volunteerism). Recent polls indicate a skew in volunteer service toward college education and business or professional employment. A Gallup poll recap noted that recruitment and maintenance of volunteers were most successful when:

1. Prospective volunteers feel the goals of a particular project or activity are valid and meaningful;
2. They feel their efforts will contribute significantly toward reaching these goals; and
3. They are recognized or rewarded (in some nonmonetary way) for their work.*

Given the time and expense devoted to recruiting and training volunteers, many NFPs could be much more cost effective by paying attention to the *continuing* need for rewards. While some EDs are innately capable of remembering to thank volunteers both in tangible and intangible fashion, most executives and organizations must develop a systematic recognition and reward system.

With religious organizations, Scouting, and Y's, recruitment and training are continuing facts of life. The NFP relying largely on volunteer implementation can be either very successful or fail totally. Since repeated failure usually results in a Darwinian loss of existence, it might be better to note that many local NFPs fluctuate between mediocrity and success. Rewards, recognition, involvement, and success begetting success are all motivators which, though more easily and directly controlled in business organizations, are most effective tools with NFP volunteers.

National organizations such as the Boy Scouts have developed systems which guarantee a certain amount of recognition. Elements as basic as an annual registration or membership (for which the volunteer pays and receives a registration card), a lapel pin or a uniform are automatic and, with the pin or uniform, easily visible. Years of service are stressed, with long-term service always recognized. Special levels of recognition, plaques and trophies in many shapes and sizes, public relations releases, award dinners, and a host of other

---

*Copyright Field Enterprises, *1981 San Diego Union*, December 6, 1981, p. A-40.

devices provide an effective array of volunteer rewards. These some-what mechanical though extremely important devices, however, do not make a total reward system. The personal phone call, the hand-written letter (better than word processing, which is much better than nothing), and the honest thank-you are just as important as the trophy on the office wall or front lobby.

The importance of the intangible or modest "reward" cannot be overstressed. Even in the rare organization that wrongly spends half its time as a mutual admiration society, no one ever turns down a public award. One local cultural relations NFP studied holds monthly luncheons, at which several community leaders and visitors are recognized. Over a year's time, literally hundreds of people receive plaques and trophies.

Annual mementoes, whether they be art works for multithousand-dollar "heavy hitter" donors or certificates of appreciation for the $25 family membership, should be a constant for most NFPs. Else-where we discuss publicity as part of an NFP's marketing program, but the value of a comprehensive program "covering all bases" is reinforced by success in all areas. Publicity about a membership drive gives recognition to the volunteers, helps raise money, and brings attention to the NFP mission (service delivery or whatever) all at the same time.

Just as the IRS should be taken into consideration in a configur-ment of staff compensation, an NFP should remind all volunteers of appropriate tax deductions. Where the average businessman might have his company cover his NFP expenses, many volunteers overlook routine, legitimate tax deductions. An annual pre-April reminder of deductions in general, assistance on record keeping, emphasis of the deductible portion of a fund-raising event, and periodic recaps of contributions are all useful.

Board Rewards and the Role of Volunteerism

Regarding the question of rewards at the board level, it must be emphasized that NFPs have an additional dimension, the volunteer trustee. These volunteers should be led and motivated by the ED. To the extent that volunteers are trustees, this leadership and motivation between the ED and the trustees can be described as circular. The perceived value of an NFP mission may be vital to the trustee volun-teer. Where that mission can be clearly identified, the fulfillment of the mission may by itself be the prime reward for the volunteer trustee. This is especially common in religious organizations and was borne out in the noted Gallup poll.

As with the boards of directors, the boards of trustees can provide a trustee with a sense of power. The BOT can also surpass the private sector's access to the public eye. That access provides the public recognition which is an additional motivator. While the homogeneity of a business board can give it operating strength, the breadth of contacts provided by an NFP board can be a tangible reward. Some would-be trustees openly seek board seats for the opportunity to "rub shoulders" and develop contacts leading to future monetary rewards.

Of all the rewards available to the BOT, however, the study suggests that the NFP mission is the overriding concern and foundation of BOT rewards. Although volunteers have even suffered for missions, the reward of the mission by itself may not be enough to sustain a local NFP. The integration of the total reward system into strategic planning should enhance the ability of the NFP to sustain itself and achieve its goals.

In practical terms this means that the volunteer trustee must receive the recognition, involvement, and training opportunities accorded the average volunteer, along with all the duties and honors appropriate to a trustee's position. Although a trustee may accept recognition with modesty, rare is the individual who will turn down a public pat on the back or another memento of service.

In approaching the reward question, the "golden rule" is especially appropriate. Where a board chairman has a good working relationship with other trustees, friendship and mutual admiration are often present or develop. The only justifiable surprises they should give each other are periodic recognition. In every other respect, they must consciously review reward systems with each other prior to bestowing symbols of recognition and accomplishment.

Disincentives

While penalties are just as appropriate, though hopefully not as common, as rewards, an NFP must minimize inadvertent disincentives. One glaring example is in the risk management area. Although schools, hospitals, and many business organizations are painfully aware of the need for directors' and officers' liability insurance, malpractice protection, etc., the number of unprotected NFPs in our litigious society is in our judgment high. Increasing numbers of corporate directors are sensitive to the potential liability question. That same businessman may avoid trustee service (or move to an honorary position) if he believes his trusteeship would be a personal risk.

Other inadvertent disincentives are those promulgated by bad management, such as too many meetings, time wasted, difficult meeting times, unclear duties, and so on. The perceptive executive director and board chairman accentuate the positive and minimize or eliminate negatives which can literally cripple an NFP's effectiveness.

PUNISHMENTS

Disciplining an executive director can be done openly or quietly, correctly or incorrectly, with a sledge hammer or a scalpel. Just as rewards should be objectively and quietly considered before being established, punishments deserve even more deliberate consideration, both as to their specific objectives and potential range of expected impact.

A reduction in pay, a reduced or eliminated bonus, or a deferred pay raise might be considered the most obvious forms of disciplining an executive director or staff member. However, they're not necessarily the most visible or effective. Limiting an executive director's responsibilities can be a very specific punishment, especially appropriate if the new limits are imposed in performance areas where the ED has failed to achieve mutually agreed upon objectives or procedures. Examples of limits that boards have placed on EDs include:

- Check-signing authority
- Ability to hire/fire staff
- Establishment of staff pay levels, incentives, and work rules
- Hiring of business manager for certain administrative responsibilities

These limits may be temporary or permanent. Action may require the concurrence of the board chairman, a designated trustee with special skills, or the confidence of the board, an established committee, or, the most unwieldy, the board as a whole.

A less severe discipline than limiting an ED's authority is one that can be tied to such limits or stand on its own—that of increasing staff reporting requirements. Ideally a comprehensive reporting and control system is well established on its own merits for normal staff and board functioning. Sometimes, however, the impetus is board discomfort over real or potential staff action which conflicts with board-established directions.

One device used by some boards which the authors don't encourage (unless temporarily when the board is deciding upon a personnel question affecting the executive director) is the exclusion of the executive director from board or executive board meetings. At the point where this degree of confidence in the executive director is lacking, it is usually an indication that the executive director should be replaced or the board should rethink its procedures.

In varying degrees of subtlety or openness, other disciplines can be imposed—when appropriate by board decision—on an executive director or other key staff:

- Use of outside consultant or trustee for selected "staff" responsibilities
- Reduction or undesired change in office space
- Elimination of individual secretary for executive director
- Reduction in holiday time
- Change of title
- Temporary suspension

Disciplining or Disposing of Trustees

As has been previously discussed, extreme penalties can be separation or nonrecognition. Although there is no magic term of service for trustees, a typical pattern is for terms of two to three years, with reelection allowed two or three times. This allows for strong trustees to continue their efforts over several years, but also allows for the quiet dropping of inadequate trustees. Where board service is gradually and regularly rotated, it is much easier to "steer" the organization than in conditions of minimal or maximum turnover.

Just as executive directors should have well-specified or gradually assumed responsibilities, so should board chairmen and trustees. The trustee that interferes in staff affairs can be just as negative a force as the executive director who oversteps his or her duties. It's rare for large national NFPs to have board/executive director conflicts in public, but it has happened. In recent years one of the most painfully visible was a situation in which a board chairman went beyond her responsibilities to suspend an executive director. On a day-by-day basis the national press chronicled the board's reversal of the chairman's action, the reinstatement of the executive director, and the ultimate major restructuring of board responsibilities.

As in the corporate world, committee assignments, titles, seating arrangements, and a host of large and "seemingly" small items can be powerful rewards/motivators or penalties/disincentives. Rewards such as receptions with guest artists, special tours, and attendance at symposia are all positive reinforcement, and conscious exclusion from same can be a subtle or not-so-subtle message to an unproductive trustee.

CONCLUSION

For a mystic on a mountain or a pilgrim on a journey, the mental or physical mission may be a reward unto itself. Most mortals, however, can be motivated or "turned off" by an array of tangible and intangible signals. Because of the greater public approval of most NFP missions and need for nonmonetary compensation, it's actually easier to develop an innovative reward system for an NFP. Creativity in selecting reward and recognition devices should thus be encouraged.

As with business management in general, however, "gaps and overlap" must be eliminated. Only a comprehensive reward system, with elements checked off systematically, can assure that volunteers and professional staff are fairly compensated, and motivated as much as is feasible. Thoughtful consideration in advance and an appropriate, timely thank-you far outweigh in power the belated or haphazard acknowledgment of "services rendered."

10

The Executive Director

THE "GLASS BOOTH"

Virtually every manager in the private sector and public sector alike is faced with a continuing array of time demands and job pressures. Management, by one definition the skill of achieving goals through and with other people (above, below, and at the same level), implicitly includes the tasks of regularly dealing with countervailing "people interests." Subordinates, peers, boards, customers, competitive forces, regulatory bodies, and a host of other "people" or "publics" affect both the long-term focus and the day-to-day (and minute-to-minute) activities of the manager. The public official, whether elected, appointed, or hired, usually has a clear charter or past precedent to guide his work. The public sector manager may face a finite term in office or a public board of supervisors, but there is usually no doubt about the source of his power or charter of responsibility.

Many private sector business managers may function with similarly (or relatively) precise authority, and often escape any significant public scrutiny. For some businessmen, especially the entrepreneur/owner, the discipline of the marketplace (especially competition) may be the only demanding public. Government regulation and, of course, taxes are assumed to be constants of recorded history. Even in the largest and most complex corporations, the CEO reports in name if not always in fact to a board of directors whom he sees only periodically at a quarterly meeting, an occasional lunch, or a special committee meeting.

The nonprofit executive often has the worst of both worlds. At the local level the not-for-profit executive is the man or woman in the "glass booth." Every action or inaction may be observed by staff or volunteers who are directly or indirectly related to the NFP executive's board of trustees; and the community as a whole keeps him and his staff and volunteers in that same "glass booth," day and night. We have already noted the difficulty, when trustees provide volunteer services, of an executive director being both superior and subordinate alternately. Since community interaction and responsiveness often "go with the job," the executive director, especially in the small NFP, finds it extremely difficult to manage his own time, let alone that of his total organization.

BACKGROUND BIAS

Through much of this book, we have followed the theme that not-for-profit leaders are different from private sector chief executives, in management training and education, if in nothing else. The "glass booth" disadvantage (one cannot please everyone all the time) is compounded by the executive director's general lack of management training. Eleven years of medical training, four years of social work schooling, 31 years of running a church, or 20 years of directing an orchestra usually provide less management *teaching* than the local community college's two-year business program. Only in the past few years, in fact, have some professional schools and NFP trade associations begun to offer management training in areas such as financial management, marketing, time management, and a host of other broad functional overviews and relatively specific techniques. For example, the Graduate Theological Union (representing many different faiths) in Berkeley is planning to offer its first program ever in strategic management in 1984. Consider the contrast between the NFP manager and the business executive who may have received formal business training, most probably also entry-level management training, and very likely continuing education either formally or informally (the latter via superior or peer examples, trade magazines, industry contacts, customer and supplier interaction, etc.). Medical school or Julliard can bestow and enhance professional or artistic skills, but may not teach how to read a balance sheet.

From a devil's advocacy standpoint, one could argue that management people are not that different. Although not an everyday occurrence, the top business executive today may be a state or federal cabinet officer tomorrow, and then the executive director of a museum when he or she takes early retirement from the corporate world. A retired Army or Air Force general can be a successful CEO of a consulting firm or an insurance company. The president of an automobile company can also head the Defense Department or a graduate business school ... or another cabinet post, or the International Monetary Fund, etc. A public official can also successfully become CEO of a major corporation.

At the smaller organizational focus, the entrepreneur starting a small business (at a minimum, lacking depth of support) may not be that different from the local NFP director with little or no specialized full-time staff. The entrepreneur or small NFP director must know everything that is "going on" in his organization, and is often the only one who can manage key activities. In the business world the entrepreneur has the checkbook in his pocket; and money flows (or doesn't flow) from one pocket to another. His NFP counterpart may or may not similarly control the checkbook. Two signatures might be required and one signer could be out of town for the month.

The weight of evidence suggests that both the career priorities and the resulting career progressions do make the business manager different from the NFP executive. We strongly believe in the transferability of management skills across the business, NFP, and government sectors. The successful career shifts of current leaders such as Gavin, McNamara, Rumsfeld, current cabinet members, and a host of others support this concept of transferability.

In general, however, early career training reinforces differences; and this is borne out in our own studies referred to in our introduction. NFP executives tend to rate high on dedication to mission and social consciousness, but comparatively lower on management ability. Those with business backgrounds are usually rated in reverse order. Part of this may be due to a positive or negative "halo" based on a "social value assessment" of NFPs versus business in general. At times in the past two decades, in fact, it was fashionable for the school principal or social worker to be both "anti-business" and "anti-sales" within their professions. We believe early career training puts substance behind these perceptions. In our introduction we noted the case of the "damned good" social worker promoted beyond his management ability (not capability). Equally common is the physician with 15 years of medical training but no training in administration or negotiation. When promoted or transferred to a chief administrative role, he is suddenly called upon to negotiate million dollar programs with private insurance or government managers whose interests and priorities often differ from those of the hospital. Our recent experience has shown that such doctors are as poor negotiators as other professionals thrown into management. In contrast, the businessman is much more likely to have management techniques taught to him and practiced regularly, then monitored and controlled in the workplace. As noted, at a minimum, the latter's trade journals and other job-related reading and training will reinforce the business education with which the manager started.

In one region studied a group of high school principals believed that there was a significant difference between being an "administrator" and a "manager." They went on to define an administrator as one who "takes what he has . . . and works with it." The administrator "handles paperwork and keeps others free to perform professional duties." In contrast, they defined a manager as one who "saves money . . . fires people . . . cuts wages . . . requires more paperwork of everybody. In turn the manager cuts performance and resources and makes life impossible." In their minds business management was clearly something negative. Semantic disagreements aside, it's clear that the economic belt-tightening of the past few years is viewed from conflicting perspectives.

Obviously and unfortunately, the language varies from sector to sector. Apparently, with no apologies to English language scholars, "linkage," "interface," and "where you're at" mean different things (or nothing, which might be quite astute) to different fields and professions.

"X", "Y", and "Z" will likely be the last letters in the alphabet to the NFP technician, while the newly hired employee from business school will actually be ahead, on the average, of his superiors in understanding management theory.

A Bit of Digression on "X", "Y", and Management Theory in General

Depending on the type of organization, management training can be successful or detrimental. With no overall evaluation of the appropriateness of certain "training for an organization," there is a real risk that more harm than good will result. Devices such as "T" groups (for training, sensitivity, confrontation, therapy, touching, or whatever) may fall into the more harmful side of the equation (for example, Polaroid went from very positive short-term results with T groups to a very negative viewpoint). Good listening or fast feedback might produce a net positive half of the equation, but can't be expected to be cure-alls in themselves.

No one approach is a magic solution. Our strongest recommendation possible is that the NFP must be aware of current management theory, the varying styles of the NFP's leaders, and how those styles mesh or conflict. "X" and "Y" are worth special mention because they attempt to catalog and differentiate in general terms significantly different approaches to management. Whether directly useful or not, the study of these differences and other management approaches by an NFP will give that NFP a better frame of reference to gauge its own management styles.

Theory X and Theory Y

In the 1950s psychologists formulated ideas about key choices a manager might make in managing his workers. These were synthesized into two fundamental management patterns, "Theory X" and "Theory Y."

Theory X embraces the idea that people, and specifically workers, are basically lazy and dislike work. Motivation requires both carrot and stick, specific, and very significant rewards and punishments. Theory Y, in contrast, assumes that all people want to achieve goals, take responsibility for themselves, and in turn experience a sense of satisfaction or fulfillment. Although this description oversimplifies what was 1950s and 1960s development thought, various descriptions of X and Y thinking are useful to keep in mind.

The original proponent (or cataloger) of Theory Y acknowledged in later years that this theory didn't work. As executive director of an NFP, he found that a permissive "Y" style was not a satisfactory answer. Certain organization and responsibility had to be structured for a group of people to achieve specific goals.

Subsequent years have shown that the type and complexity of industry, the profitability or resources of a business organization, the degree of structure (rigidity, flatness, etc.), character of peer and vertical relationships, and the CEO's own style and character (task and/or people orientation) all influence the degree to which a permissive Y or rigid X approach might work.

Japanese Management and Beyond— With an American Model

With the economic return of Japan to its pre-World War II growth line and the success of a statistical approach to quality control overlaid on Japanese society, we have seen Japanese management style become a major focus in the past few years. We have also developed a greater respect for well-established, paternalistic companies such as IBM, Procter and Gamble, Jewel, and younger firms such as Hewlett-Packard.

Over the years the authors have consulted and worked with a large number of New York, Southern California, Kansai, and Kanto-based Japanese operations. The elements that are derived from Japanese culture or newly developed quality improvement programs have certain counterparts in American management. Among these are:

Japanese Model	U.S. Version or Preference
Security of lifetime employment to age 55 (in top tier companies that stay in business; lifetime employment is of no value in the companies that fail)	Implicit lifetime employment, contractual protection, and portable pensions
Management by consensus (even though everyone knows who is boss, who is really the decision-maker, and who will take responsibility for certain decisions)	Consensus, "sign off," having a voice in the decision
Belief in and commitment to the company	Belief in the mission and "culture"
Paternalistic care for the employee and his family, combined with employee acceptance of his station	Paternalistic care with American sense of individuality (where unions are not present)
Greater stress on training as "generalist"	Greater functional specialization
Dealing with outsiders of comparable rank	Greater social mobility

The comparisons can go on indefinitely, from *amokdori* ("para-chuting from heaven") versus "kicking upstairs," to honorifics versus informality, to *okyakusama* ("customer" and "guest" the same) versus knowing the needs of the customer, to centralization versus geographic dispersal, etc. The key message for the American NFP or the American business is that they be aware of what management techniques work under what circumstances. What may be exceedingly good in the Japanese culture may or may not work in the American culture. However, all techniques should be known to the executive director.

WHAT TO DO?

Good management involves several aspects of critical self-analysis, in effect the same self-analysis that produces elements of a total strategic management effort. This includes a periodic board/top management evaluation of:

Strengths and weaknesses
Current organization
Organization and staff changes, if any, required to better achieve the
    organization's mission, goals, specific action plans, etc.

Part of the assessment process involves the question of management personality and style. The common business school axiom is that a manager should be concerned about his people and, if he is not, he should pretend to be. Most of us are not "results-oriented Theory Y," or "Theory X with a hidden heart of gold." (To repeat, even the strongest early proponents of Theory Y found that they could not fully practice what they preached when given general management responsibility.) All of these can relate to people concerns versus organizational goals or questions of substance versus form. Ideally there is no tradeoff between questions of personnel management and the achievement of specific tasks. In the real world, most managers have varying styles and strengths. We can't be all one thing or the other. It is vital that we realize what our styles and capabilities are. In turn, they must mesh as well as possible with the existing or changing "fabric" of the NFP organization, its mission, its people, and its concrete goals. We must also adapt techniques to suit the personalities of the NFP board, executive director, and staff. *At best personality change is difficult, so the manager must use manage-*

ment techniques on the assumption that he can't change personalities.
The people-oriented leader must establish devices (formal or informal
controls, reminders, subordinate assistance, etc.) to keep his task
goals in focus. The "100 percent" results-oriented manager will
require comparable devices or assistance for people or personnel
needs.

In Chapter Four, we covered organization structure and communications. Once again we emphasize that continuing management
education is important in all organizations and, we believe, especially
neglected in NFP management. It is not crucial that the NFP manager
read all leading management authorities, but that person should have
an understanding of concepts such as:

- The basics of strategic planning and strategic management, and
  what this means to a leader
- The X, Y theories
- Trends in American (and Japanese and British and German) man-
  agement
- Rewards and punishments
- Achievement versus affiliation versus power
- Job enrichment and growth
- Form versus content/structure versus process
- Can structural change come only after changing or improving top
  management skills?

As long as the executive director keeps a critical perspective (that
is, takes in all management theory information with a "grain of salt"),
we believe a little knowledge is better than none. But both are inferior
to a "solid foundation" and self-understanding. The social worker who
is trained to listen may have difficulty when promoted to a management position. Early training emphasized not giving orders, whereas
the new manager is suddenly supposed to talk, act, and give orders.
In one case a medical school dean totally rebelled against the techniques of inventory control and record keeping of emergency treatment trends, and the overall concept of cost-benefit analysis. Yet, all
of these were crucial to improving his school and teaching hospital's
operations. Putting a value on life (or the cost of saving one) is a
difficult concept for most of us who by upbringing think of saving
lives at "any cost." Yet, any health science professional must regularly face decisions (or avoidance of decisions) that explicitly or

implicitly determine where resources go, and in turn, what lives may or may not be saved. Every decision has a price.

Trustee Involvement and Assessment of the Executive Director

We strongly encourage annual review of ED performance, and believe the review should be tied to both specific goals/performance and changes in compensation. (See Rewards and Punishment chapter.) A much more important facet of board responsibility, however, is the initial hiring or promotion of the executive director. The "right" choice of a supportive board is often more than 51 percent of the equation in determining the NFP's (or any organization's) success. While setting policy is always an equally important board responsibility, the right ED makes the other tasks significantly easier. In a large NFP where implementation is handled by professional staff, ED selection is crucial to organizational success. Even in the small NFP where board volunteers are an integral part of all activities, a weak executive director will divert the energies of board members and weaken performance. For example, the legally required integration of girls into Little League was very easy in some organizations and unduly difficult in others.

It should be obvious that the ED must have adequate technical skills to handle his new assignment. Less tangible are the "human" and intellectual skills required to work effectively, through others, to achieve overall NFP goals. It is difficult (if not dangerous) to "play" psychology in hiring a new ED, but we strongly encourage going beyond the proven track record of achievement in some professional field (without which, we usually wouldn't go further in considering an ED for hiring). The "personal chemistry" can be vital to the selection process. At a minimum, a candidate should describe his own personal strengths. What is good for one NFP in leadership style may not be good for another. Unfortunately, a BOT may ultimately hire or fire an ED based on some highly uncertain criteria. The people plans and decisions that lead to accomplishing the stated goals of the organization should be the guiding force of the NFP.

Personality Characteristics of Executive Directors

Although different clusters of personality traits are more appropriate for different types of organizations, or timing within an organization's evolution, it is useful to consider an ED's strengths in the context of many dimensions. The following table reflects a sampling of the relative value of some of these traits to different types of NFPs:

	NFP Perspective
Decision-making and conceptual abilities	Always important, but more crucial to rapidly changing NFP or one requiring integration of many elements. In uncertain situations, this is probably even more important to NFP world than business sector. It is especially so where some goals are not specific and the ED does not have strong board input
Authority	As with decision-making ability, crucial where people responsibility is significant and/or organization lacks discipline
Ability to relate to others	Might or might not be less important in a successful performing arts organization than an overworked social services NFP
Presence: ability to make a good impression	A union local president does not have to handle himself in public as well as a lobbyist or an NFP requiring significant fund raising
Personal habits and organization skills	On judgment, not as crucial to the performing arts as to a service group using thousands of volunteers
Values/integrity	Personal standards must fit those of the NFP, at a minimum. Absolutely critical to most NFPs

The Executive Director and a Changing Environment

For better and worse, for success and failure, organizations are continually changing. This is a characteristic, almost by definition, of NFPs. The right leader to start a new NFP or turn around a fallen one is not usually the type to keep a "gentle hand" on the organizational ship. Where one manager will enjoy the challenge and diversity of a "turnaround" situation, another executive director may prefer, or only be capable of, administering an NFP that is well established with a proven set of programs and personnel. In one NFP studied, the ED came from the private sector to replace an association executive with many years in the field. The BOT consciously rejected all public sector and NFP candidates in looking for a person willing to change the direction of the NFP, and then move on to another challenge. (Along with substantive changes in programs and people, the new ED also extended office hours and replaced decaffeinated coffee with regular coffee his first day on the job. The "12 O'clock High" approach—the general shaping up of the organization—is sometimes quite appropriate. On the other hand, in another case, a new local ED coming from a national NFP very successfully turned his new organization around with tight controls, a new BOT, and a very quiet entry into his new job.)

Another NFP in the performing arts had a strong executive director who insisted on dominating all activities (he even replaced standard "board" stationery with a revision bearing his name only and refused to be bound by "break even" financial constraints.) Upon his resignation, the board of trustees embarked on a search for a less commanding presence, and a commitment to stay within budget limits.

Money is oftentimes the source of conflict in the museum field, where "blockbuster" exhibits or "chance of a lifetime" acquisitions offer a curator or executive director a direct method of improving the museum's stature. When viewed in the context of building for the long term, it could in fact be cost effective to suffer a short-term cash outflow. Difficulties are compounded where the art director will raise money to support one element of an annual budget, possibly "drying up" or limiting overall fund-raising programs. Here, again, unified board thinking (or at least conclusions) and action are crucial. King Tut or a Vatican art exhibit might guarantee money making for both a museum and a city as a whole. Less popular exhibits are not as easily decided.

In one national minority group association, the long-term executive director had the backing of the board but clashed openly in the national press with the chairperson. The chairperson took it upon herself to suspend the executive director, and in turn, was overridden by the board as a whole. To say there was a lack of understanding of organizational direction and delineation of responsibility would be a major understatement. The chairperson, subsequently eased out of any significant responsibility for the second half of her term, and the executive director could both be faulted for a public power play and confrontation hurting the mission. The board had selected the wrong chair for the NFP, and must bear the ultimate responsibility for a month-long saga in the national press. Again, the interrelationship between the BOT and the ED remains as always a crucial one.

This leads into a subject that is generally ignored, evaluation of the BOT by the ED. Only in an NFP where the ED is in a strong position does this regularly occur, usually in the context of new trustees being appointed. If the ED is new or not secure in his position, at best he might offer a somewhat timid suggestion in evaluating BOT performance. In this case only strong board members or an outside consultant can assist in this crucial evaluation. This evaluation is vital in precluding the type of public confrontation just discussed. Furthermore, it makes day-to-day activities that much more pleasant and productive.

CONCLUSION

One does not wear the same clothes throughout one's life. The right executive director (or chairman) for an NFP at one period in the evolution of the NFP may be the wrong one at a different time. No matter how many job criteria or traits are explicitly listed, people are too complicated to profile with absolute certainty. Nonetheless, a board of trustees must agree on the shape the organization should take before, or during, the time it agrees upon who will be entrusted with the job of chief executive. Just as organizational structure follows the mission and objectives of the NFP, so should the selection of the executive director. While day-to-day management skills are important, strategic management directions can also be enhanced by an affirmation of the following:

1. The potential executive director must have a belief in the mission of the NFP. With such belief, there should be involvement in all appropriate managerial activities. In the long run, the survival of the NFP is usually dependent upon the collective belief of trustees, beneficiaries, and the community, as well as the ED, in the value of the NFP mission.

2. The fund-raising function should be defined for the executive director. As with the trustee, the responsibility may be characterized either in terms of dollars or in priority of activity.

3. The ED typically comes from a specialized professional area. Social work, the ministry, or the performing arts do not prepare the ED for an integrative approach to the organization.

4. The general managerial education of the ED should be encouraged. This may include formal professional schooling at the MBA (business administration) or MPA (public administration) level, advanced management programs, professional meetings, and in-house seminars. A few national organizations provide such programs. The education of the ED should not be limited to the technical or scientific aspects of the mission. To the contrary, managerial skills devoted to policy formulation and implementation should become a key objective of such education.

5. As with the trustee, the selection of the executive director must entail an analysis and discussion of personal value systems. Where the values between the BOT and the ED are not in congruence, strategic planning and management in general will be difficult if not impossible to accomplish.

6. The measurement and control function of the private sector may be applied to the NFP, within the limits outlined in our chapter on Fund Accounting. Although the NFP mission may not be stated in monetary terms, qualtitative measures of successive stages of performance can be provided. In addition, specific measurements should be established for the ED to guide the BOT in measuring performance or vice versa. A distinction should be made between fund accounting, where used, and management control systems.

7. The creation of team spirit between NFP professional staff and trustee volunteers is a process that can materially enhance the success of the organization. The leader can be either the ED or a trustee. However, one leader should be clearly identified to coordinate paid and volunteer staff activity and, in turn, to receive the support of all.

Formal personnel and management programs can help in this team-building process, but much of it will depend on the personalities and willingness of ED, staff, and board.

8. The success of the organization will in part be dependent upon the continuity of strategic planning and strategic management. Hence, the selection and succession of an executive director must be integrated not only with the mission but also with the strategy of the organization.

11

Not-for-Profit, Public Agency, and Private Sector Partnerships

A significant relation for all NFPs is a community partnership with business. This chapter examines the benefits and problems with the business sector, the methods to begin the relationship, and the means for continuous increased involvement with the business sector.

THE TROIKA—BUSINESS, NFP, AND PUBLIC AGENCIES

In recent years a growing national awareness of the mutual concerns within communities among business people, NFPs, and public agencies has emerged. Business firms are finding that the skills needed in modern technical industry are beyond the abilities of many high school graduates. Public agencies find their institutions underfunded and unable to meet all community needs. The NFPs and their missions have to be integrated into the specific communities they serve, and for which they provide programs. This must usually be accomplished with the cooperation of the public and private sectors.

The process and value of integrating all sectors (public agencies, community agencies, and local business firms of all sizes) of the community into working partnerships have become apparent to many executives working in each of these sectors. Some cities have developed coalitions of agencies, offering training, technical assistance, and citywide agency planning in all sectors. The development, concept, and existence of the Community Congress has evoked positive recognition from the business and NFP sectors. This, in turn, has led

FIGURE 11.1   The Partnership Business

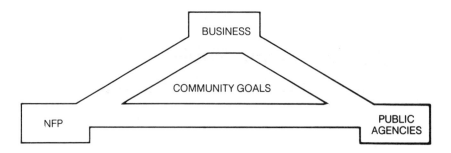

to a new collaborative relationship wherein the traditional NFP approach of asking for contributions has developed into a more mutual relationship where *money is only one of the resources.* In this process, the executives of all the sectors, representing themselves or their agencies, have learned about and relished the benefits they derive from participation. (At the federal level, one significant improvement of CETA* in the late 1970s was the move from total public administration to the use of voluntary "PICs," or Private Industry Councils.)

Purposes of "The Partnership"

For each sector of the joint venture (NFP, public agency, and business), a constellation of purposes may be served. These purposes are also covered by a conceptual framework which suggests an overall communal enhancement.

The inclusion of the business sector, along with NFP agencies and public agencies, brings to the partnership a different set of skills and experience, an added perspective, and a resource pool for collaboration in many areas.

Government budget cutting has severely limited the ability of NFP agencies to continue to meet local needs either in the accomplishment of their mission or in the delivery of community services.

---

*Comprehensive Employment Training Act.

Yet each community fully recognizes the need for the services of the NFP agencies it feels itself losing. In keeping with the current thrust of turning to the local level to develop the resources to meet needs, the inclusion of the business sector of the local community is fitting.

The Role of the Business Sector in Assisting NFPs

Local businesses within the community can be partners with NFPs and local government in effectively determining:

1. The needs of a specific or group of NFPs (or on a task force basis recommending local governmental roles)
2. Developing training programs
3. Exploring economic development projects
4. Encouraging adult educational programs (such as health) or otherwise participating in the recognition of needs
5. Steps to implement the above

Businesses and their representatives can prove a substantive source of management skills, planning know-how, and technical assistance.

Furthermore, the inclusion of the business sector in the partnership may assure a beginning of the breakdown of the mutual stereotypes of business vis-a-vis the public and NFP agencies. This very process of inclusion can lead to mutual enhancement and cooperation.

Prior History

The exclusion of the business sector from the decision-making process carried on within the community by some NFPs has resulted in resentment and, eventually, apathy by the business community. This has led to further separation between and among various parts of the community and further reinforcement of negative stereotypes. Countless NFPs have minimal or no active business/management representation.

Problems and Benefits of the Partnership

Many NFP executives may have already sought the participation of business people in partnerships. Some communities have shown creativity and innovation in attracting the business sector to the public sectors. However, there are other NFPs that have experienced severe difficulties when trying to involve business. Such difficulties include:

Historical stereotyping
"Language" differences
Personal and professional value differences
Lack of understanding of managerial techniques that are applicable
     to all three sectors
Inability to communicate (for example, via an annual report or operations plan) enough basic information on the NFP to entice business involvement

The Stereotypes

Historically, the interrelationship of business people with NFP executives has been sporadic, controversial, often antagonistic, and self-defeating. The stereotypes fostered by the media are easy to characterize. For example, the educator is described as undisciplined, a thinker rather than a doer and one who is not concerned with the "real world"; the social worker is supposedly a do-gooder with no regard for costs; the businessman is depicted as uneducated (or at least unenlightened), nonhumanistic, and interested only in the dollar sign; and the public executive is portrayed as not being a hard worker or truly concerned with the community. All of these descriptions are far from the truth, yet these misconceptions persist. The propagation of such stereotypes is paradoxical and self-defeating. It should be obvious to most onlookers that all of the executives from each of the three sectors are needed in every community. The NFPs and the public agencies would have little or no monetary or technical resources without business; and business would not find educated people to train without the assistance of educators and social agencies. Nor would business wish to be burdened by the host of human problems attended to by the NFPs.

Communication

The most prevalent problem created by cultural stereotypes, by far, is that of communication. Each sector has developed its own jargon; and frequently difficulties are encountered in speaking to someone in another sector, or in understanding what is being said.

TABLE 11.1 Cultural Stereotypes

	The Perspective of . . . Looking at	
	NFP Administrator versus	Business Manager
NFP executive	They provide a system for task assignment, flow of paperwork, psychology of time equals one year. Value = Good	People from outside the organization. Their prime function is to cut budgets and fire people. Lack of humanistic understanding. Value = Poor
Business executive	They are solely concerned with paper shuffling. "Linkage" and "networking" processes are more important than accomplishing a specific goal. No concern for use of funds. Lack management training. Value = Poor	They are people who design and implement plans for the organization to achieve stated objectives and profits. They are technically educated and trained. Value = Good
	Mission versus	Profits
NFP executive	An obligation to provide services to designated recipients.	May not exist in quantitative financial terms. Subjective benefit analysis.
Business executive	An obligation to produce goods or services for customers, suppliers, stockholders, management, labor.	Primary purpose, measurable on bottom line of profit and loss statement and related to all rewards.
	Group Process versus	Organizational Structure
NFP executive and agency	Decision by consensus, often ignoring concept of hierarchical responsibility. Value = Good	Antithetical to group process of decision making, noncreative, nonparticipatory. Value = Poor
Business executive	Lack of individual responsibility and time consuming. Value = Poor	Structure defined in hierarchical terms creating individual responsibility. Value = Good

Among the many illustrations of language barriers are the misunderstood views and judgments diagrammed in Table 11.1.

In addition to the terms illustrated, misunderstandings are found in specific words and terms such as bottom line, time spans, span of control, participation, stakeholders, payoffs, cost of capital, and cost/benefit.

There are also other stereotypes of cultural differences relating to personal behavior and group values, a few of which are presented in Table 11.2.

Typically, the most mysterious phrases for NFP professional staff are those relating to the managerial techniques used in business. These could include:

"Decision trees"—Methods of analyzing risks and propensities while making decisions.

Market research—Use of pre-testing, tracking, etc. (See Marketing chapter.)

Managerial accounting—What is behind the numbers; what do the numbers mean?

Cost control systems—What do services or products "really" cost?

Information systems—What timely data are important to whom?

Managerial training

Strategic management

Negotiation techniques

Value engineering—How refined can or should cost accounting be?

TABLE 11.2 Behavioral Stereotypes

NFP Executive	Business Executive
Even pace	Rapid pace
I'll wait until you come to me	We have to go out and get
Body language slow or studied	Body language staccato
Decision making = time consuming	Decisions made today
Try not to risk	Risk each day
Time not computed in terms of total cost	Time and opportunity costs meaningful

TABLE 11.3 Organization Structure

	Public Agency	NFP	Business
Policy level	Board of Supervisors, councilmen	Board of trustees	Board of directors
Chief executive	Mayor, city manager, county executives	Executive director	President
Highest operational level	Director of a division	Assistant director	Executive vice president
Decentralized leaders	Manager or supervisor	Project leaders	Vice presidents
Supervisory people	Department heads	Professional workers	Section or division manager
Working level	Citizens	Recipients	Labor, customers, and suppliers

Critical path ("CPM" or "PERT")—What actions must be taken when to keep projects moving on schedule?

Operations audit—Keeping accounting records is not the only audit function of a board.

Many of the national NFPs are currently directing themselves to the areas listed. However, local NFPs rarely address themselves to these business techniques. It is possible, however, to point to similarities among the three partners and to stress those similarities rather than the differences. For example, organizational structure and titles can be categorized as shown in Table 11.3.

Contrary to the assumptions of the professional staff of many NFPs, it is significant to bear in mind that every business person is a human being first, and a business person second.

Despite the differences of culture, language, and professional motivation, the business person has many, if not all, of the personal and emotional needs of the NFP executive and public servant. An adversary position toward the business community could lead only to a negative response. A collegiate approach and attitude will create the environment for a successful partnership.

Benefits

Despite all the various problems outlined above, the benefits inherent in the partnership of the business sector with the NFPs of a community may be as important to business people as it is to the community agency people. What follows is a brief listing of some of the benefits that can be derived by business people from such a partnership:

1. Individual self-realization, personal enrichment, and a sense of ethical fulfillment that stems from community recognition that the businessman contributes more than an economic function.

2. Community awareness of business input into the joint venture provides business with a positive public image.

3. Through participating in NFP programs, businessmen can have an impact on major problems such as youth unemployment, quality or forms of education, community health, crime, etc. Companies need a well-trained, educated potential labor force. For example, through collaboration and participation, business can directly affect the kinds of vocational training young people have available.

4. Local business is becoming increasingly aware that it pays a heavy part of the costs of social ills through taxation. Business should certainly be interested in having a more active role in determining how tax monies are spent, especially as many federal supports are cut or eliminated.

5. As business becomes more involved, community interest in companies is aroused, thus providing potential customers, suppliers, management personnel, etc.

6. Participation for any particular business or businessman enables that firm or person to become involved in a network including other businesses, and may increase stability within the local setting.

7. Employees of both the private and public sectors often become bored with their traditional tasks. NFP community involvement can prevent disaffection from the firm or public employer.

8. Participation in the partnership can be viewed as a training ground for beginning managers.

9. Working cross-culturally, employees can improve understanding of the other sectors and their language, or jargon. Both of these benefits can prove profitable for a business.

10. Neighborhood involvement creates a natural data base (or at least a subjective early warning system) for market research, which has also been found to be profitable.

Summary

It is evident that there is a spectrum of difficulties in relationships among public sector executives, NFP professionals, and business people. Prior experience suggests that NFPs and public sector agencies have been successful in their joint efforts. There is no doubt that the business sector can also benefit significantly from participation in the partnership, as well as enhancing the multiple objectives of the public and social agencies within the community.

HOW CAN NFPs REACH THE BUSINESS COMMUNITY?

Start from within. For educators and social workers to involve the business community, it may be necessary to adapt many of the effective techniques of business and to study the culture and language of business.

How to begin to reach the business community?

1. Reach into the NFP and identify the business and professional needs of the organization that might be met within the NFP. These should include:

- Members of the board of trustees
- The suppliers of services and equipment such as printing, furniture, office equipment, etc.
- Professional services, such as accounting, law, medicine, etc.
- Friends and relatives of all the employees and/or volunteers of the NFP

2. Explore the immediate surrounding environment through:

- Street-by-street canvassing
- Booths at shopping malls
- Selecting local advertisers from local newspapers

3. Indirect referrals can evolve from:

Lawyers or the local bar association
Accountants, real estate brokers, insurance salesmen
Doctors and dentists
Bankers

4. Reaching further afield would include contacting local business organizations such as the chamber of commerce and service clubs such as the Rotary, Lions, Kiwanis, etc.

5. The miscellaneous category could include church groups, economic development associations, alumni groups, etc. Local politicians should not be neglected.

Once the initial contact is made, it is necessary to branch out, using the following procedures:

1. Use the referral network or tree-branch system to obtain the names of people who may want to become involved.

2. "Homework" must follow in order to have a clear understanding of the person and the business organization to be approached.

3. Use an organized telephone technique to achieve appointments for personal meetings; for example, always be the caller, not the "callee."

4. Prepare a motivating sales presentation exploring the benefits of the partnership to the business. This should include specific prose describing mission, track record, etc. Hard data describing past results, future goals, and budget levels are always important.

5. Prepare a series of questions designed to obtain positive responses and closure.

Marketing

Marketing involves a number of different techniques:

a. Market research; for example, customer needs
b. Market identification; for example, demographics
c. Advertising; for example, direct mail
d. Promotion, publicity, etc.
e. Selling; for example, fund raising

f. Negotiation; for example, noncollective bargaining
g. Service or "product"
h. Evaluation of results

This list includes only the highlights of a marketing program or mix. (See chapter on Marketing for more complete discussion.)

One of the more misunderstood management tools is the process of negotiation. All of the participants in the partnership must constantly negotiate with each other, either formally or informally. Negotiating techniques and skills are absolutely crucial in transactions with community members when goals and values may differ significantly.

Control and Information Systems

Typically, NFPs, public agencies, and businesses are locked into tight budgets. Control (quantitative) and information (qualitative) systems are necessary as operating tools. From the top of the hierarchy to the bottom, every person should be able to ascertain what is happening to the partnership. Simplified records or key summaries may show evidence of vital problems.

The results, not the words, demonstrate the trends of all activities. Monthly or especially seasonal and annual reports may be developed too late to make necessary changes. Control and information systems, plus the use of the computer, can be designed by the participating business people in cooperation with the other partners. These may be formal, monthly unaudited accounting statements, a handwritten note from an executive director, or an "as needed" verbal briefing of key community leaders.

Evaluation Criteria (See Strategic Plan of the Economic Development Corporation, Appendix)

The control system has little meaning unless criteria are established and an evaluation procedure is instituted. Criteria should be clearly defined at each step of any operation. Such criteria must relate to the objectives of the partnership. It is relevant to establish all criteria prior to the beginning of the partnership. If not, an ad hoc situation exists and subjective evaluations may lead to discord.

In creating the systems:

a. Establish a time frame for each step.

b. The more steps defined, the easier it becomes to adjust to any problems or stopgaps.

c. Create some quantitative and qualitative benchmarks based upon prior experiences. As the program proceeds, it is then possible to adjust (up or down) the quantitative objectives.

d. Start with basic ideas and then add new ones that are derived from the new partnership.

e. Criteria will become worthless unless there is a system designed to update them.

f. Some examples of criteria for the project evaluation are:

(1) Relationship to overall organizational goals and programs

(2) Number and type of co-sponsored events

(3) Number and association of regular council members

(4) Number of contacts by professional or public executives with business

(5) Contacts and nature of involvement made with businesses other than the business partner

(6) Number of activities between business and public agency and NFP which have employees involved, and/or such processes as compensatory time or release time which allow employee involvement in joint programs

(7) Number of new business partners

(8) Number of community and project planning sessions involving all partners

(9) Development of a philosophy statement and/or goals representative of business's involvement with the public agency and NFP

(10) Number of meetings of service clubs, chambers of commerce, etc., attended by public agency and NFP personnel

(11) Recognition of benefits of partnership for NFPs/agencies in: management skills (the how–what process); special resources obtained from businesses; cost efficiency of the NFP.

(12) Increase in the number and quality of service or mission delivered to the community while eliminating duplication.

(13) Increased knowledge by business of community needs through a demonstrated process to work toward assisting these needs in the partnership.

(14) Increased use of the public agency and NFP facilities as a human resource center.

(15) Positive attitude of business employees reflected in increased rapport with NFP role in the community.

Strategic Planning and Strategic Management

By far the most significant management tool available to the partnership is strategic planning and management. Administrators and executives are "deceived" into believing that a fiscal budget is a "plan" by itself. Experience has proven that is not the case. Budgets are important, but they are only one element of a strategy. Given two sets of community partnerships with an equal amount of funding, it is quite conceivable that one project will succeed and the other fail.

Such difference in results may be attributed to the lack of understanding of strategy. The strategic framework includes:

Environmental opportunities and risks
Resource assessment of strengths and weaknesses
Value system of the decision-makers

The analysis of the listed areas and systems evolves into a set of objectives and goals, or missions. This set may be called *strategic planning*. However, no plan has any meaning unless it can be successfully implemented. The continuous control and process of implementing the plan is called *strategic management* (most organizations have not used any formal programs for this area of management). Strategic management includes a set of systems for getting things done. Some of these systems are organization and structure, control and information, rewards and punishments, selection and training, negotiation, and formal evaluation of the totality.

It has been said that strategic management is a "holistic approach to the whole" organization. This management tool should be the starting point of every partnership.

For example, a pre-engineering program at a high school receives teacher training from General Motors, the loan of 10 personal computers from IBM, and guest lecturers from the local electric utility. At other schools, local hospitals are supporting a health professions program; a local advertising firm is helping with communications courses; hotels are helping train future hotel managers and chefs; and banks are supporting training in business and finance. In all, the NFP has secured $2.5 million worth of private-sector support in the last 18 months for various school projects.

CONCLUSION

Given the awareness of the budgetary limitations of most NFPs, a partnership with the business community and with public agencies is the wave of the future. It should be obvious that the business sector can provide management techniques that are usually not practiced by many NFPs in the public sector, particularly in the smaller organizations. Of equal significance is that while doing so the business executive can also learn the professional techniques of the NFP and public sector executive. Differences in values can be recognized and, in turn, accommodated as much as possible.

12

Conclusions
— Axioms for NFPs

There are no magic 3 or 13 or 23 steps to better NFP management. The very nature of most NFPs is that they are all highly individualistic. Therefore, we suggest guidelines which apply to most, but not all NFPs as they work to improve their operations, from the initial stages of strategic planning through the never-ending cycles of managing for worthwhile achievements.

1. The basic theme for the existence of any NFP is the mission. In selecting a potential trustee or executive director, it is necessary that he or she have a thorough belief in the mission of that NFP. Without such involvement and belief, all management action is futile.

It goes without saying that few NFPs can afford to pay (or should pay) executive directors for overtime work and other "above average" commitments. Moreover, a significant part of board of trustees work is done on evenings or weekends. This means that the personal and family life of the trustee or executive director must pay a certain price for the many hours devoted to the NFP. Such devotion is only acceptable when the mission is one embraced by all involved. The ED who works 9 to 5 is not the right person for most NFPs, or perhaps shouldn't be involved in any. The ultimate goal or bottom line is the accomplishment of the mission.

2. A potential trustee should receive in writing the minimum number of days and hours per month that is expected. In return there should be an *honest* commitment by the trustee to the time schedules outlined. By the nature of the selection system, most

trustees are busy people prior to being selected. Therefore, one new board membership or assignment may not be feasible given the reality of time limits. A trustee should often refuse the obligation or opportunity to serve unless a current commitment is reduced.

The authors find it inexcusable that private business boards of directors (BOD) manage 90 percent attendance, while board of trustee (BOT) attendance averages 50 percent. This is not fair to the NFP as a whole, other trustees, or staff. A few trustees may be appropriately fulfilling their duties with minimal attendance, if their prestige, heavy financial gifts, or some other attribute makes attendance less obligatory despite their supposed commitment. Most trustees don't fit that mold.

It is all too easy for one's ego to encourage taking on more memberships than can be effectively "digested." This leads to embarrassment for the trustee but, more importantly, poor performance by the NFP that is relying on that trustee. An old Swedish proverb cautions:

> Man should not take more responsibility than
> he can hold in the palm of one hand.

An honest "no" is preferable to an absent trustee.

3. The number of trustees involved in policy setting should be limited to fewer than 10 people. They should be selected and reappointed on staggered, continuing bases. There can be additional board members who can be labeled with euphemisms such as "honary trustees," "committee members," "auxiliary trustees," "advisory trustees," "associate trustees," "council advisors," "guild chairmen," "area chairmen," "district commissioners," and "functional chairmen" (finance, marketing, personnel, etc.).

Such nomenclature can involve 50, 100, or more so-called "trustees" for their political influence or the potential size of their donation. Donation or development categories can also be creatively broken down into founders, benefactors, patrons, sponsors, leader donors, sustaining donors, century fund donors (that might be 100 years worth of giving or only $100), memorial donors, etc. The list on and on, limited only by the inventiveness of development people.

What is clear, however, is that not all donors or volunteer leaders are decision-makers. Only the key policy-makers should, in fact, be given the authority to make policy decisions. Other groups can serve many useful purposes in assisting decision-making, and at times make very valuable suggestions. There is nothing wrong with an "honorary board" whose "only" honor is that they provide most of the cash necessary for an NFP to accomplish its mission. It must be clear, however, that the "policy trustee" or "executive board" or, refreshingly, the "board," is one which truly sets policy and selects the chief executive.

4. The fund-raising function and responsibilities should be defined in writing for each of the trustees and the executive director. Such responsibilities may be characterized in terms of dollars and/or action. It is prudent for the trustee to make a commitment in writing at the start of the term of office. Furthermore, there should be some understanding of the degree to which the trustee will seek the help of friends, contacts, or corporate resources. This may be crucial to the selection of political figures on a board. Most politicians or other public servants are willing to lend their names, but equally unwilling (or unable by law in the case of certain judges) to raise money or give a significant amount of their own time or money. Especially eager for exposure but unwilling to solicit funds is the politician at election time. They can't ask the same person for a political contribution and an NFP donation at the same time. What a public official can do, however, is often make available local government equipment, supplies, and other resources to an NFP at modest or no cost.

Sports and entertainment figures are often called upon to lend their name and time to boards or special events. Their time is often as limited as that of the public official; and NFP boards should use them wisely. Such indirect contributions, either public or private sector in origin, may be quite significant.

5. In the fund-raising arena, we have found that "professionals" (especially in education, medicine, and social service areas) wash their hands of all fund-raising activities. To them this comes under the title of "selling." This attitude must be explored before hiring or promoting anyone to a job in which the fund-raising function is a modest or major duty. There is no reason an executive director and managerial staff should not help in any appropriate way. Good examples of the opposite end of the spectrum from reluctance are artistic directors in the performing arts. Because of their professional talents, and in a

few cases charismatic personalities, they often can raise large sums in a community where others would achieve less.

Even those executive directors or artists (or "professionals") who don't like fund raising can be of assistance with their mere presence. How much would you pay at an auction to have dinner with Beverly Sills, or Jonas Salk, or Leonard Bernstein, or three Nobel prize winners?

6. The management education of the executive director and key staff must be encouraged. Social work, the ministry, or the performing arts may not prepare the ED for an integrative approach to the organization. Most EDs start their education in professional schools, where in past years management skills were never considered. Case studies of patients were the norm, but case studies of the organizations serving those patients were rare. A partial solution to the lack of managerial skills is provided by continuing education, from weekend MBA schooling, advanced management seminars, and in-house programs to outside trade association activities, government-sponsored programs, and a host of other programs that must be analyzed and *budgeted for.*

Encouraging signs in improving management skills include the YMCA's effort to enhance and implement strategic planning at all levels. There's also a growing trend in some theological groups to worry about church finances along with pastoral counseling. For example, the Graduate Theological Union in Berkeley has established an interdenominational summer program in church management.

It is important to remember that continuing education is not something to be limited to schools and universities. Acquisition and maintenance of management skills must be a key objective of the executive director, for himself, his professional staff, and key volunteers.

7. The organizational management education of trustees cannot be ignored either, especially in the "nuts and bolts" of the NFP itself. When a trustee first takes office, that person should be briefed in writing and in person on the past and current activities of that NFP. Ideally, a sound annual report, development materials, and a strategic plan (see San Diego Economic Development Corporation excerpt in Appendix) already exist to quickly provide the trustee with an effective base of knowledge.

The managerial education of trustees is equally crucial. Now that 50 percent of American women are actively working or volunteering, more are serving on NFP boards. Although women are now acquiring management skills more frequently via professional schooling (for example, increasing from virtually zero to more than 25 percent in MBA programs), the social worker, teacher, or nurse (male or female) without any management training is not unusual. They cannot effectively guide an NFP's business affairs without a frame of reference. Especially in finance and marketing, the clergyperson, physician, or, sometimes, lawyer, working his or her way in a community to trustee positions cannot be expected to have the managerial skills we're asking of the executive director. At a minimum, though, they should know what those skills are and why they are important.

At the national level a few NFPs now provide trustee courses. Such programs should be available at the local level where there may be a greater need for such education. Because of time constraints and reluctance of many trustees, a periodic half-day of training may be the maximum feasible. It is suggested that basic accounting, marketing, finance, and organizational behavior be studied. Although trustees are reluctant to take time for this instruction, regularly scheduled education can be productive in limited "doses."

8. With the exception of large NFPs, the lack of a library of key historical files and educational materials is a glaring deficiency. Ideally each NFP should have a notebook or bound volume which accurately describes each past year of operation. In a more general sense a small library of management books can be most valuable:

- Books, audio cassette tapes (and video if affordable) on management techniques
- Self-study courses
- "Industry" trade journals, books, magazines
- NFP-related publications (such as Taft Corporation's "The Nonprofit Executive" newsletter)

9. Executive director and trustee selection must include analysis, evaluation, and plain general discussion of personal value systems. What is significant is the clash or harmony of BOT and ED values. Where these values are not held in common, significant problems usually arise, all to the detriment of the mission of the NFP.

The stronger the variances are in value systems, the greater the potential for conflict. The artistic director or curator moving into the twenty-first century may not be the right person for nineteenth-century art, or a nineteenth-century trustee. In selecting new executive directors, trustees usually focus on professional and educational background, often overlooking the importance of potentially different value systems.

Finally, value systems should not be confused with attitudes toward the NFP mission. These are two separate elements. While two different value systems might support an existing mission, they might differ dramatically on how to fulfill that mission, or adjust it if circumstances force or encourage a change. If an NFP hospital is confronted with difficulties in containing medical costs, it could lead to solutions ranging from modernized expansion to curtailment of emergency services to decentralization to outright closure or sale to a profit-making organization. Any of the options might help fulfill a general mission of improving regional health care, but different trustee/executive director values would lead to markedly different strategies. In the performing arts an artistic director might believe it's more important to improve "reputation" than to balance the budget.

10. Virtually all management and control techniques of the private business sector may be adapted and applied to NFPs. Although NFP missions are rarely stated in monetary terms, key quantitative measures must be established and used. Membership growth, new chapters, turnover/attrition, number of patients treated, and a host of other benchmarks can be established to manage, report on, and control the varied elements of NFP operations. Qualitative concerns are important; undue pressure on "head counts" can cause more harm than good. Nevertheless, in addition to basic financial results, the use of quantified, meaningful performance measures is imperative to sound NFP management.

Specific measurements should also be established with the consent and cooperation of the executive director in order to guide the BOT in measuring the executive director as frequently as regular board meetings. At the time of annual reviews or contract renewal, such concrete benchmarks are all the more important. In fact, in some NFPs, the stronger executive director often takes the lead in establishing performance goals.

One of the most difficult management skills is that of self-evaluation; and executive directors are, at best, no worse than the average professional. Sound evaluation criteria can help.

11. Although belief in mission and agreement on time commitments are vital in selecting trustees, trustees should not be clones of one another. There should be honest disagreements; different trustees will offer a variety of strengths to the NFP.

The potential trustee who may not make a strong time commitment may also have a role. Economics, power, prestige, and self-esteem are all motivators for involvement. Do not overlook these factors in BOT selection. Rather than reject such volunteers, recognize the contribution they can make, and if that includes a trustee role, or some lesser title, make use of it.

12. Use care in the selection of board volunteers for the strategic management committee. It should be limited to five to ten people.

Each person should be capable and experienced in a skill of value to the planning process, for example, finance, control, fund raising, marketing, etc. Incorporate these areas of specialization into the NFP plan. The mission and values *of the NFP as a whole must be recognized* in the planning group's work. An attempt to incorporate these diverse values into the NFP plan should be made.

13. In selecting trustees, money alone may be an appropriate reason for board membership. Such trustees should be balanced with trustees offering total commitment and management skills and/or the support of their private sector corporations. As noted, corporate leaders can also augment their value by using non-monetary resources of their organizations. Examples include computer time-sharing, printing support, secretarial support, word processing, mailing services, and loaned executives.

14. The area of special funds cannot be left solely to the BOT. Assign a designated trustee or professional fund raiser the task of organizing both short-term and long-term systems for major donations. There is nothing wrong with professional fund raisers per se; they oftentimes are crucial when schools or hospitals embark on major capital acquisition programs.

Unfortunately, there are also cases of junior business groups or athletic organizations that have relied on "professionals" (not the professionals used for million dollar or $100 million building programs) to sell plastic bags, jams and jelly, or athletic event tickets, and give up 90 percent of the proceeds. The ultimate responsibility, however, is always that of the board of trustees.

15. The use of large grants from foundations, bequests, and other special gifts offers dramatic opportunities for the NFP. What is often forgotten is that these opportunities carry risks. Diversion of such funds to normal operations could leave the NFP vulnerable to future budget cuts. Special short-term projects, capital expenditures, and seed money for future projects are all appropriate uses. The BOT role as financial planners is especially crucial. Most NFPs seek financial security through endowment funding and other fund-raising programs. However, only the successful ones set aside part of their current funds to provide for long-term financial stability.

One regional health care group set a major goal of reducing the amount of federal money it received. At the point this goal was set in 1974, federal support covered 85 percent of the NFP's budget. By 1982, it dropped 15 percent, while total budget and service delivery more than tripled. Stepped-up fund raising and the initiation of a sliding scale for patient charges were both used effectively in this process. Finally, the board and executive director withdrew from all federal programs, both because of their self-sufficiency and the year-to-year risks (and strings) of the federal support.

16. The NFP needs to fund its operations from one or more sources. Given changing tax laws and tighter public budgets, the BOT must address finances realistically. The NFP which conservatively avoids optimistic projections of income in turn avoids drastic year-end cutbacks. Devil's advocates in the budget process are useful counterpoints to bubbling optimism.

The concern for the bottom line is universal in the U.S. business world. Yet many NFPs have begun "outlandish" projects without concern for questioning the budgetary impact of such programs. The individual silence of a trustee does not necessarily mean approval.

Trustees should avoid conflict related to "pet projects" where financial impact is significant, or potentially significant in the future. When such expenditures are not truly resolved at an early stage, the resulting conflict from project failure can be disastrous.

17. Use bonus and other incentive systems common to private business with the ED and other professional staff. The criteria for such incentives should be largely related to measurable performance. The kinds and amounts of such bonuses should be openly negotiated by the ED with a small trustee executive or compensation committee.

18. The creation of team spirit between NFP professional staff and trustee volunteers is a process which can materially enhance the success of the organization. The leader can be either the ED or a trustee. However, leadership must be clearly identified to coordinate paid and volunteer staff activity, and in turn to receive the support of all.

19. The success of the organization may be dependent upon the continuity of strategic planning and strategic management. Hence, the succession of trustees and the selection of a new ED should be intertwined not only with the mission but also with the strategy of the organization.

20. Contrary to popular belief, trustees, even in church groups, are fully responsible for the activities (and in certain states) the legal debts of an NFP. Wherever feasible, directors' and officers' liability insurance should be purchased. (This still doesn't release a trustee from the aggravation and court time if, in fact, the NFP is sued.) This insurance, however, in no way reduces the moral obligations of the trustee to accomplish the NFP mission.

21. The process of training volunteer trustees to use strategic management has generally not been pursued. Serving as or using outside consultants, the authors have observed a variety of successful approaches to the planning phase of the strategic management cycle. The following approach can fit most trustees' schedules. It has ranged in success from, at worst, a good interchange of ideas to, at best, the establishment of a meaningful, ongoing, strategic management program:

a. Hire experienced consultant.
b. Each trustee is interviewed to discuss values, goals, problems, and potential resolutions.
c. The consultant designs a seminar, with an agenda to integrate as a group the ideas considered individually.
d. Each trustee is then assigned a particular functional area of planning.
e. Such plans are exchanged among the trustees.
f. Another three-hour meeting is then held to evaluate each of the areas to develop a final, coherent plan. Criteria for evaluation must be established.
g. Some months later a follow-up meeting is held to evaluate progress and move on to appropriate next steps.

Although the Appendix (San Diego Economic Development Corporation plan) contains most elements of such a plan, it should be emphasized that only "half the battle" is complete when the plan is first drafted. It must be implemented by specific people doing specific tasks on a specific timetable. And, at the same time, a team spirit must unify this individually accountable effort.

Plans Don't Do Anything
People Do

CONCLUSION

It is apparent that business executives who become trustees do not apply their managerial expertise to their NFP volunteer efforts. Most executives work long hours to create wealth, which in part is then donated to NFPs. It is ironic that they fail to exercise anywhere near the same effort as a trustee as they watch their donations "vanish into empty air."

This void in management is most apparent in the formulation and implementation of strategy. Factors such as size, continuity, time, and lack of measurements might be used as excuses to limit the utility of private sector managerial tools. However, managerial tools can be structured to work for the NFP sector without impairing the spirit and substance of the NFP mission.

Where cases cited strike you as being close to home, be assured that the NFPs studied cover a wide range of geographic and functional areas. Whether the comparisons be pleasurable or painful, the message is that thousands of NFPs share many of the same problems and satisfactions. Although we have focused on the strategic management deficiencies of the NFP and concomitant challenges, our own service record supports a strong faith and appreciation of volunteerism within the NFPs throughout America. We also salute the trustees and executive directors who support and manage hundreds of thousands of not-for-profit organizations with their own faith and resources.

Appendixes

Appendix I:
Community Services for
the Disabled, Inc.
— A Case Study

On the evening of September 3, several people were gathered in Suite 10 of the Community Service Center for the Disabled's (CSCD) suite of offices in downtown San Diego. Several more people straggled in over the next half-hour. They had all come for the monthly Board of Directors (BOD) meeting for CSCD. The suite was large and well lit, with sunlight pouring in through the large windows at both ends of the room. Several conference tables had been pushed together to create one very large table around which everyone sat. The atmosphere was one of informality. The Chairperson, Dr. Cathy Johns, called the meeting to order shortly after 5:00, approximately 20 people were present.

After the routine business of the approval of the minutes and general introductions had been discharged, Ray Zanella, Co-Executive Director (ED) of CSCD, passed out copies of an undated, handwritten budget proposal. (See Exhibit 1.) After board members questioned the purpose of the proposal, it was pointed out that it was a budget worksheet for the fiscal year which started October 1. The next hour or so was consumed in discussing this budget, with Mr. Zanella providing most of the input. After an hour of questions and answers, it was apparent that few of the directors understood the budget proposal.

The budget worksheet listed nine sources of revenue (many of which were grants) and seventeen line items. There was an operating deficit of $34,927 and a possible total deficit of nearly $70,000. The difference between the two hinged on the $31,500 allocated for personnel from a potential grant from the state for Comprehensive Service Centers (AB 2687).[1] It was unclear to the directors exactly why this was so. The possibility of employee layoffs in general was mentioned. However, Ray Zanella optimistically forecast the deficit to be $35,000, $20,000 of which included costs of rent, utilities, and office maintenance.

This case was written by Deborah Ford, Research Assistant , under the direction of Dr. Israel Unterman, Professor of Management, College of Business Administration, San Diego State University, San Diego, California. It was prepared as a basis for class discussion, rather than to illustrate either effective or ineffective handling of an administrative situation. Copyright 1983 by Dr. Israel Unterman, San Diego State University.

EXHIBIT 1 Community Service Center for the Disabled, Inc.—
Budget Worksheet Presented to Directors at September BOD Meeting

	State ILC Grant	City Revenue Sharing	County Revenue Sharing	United Way De-Inst Grant
PERSONNEL				
Salaries	418,260	14,436	6,456	14,840
Fringe Benefits/Taxes	57,035	2,598	734	2,375
Subtotal	475,295	17,034	7,190	17,215
ADMINISTRATIVE				
Unallocated				
Space Costs	41,193	2,330	939	2,100
Telephone	8,000	900	147	490
Supplies	3,000	264	33	145
Postage	2,000	96	5	140
Painting/Publication	6,000	72	15	
Travel	2,000	252	197	210
Van Insurance	3,000			
Vehicle Maintenance	2,000			
Equipment				
Equipment Maintenance	500			
Interpreter Services	500			
Accounting Services	2,000		330	
Product Liability				
Consultants/Training	500			
W/C Inventory				
Miscellaneous (Interest, Fees, etc.)				
Subtotal	70,693	3,914	1,666	3,085
TOTAL	$545,988	$20,948	$8,856	$20,300

DR CBA Grant	United Way ILP Base Allocation	Wheel-chair Repair Program	Dues, Fees, Dona-tions	AB* 2687-CSC	Total Revenue	Total Expense	Balance
21,948	13,992	35,800		28,125	553,857	553,875	
2,853	1,679	6,086		3,375	76,735	76,735	
24,801	15,671	41,886		31,500	630,592	630,592	
			4,000		4,000	4,000	
4,200	3,000	13,800		5,500	73,062	92,644	(19,582)
2,100	1,734	1,200		3,000	17,571	17,400	171
600	600	2,400		100	7,142	9,000	(1,858)
250	300	1,200		200	4,191	6,000	(1,809)
	100	5,600		100	11,887	18,000	(6,113)
2,850	150	2,000		1,000	8,659	10,000	(1,341)
		2,200			5,200	4,400	800
		3,600			5,600	6,000	(400)
		14,870			14,870	14,870	
	100	1,800			2,400	2,400	
175	100				775	1,200	(425)
	600	3,600		500	7,030	11,400	(4,370)
		4,500			4,500	4,500	
		2,500		100	3,100	3,100	
		18,200			18,200	18,200	
		200	6,000		6,200	6,200	
10,175	6,684	77,670	10,000	10,500	194,387	229,314	($34,927)
$34,976	$22,355	$119,556	$10,000	$42,000	$824,979	$859,906	($34,927)

**EXHIBIT 1 A Community Service Center for the Disabled, Inc.—
Explanation of Items on Budget Worksheet**

Revenue Sources:

State ILC Grant—A state grant, administered by the Department of Rehabilitation, for Independent Living Centers.

City/County Revenue Sharing—These grants originated from funds distributed by the state to cities and counties. The funds were then distributed by the cities and counties to social service agencies.

United Way De-institutionalization Grant—A one-time project grant to assist in the de-institutionalization process of disabled people. See Note 11.

DR CBA Grant—A Community Based Advocate grant from the Department of Rehabilitation. This staffing grant provided for one advocate and one clerical position. The advocate acted as the regional liaison between CSCD and the State Department of Rehabilitation.

United Way ILP Base Allocation—A grant, by the United Way, to provide independent living services to the community.

Wheelchair Repair Program—The Spoke Shop, a wheelchair repair shop, was a business subsidiary of CSCD. The BOD had previously requested that all financial information for the Spoke Shop be prepared and presented separately.

AB 2687 CSC—A potential grant to develop a Comprehensive Service Center. See Note 1.

Line Items:

Unallocated—Those monies that had no restrictions placed on their use.

Interpreter Service—To provide interpreters for hearing-impaired clients or board members.

Consultants/Training—To provide for workshops and/or seminars.

W/C Inventory—Wheelchair inventory for the Spoke Shop.

A point that was brought up during the budget discussion was a need for an additional full-time bookkeeper to assist Bobby Williams, the accountant, and the current part-time bookkeeper, Virginia Harper. No one mentioned how this addition to the staff would be funded.

Even though there were still questions in the minds of the board members, and at least a $35,000 deficit, it seemed important to Zanella, Williams, and Bill Tainter (the other Co-Executive Director) that the Board approve the proposed budget. This the Board was not willing to do. Instead, Rod Tompkins, a board member, suggested that solutions be found to offset the deficit, and that the budget be reintroduced for approval at the next BOD meeting. To this end, the Chair requested a committee of board members be formed to assist Zanella, Tainter, and Williams with the budget and finances. After three volunteers had been elicited from the group, the discussion of the budget began to wane.

All of the people present seemed to be friendly, interested, and dedicated to CSCD. The group was comprised of board members, staff representatives, and key CSCD personnel. Many of them apparently had non-business backgrounds. This seemed evident by the questions that were asked, and the answers that were given, during the budget discussion. Having so many people present, while broadening the base, seemed to add to the length of the discussion.

There was a unique feature to the BOD membership: the Chairperson was physically disabled.[2] In fact, over 75 percent of the people present had very noticeable physical disabilities of one form or another.

History

Two days after he moved to San Diego, Ray Zanella attended a meeting at San Diego State University (SDSU) where about 30 people had gathered to discuss the development of an ILP[3] in San Diego. Zanella was elected as chairman of the task force to develop the ILP.

Before coming to San Diego, Zanella, a hemophiliac, had been very involved in the Independent Living movement. He, along with Betty Bacon and others, was instrumental in developing the Disabled Student Union at San Jose State University (SJSU). Later, while still an engineering student, Ray worked as the Disabled Student staff advisor. The movement accelerated. The Center for Independent Living (CIL) Berkeley was started by Ed Roberts and other disabled activitists. After graduating, Zanella went to work for CIL-Berkeley as a benefits counselor. As Zanella and Bacon were leaving for San Diego, Ed Roberts was leaving for Sacramento to become the new Director of the State Department of Rehabilitation (DR).[4]

Zanella had been told by Roberts that DR was planning to set aside $600,000 of "innovation expansion monies" for the development of ILPs in California. He also knew that his task force in San Diego would have to incorporate to get any of it. CSCD was incorporated in March of the following year. The task force had by that time dwindled to just a handful of people. Almost word for word, Ray based the bylaws and articles of incorporation on CIL-Berkeley. He and Betty Bacon did most of the work on the grant proposal to DR, often working through the night. They had been told that the average grant would be $70,000. Since they didn't want to underfund CSCD, they requested $88,000. The grants were a 90/10 percent match. They had to come up with 10 percent of the $88,000 before they got any money from DR. The DR grant money would be available to them if they had the match money.

At this point CSCD still had no office and no staff. There were nine directors, both disabled and able-bodied, all of whom were dedicated to the independent living concept. Ray was elected Chairman of the BOD. As required by law, all were volunteers. These volunteers, particularly Ray and Betty, canvassed local agencies and businesses for the $8,800 they needed. They had four months to get the money, or forfeit the State-DR grant. Though CSCD received moral support for what it was trying to accomplish, only National Cash Register came up with any money. That $300 was used for supplies and postage. By September, time was getting short and everyone at CSCD was desperate. Finally Ray took CSCD's idea for an ILP to the Easter Seals Advisory Board. This was made possible by a referral to Dale Williams of Easter Seals. He pushed CSCD's application through. Rod Tompkins, then Chairman of the Grants Subcommittee of Easter Seals, believed in the idea. CSCD received $8,500 from Easter Seals in time to meet the deadline.

Ray resigned as Chairman of the BOD and was appointed the Acting Executive Director. He was attending graduate classes at SDSU and was not certain that he wanted to commit most of his time to CSCD. Therefore, he asked his old friend from SJSU, Bill Tainter, to travel to San Diego and share a joint executive directorship with him. Tainter, a post-polio victim from the age of 13, was then involved in developing an ILC in San Jose. He decided to accept Zanella's offer and, in November, the BOD hired Tainter and Zanella as the Co-Executive Directors of CSCD. CSCD opened its doors that next February with three employees: Bill Tainter, Ray Zanella, and Julie Witcoff (as secretary).

Mission

Zanella defined the mission of CSCD in its first year as "to provide a support service mechanism where people with disabilities could have more opportunities for independent living."

The concept for independent living grew from the activism of disabled persons in the late 1960s and early 1970s. Many disabled persons did not want to be the recipients of pity or to be considered helpless and useless. Many felt that their needs were not being adequately recognized or met by the various existing agencies. There were about 30 agencies in San Diego that served the needs of the disabled. However, each one served either a specific need or a specific disability. By that time, CSCD had 43 members,[5] 31 of whom were disabled. The members wanted the organization to provide comprehensive independent living services to the disabled population in San Diego.[6] The members felt that having a constituent-controlled and operated[7] organization would provide the necessary "inside" knowledge to make CSCD a valid and viable organization.

Five years later, the official mission statement of the organization defined the mission of CSCD as "to establish and operate a comprehensive service organization, controlled by persons with disabilities, which promotes their self-determination in independent living by providing supportive services, promoting a barrier-free environment, and advocating for their civil rights."[8] Though the wording varied, the staff and directors interviewed all gave basically that same definition, with one exception: Zanella, Tainter, and Cathy Johns were the ones who identified advocacy as part of CSCD's mission.

Most people felt that the key way of achieving the mission of the organization was by hiring the appropriate staff to provide the various services to the clients. Bill Tainter and Rod Tompkins felt that a formalized method for measuring the success of CSCD was needed. Basically, the criteria used were the growth of the agency in terms of budget and clients served, and client feedback on the quality of services.

Services

The objectives of CSCD were considered to be specifically related to a service or department. Section 19801 of AB 204 required that an ILC:

> Provide, but not be limited to, the following services to disabled individuals: peer counseling, advocacy, attendant referral, housing assistance and other referrals. [And] provide other services and referrals as may be deemed necessary, such as transportation, job development, equipment maintenance and evaluation, training in independent living skills, mobility assistance and communication assistance.

Some of the services provided by CSCD were the following ones included in an undated paper by Bill Tainter and Ray Zanella,, "The Independing Living Program in America's Finest City":

Housing Services	Accessible apartment lists, moving assistance, rent subsidy programs, emergency housing assistance
Counseling Services	Assertiveness training, personal adjustment counseling, pre-employment and life counseling

EXHIBIT 2 Community Service Center for the Disabled, Inc.

TABLE I Community Service Center for the Disabled, Inc.—
Number of Clients Receiving Services*
(July 1, 198- to February 28, 198-)

Month	Client Contacts	Community Contacts	Total Contacts
July	540	560	1100
August	599	523	1122
September	583	562	1145
October	611	458	1069
November	508	405	913
December	611	403	1014
January	662	425	1087
February	658	490	1148
Total	4772	3826	8598

*Unduplicated.

TABLE II Community Service Center for the Disabled, Inc.—
Number of Clients Receiving Services by Components
(July 1, 198- to February 28, 198-)

Service Component/ Month	July	Aug	Sep	Oct	Nov	Dec	Jan	Feb	Total
Attendant referral	352	253	314	271	253	281	234	257	2215
Housing referral	121	180	137	155	155	144	163	205	1260
Transportation	22	25	23	24	19	25	24	27	189
Counseling	81	112	180	224	189	214	268	251	1519
Financial counseling	28	60	21	46	48	52	69	85	409
Benefits counseling	52	86	117	129	101	104	96	150	835
Personal advocacy	113	136	147	144	114	111	187	189	1141
Employment	218	202	202	254	181	226	206	243	1732
Total	987	1054	1141	1247	1060	1157	1247	1407	9300

Source: "Application for AB 2687, Comprehensive Service Center, Pilot Project: Phase I," submitted by Community Service Center for the Disabled, Inc.

Employment Assistance	Job seeking skills, job and resume bank, placement assistance, job development
Benefits Counseling	Financial assistance programs, paralegal services, community liaison
Personal Helper Referral	Attendants/housekeepers screening and referral
Disability Awareness	Awareness training and sensitization services for educators, rehabilitation professionals, students, employers, and community groups
Nondiscrimination and Affirmative Action	Consultation on barrier removal and employment practices to assist in the implementation of Section 504, Rehabilitation Act of 1973

See Exhibit 2 for statistics related to client usage of each service component.

Funding

CSCD's major sources of funds were from government and private grants.[9] In their fifth fiscal year they were administering seven grants totaling $750,000; $550,000 was from the State Independent Living Center grant AB 204. Other grantors included City and County Revenue Sharing and the United Way.

CSCD had to submit applications for grants on a yearly basis. However, many of the grant sources had an "unwritten" policy to continue funding the organization. Mr. Zanella estimated that they were able to forecast approximately 80 percent of their funds due to this policy. However, he was quick to point out that there was an ever-present danger of changes due to government cutbacks. These grant contracts had termination clauses: 30 days for the State of California and 72 hours for City/County Revenue Sharing.

The funding process was a complex one at CSCD. The grants could differ in the way the monies were received. Some provided advance operating money, but most were on a reimbursable 90/10 percent match.[10] Additionally, each grantor required monthly expenditure reports and reimbursement requests. (See Exhibit 3.) Since the grants operated on a pro rata basis for the costs they shared, cost allocation was necessary. Some grants were very specific in purpose and did not provide for all costs (for example, staffing grants, project grants,[11] etc.).

Zanella, Tainter, and Williams determined the cost allocation in two steps. First, they calculated the number of employees that shared in a similar benefit,

EXHIBIT 3 Community Service Center for the Disabled, Inc.—Expenditure Report Request Form
for the State Department of Rehabilitation

STATE OF CALIFORNIA
DEPARTMENT OF REHABILITATION

OPERATING EXPENSE BUDGET EXPENDITURE REPORT AND PAYMENT REQUEST

PAYMENT TERMS NET 30 ☒ OTHER

FACILITY NAME AND ADDRESS
Community Service Center
1295 University Avenue
San Diego, CA 92103

PERIOD COVERED FROM 11/1/81 TO 11/30/81

THIS REPORT INCLUDES
BUDGET REVISION ☐ MAN ___ I ___ DATED 10/1/81

PAGE 1 OF 2

PAYMENT BENEFIT NUMBER 8864

A BUDGET LINE NUMBER	B QUANT	C DESCRIPTION OF EXPENSE ITEM	D DATE	E TOTAL AMOUNT BUDGETED	F AMOUNT CLAIMED REQUEST	G AMOUNT CLAIMED THIS PERIOD	H ATTACHED INVOICE NUMBER	I TOTAL CLAIMED TO DATE (F + G = n)	J AMOUNT OVER UNDER BUDGET
1		Van Insurance		3,500	3400	0		3400	100
2		Insurance		2,000	55.29	0		55.29	1044.71
3		Van Maintenance		2,000	1300.81	133.30		1434.11	575.49
4		Office Maintenance		1,000	0	0		0	1000
5		Rent		49,693	25,941.88	5,232.81		31,174.76	19,518.24
6		Consultants		500	0	0		0	500
7		Telephone		10,000	5,016.16	1,763.64		6779.80	3220.20
8		Accounting		2,000	21.99	0		21.77	1978.23
9		Travel		4,500	1456.33	1208.91		2665.02	1834.95
10		Equipment Maintenance		1,000	683.61	32.68		715.81	284.19
		PAGE TOTAL		76,193	37,875.65	8370.91		46,246.56	29,916.44

ACCUMULATIVE TOTAL

PROJECT BUDGET 100 %

CONTRACT | CONTRACT TOTAL | TOTAL EXPENSE | AMOUNT REQUESTED | DISCOUNT IF APPLICABLE | NET AMOUNT REQUESTED | **PAY THIS AMOUNT**

REIMBURSEMENT RATE 100 %

REIMBURSEMENT APPROVAL

DEPARTMENT OF REHABILITATION ACCOUNTING SECTION USE ONLY				DATE	SIGNATURE OF CLAIMANT
SPECIALTY	PROGRAM	SOURCE	FACILITY		

STATE OF CALIFORNIA
DEPARTMENT OF REHABILITATION

OPERATING EXPENSE BUDGET EXPENDITURE
REPORT AND PAYMENT REQUEST

FACILITY NAME AND ADDRESS
Community Service Center
1295 University Avenue
San Diego, CA 92103

PERIOD COVERED FROM 11/1/81 TO 11/30/81
THIS REPORT INCLUDES BUDGET REVISION
MAN DATED 10/1/81

PAGE 2 OF 2
PAYMENT BENEFIT NUMBER 8864 / 5

PAYMENT TERMS NET 30 X OTHER

A BUDGET LINE NUMBER	B QUANT	C DESCRIPTION OF EXPENSE ITEM	D DATE	E TOTAL AMOUNT BUDGETED	F AMOUNT CLAIMED REQUEST	G AMOUNT CLAIMED THIS PERIOD	H ATTACHED INVOICE NUMBER	I TOTAL CLAIMED TO DATE (F + G = n)	J AMOUNT OVER UNDER BUDGET
11		Supplies		3,000	1,881.54	556.47		2438.01	561.99
12		Postage		3,000	1,457.19	198.31		1655.50	1344.50
13		Printing/Publication		6,000	4,904.07	309.03		5213.10	781.98
14		Interpretor Services		500	0	0		0	500.00
15		Client Transportation		500	75—	15—		90—	410.00
PAGE TOTAL				13,000	8,317.80	1078.81		9346.61	3603.09
ACCUMULATIVE TOTAL				89,193	46,193.18	9449.72		55,643.07	33,549.83
PROJECT BUDGET 100 %				89,193	46,193.18	9449.72		55,643.07	33,549.83

CONTRACT

CONTRACT TOTAL	PRIOR EXPEND	AMOUNT REQUESTED	DISCOUNT (IF APPLICABLE)	NET AMOUNT REQUESTED
		9449.72		**PAY THIS AMOUNT**

REIMBURSEMENT RATE 100 %

REIMBURSEMENT APPROVAL

DEPARTMENT OF REHABILITATION
ACCOUNTING SECTION USE ONLY

SPECIALTY	PROGRAM	SOURCE	FACILITY

SIGNATURE OF CLAIMANT

DATE

such as rent. Then they broke that down on a pro rata basis for each grant. This was necessary because of the "fair-share"[12] doctrine employed by CSCD funding sources.

Searching out new sources, writing grant applications, and monitoring existing grants was a time-consuming and continuous process at CSCD. Grant applications could vary in length from one page for a continuing grant, to 100 pages for a project proposal. Many hours were spend on researching and developing potential money sources. For example, preparation of the project proposal for a Comprehensive Service Center involved five staff members and a total of 100 hours. Zanella and Tainter worked on these things year-round, because grants could be awarded at any time during the year.

Personnel

In November CSCD had 35 employees, two-thirds of whom were disabled. Of those 35, five had undergraduate degrees and 13 had advanced degrees, primarily in the social sciences. Many of these people had known each other for many years, particularly the key executives. There was a decidedly friendly and informal atmosphere at CSCD. Employees, executives, and board members were all on a first-name basis.

The agency was organized into four major departments. (See Exhibit 4.) The five-member management team was comprised of the heads of departments and the executive directors. Because Ray and Bill shared the position of executive director (only one position was funded), they each assumed another half-time position. Ray became the Deputy Director, and Bill was the Program Manager in charge of administrative services.[13] Such distinctions were made for funding purposes only.

Bill and Ray were directly responsible for all the personnel at CSCD. The managers did their own interviewing. Their selections were then interviewed by Ray and/or Bill. The managers examined the applicant's listed qualifications. Ray and Bill concentrated on his/her philosophical 'qualification' in regard to disability and the independent living concept. This was done in an effort to have CSCD operate as a cohesive unit of people.

CSCD was an Equal Opportunity (EOP) employer with an Affirmative Action (AA) program.[14] CSCD made an effort to recruit ethnic minorities, women, and disabled individuals. Job announcements were sent to 494 agencies and/or individuals in the county that served these populations. Bill felt that the agency was "too skewed towards male dominance in key executive positions." He wanted CSCD to have a dynamic disabled woman in a key position.

California Law AB 204 required that a majority of board members of ILCs be disabled. It further required that as many employees as possible be disabled. Having personal experience with disabilities was a qualification for all positions

**EXHIBIT 4 Community Service Center for the Disabled, Inc.—
CSCD Organizational Chart***

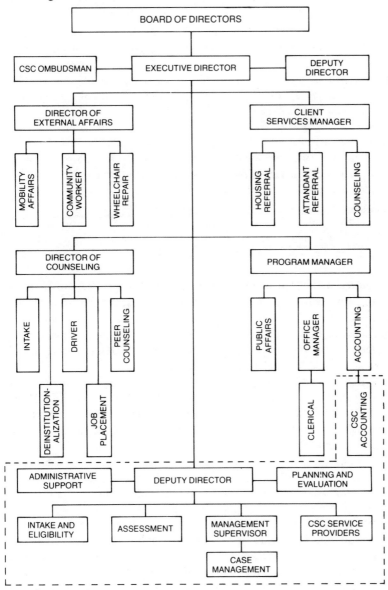

*The areas within the broken lines reflect potential additions if AB 2687 is funded.

Source: Company records.

at CSCD. The EDs hired the most qualified person for the job; however, there was a decided preference to employ disabled people. Ray said that some able-bodied people tended to get angry at this means of selection. (This casewriter was treated with respect, courtesy, and friendliness, yet still felt at a disadvantage because she was able-bodied.)

CSCD utilized volunteers, but had no formal volunteer program. Volunteers came to CSCD in one of two ways. Some were referred by the municipal court to work off a misdemeanor fine at $5/hr. These referrals came from a variety of career fields, such as lawyers, rehabilitation counselors, construction workers, etc. The major source of volunteers, however, came from disabled people who wanted something to do. When they contacted CSCD, they were referred to Julie Witcoff. Julie showed these people around the organization and asked them what they wanted to do, "so they would be happy." She then sought to discover where that volunteer could be useful. Approximately 25 potential volunteers came through the agency in one year: six were referred by the court and the remainder were disabled people who wanted to help out.

CSCD had one clerical volunteer who had come in daily for more than a year. Four others came in on a regular bimonthly basis, and three or four others could be called in to help out with special projects. The majority of the work was clerical in nature. The use of volunteers was a very informal process and no official records were kept.

Bill Tainter wanted to initiate a more systematic volunteer program. He wanted to identify what staff needs were, write job descriptions, and advertise for persons who wanted to volunteer for the work. He had no target number in mind. His idea was to provide operating support for the agency. A board member had suggested the business internship program at SDSU[15] as a source of volunteers. No action had been taken along these lines.

Julie Witcoff hated to see the volunteer 'program' become bureaucratic. She felt that the casualness of the agency was a fringe benefit that some people may not have recognized. For example, one person brought a baby to work and another brought a dog. She thought that this informality did much to relieve some of the tension at CSCD.

In the spring of that year, there was a great deal of tension in the organization. It had inadvertently come to a few of the employees' attention that management was planning some type of reorganization. Due to funding cutbacks, some positions would be eliminated. The unofficial phrase was "justify your position." Many of the employees wanted to have some input in the decision. An ad hoc committee was formed to address management on the issue. This committee later decided to send a memo to the BOD requesting that they be informed about the situation. Copies were also sent to all staff members. The employees requested that an official staff committee be formed. The tension at CSCD mounted.

Prior to this employee involvement, the decision regarding which positions to cut was to be made by Ray and Bill. After the staff memo was distributed, it was decided that this was a policy issue for the BOD. There was no established criterion or procedure to follow to make such decisions. Therefore, the BOD had to establish a policy. After much discussion by both staff and BOD, the decision was made to eliminate two positions. The staff voted to forego salary increases in order to save a third position.

Although the 'personnel crisis' was over, morale continued to present a problem at CSCD. Bill Tainter and Ray Zanella thought that the issue was vertical communication. Some staff did not think the executive directors receptive to their input. Some staff were also confused about their job descriptions. In an effort to rectify this, the EDs had requested that each employee write his/her own job description. The employees were to write these descriptions in conjunction with their supervisor. It was felt that this would help everyone understand the responsibilities and expectations associated with each position. Job descriptions could also make the process of staff evaluations "more meaningful and effective." The executive directors, themselves, had not considered their own job descriptions. However, they thought it might be a good idea to do so, as there was no formal method available by which the BOD could evaluate their performance.

Another factor contributing to low morale was the assumption of many of the able-bodied employees that they could never "really fit in." They were not disabled and could not be vitally involved in the disabled movement. Some sensed a strong protectiveness among many of the disabled employees. Other contributing factors were those found in many organizations: low pay and high-stress workloads.

Executive Directors

Bill Tainter and Ray Zanella both thought that their collaboration as co-executive directors had been very successful. They shared the same general philosophy about the organization and the political disabled movement. They were able to motivate each other by sharing ideas and providing valuable feedback for each other. Ray believed that their trust in one another and their ability to communicate without many words were key reasons for their success. Bill included another advantage of this co-leadership: "We don't have to worry about the place falling apart if one of us is away."[16]

Julie felt that the co-executive directorship worked very well. She thought that Ray and Bill did complement each other effectively. "Ray was excellent in working with the budget and managed things well. Bill excelled in verbal skills and grant writing; he managed people well." Whenever the two EDs disagreed about something, they discussed it until an agreement was reached. Julie agreed with Ray and Bill that there were no significant problems with the relationship.

There was no clearly defined separation of duties for Bill and Ray. What they did was based primarily on their own preference and their experience with a particular activity or agency. Ray's interests lay more with the physical aspects of the office and building. He was concerned with barrier-removal consulting for other organizations.[17] Bill was more interested in community relations and activities, such as speaking to groups and meeting with influential people. These activities, however, constituted only a small percentage of their actual workload.

The majority of their time was occupied with administration—supervising staff functions, program development, hiring, monitoring grants, developing new grant sources, and completing the mounds of required paperwork. They also worked on board-related issues when necessary. (See section on BOD.)

The largest percentage of their time spent on administrative tasks was occupied in obtaining and monitoring funding. Bill went so far as to say:

> My primary role here is to keep the funding coming. . . . Most of the money coming into this organization is a result of Ray and I. . . . I try to get away from the things that I think are somewhat routinely related to contract administration. I think it's necessary that I take an active role in assuring that things appear to be going the way they should in terms of grants, but I don't think that's an activity that I should spend as much time on as I have in the past. I would like to phase some of those activities down to make time for things related to promoting the agency in the community.

Although Ray and Bill each monitored several grants and worked on different projects, there was no clearcut way to describe how their duties differed. They worked independently of each other on several things, yet managed joint decisions or concurrence on nearly everything. Ray attributed it to their complementary talents.

Budget

The annualized budget of CSCD grew from $88,000 to $750,000 (excluding the $120,000 for the Spoke Shop) in five years. Bill Tainter and Ray Zanella, with assistance of Controller Bobby Williams, would start working on the budget two or three months prior to the end of the state fiscal year, June 30. This was the time when their contracts were renewed.

Bill and Ray started the process by gathering operational information from the managers and financial information from Bobby Williams. There were basically two different aspects to preparing the budget: first, the EDs determined how many dollars they would have, and what services they had to offer according to AB 204. Then, they had to see how the funds they were assured would allow them to provide these selected services. They looked at the fixed costs and, based upon their experience, chose a level for operating costs. Salaries had been fairly standardized and they worked with the BOD to set cost-of-living and merit increases. This became their historically-based budget. The other aspect to preparing the budget was to decide on what potential services they would like to offer, yet couldn't afford. They then attempted to develop a plan for obtaining the money.

After a budget had been determined, it would go to the BOD for approval. (See Exhibit 1.) As Ray explained it, "It's kind of moot, because most of our money is in the form of contracts (grants). If the BOD approves the contracts, they've already approved that portion of the budget." Because of the fair-share doctrine, CSCD had to prepare individual budgets for each grant. These budgets, usually prepared by Bobby Williams, were included in the contracts. Internally, these data were used by Bill, Ray, and Bobby to monitor grants. If, during the year, CSCD either acquired new funding or lost existing grants (defunding), the budget(s) had to be revised. Thus, budgeting was a never-ending process at CSCD.

Administrative Services

Accounting

The accounting department at CSCD consisted of one accountant, one full-time bookkeeper, and one part-time bookkeeper. Bobby Williams described the function of his department as "to account for all the money coming into CSCD, to make sure we remain solvent, and to take care of any kind of financial transactions in the agency." Bill Tainter described the function as "to ensure that funds are adequately and appropriately accounted for, that adequate budgeting procedures are followed and that we're adhering to the requirements of the grants."

In order to assure compliance with grant requirements, CSCD used a fund accounting system.[18] Each grant, if required by the grant source, had its own separate fund. One fund was used for those grants that did not require separate accountability. In addition, CSCD had a General Fund to account for monies that did not come from grants.

CSCD utilized two computerized accounting services. The California First Bank Computer Payroll Service was used for the monthly payroll. Bobby monitored all of the time sheets, made inputs of the data to the bank, and monitored the output. The disbursements and receipts general ledgers were coded to the Accounting Corporation of America computer service. Bobby sent out reimbursement forms for each grant every month. (See section on funding.) He then monitored the incoming receipts to make sure the agency was receiving the proper amount of money. He also monitored the reimbursements to ensure that

CSCD. was within the allowable limits, according to the budgets. All checks drawn for disbursements required source documentation of either an invoice or a CSCD purchase order.

The accounting office was extremely unorganized when Bobby came to CSCD nearly two years before. This was primarily due to the prolonged illness and subsequent death of a previous accountant. Bobby undertook to organize the office and get it to operate efficiently. It took over ten months to consolidate the old records. This workload, in addition to the current workload and a limited staff, made it impossible for Bobby to utilize the computer services to their fullest potential. There was no time available to input data for the computers. Manual subsidiary ledgers were used to prepare the reimbursement reports. Monthly statements were 35–45 days late. The end-of-year statements had been 8–10 months late for each of the previous two years. Bobby estimated, however, that the current end-of-year statements would be on time.

CSCD did not have an annual report. The routine financial statements prepared by the accounting office were balance sheets. (See Appendix B.) Other statements were prepared at the request of the EDs. For example, Bobby had prepared three cash flow statements that year for the EDs. Bobby also generated various reports and statements for the BOD. These statements were frequently unsolicited by the BOD. According to Rod Tompkins:

> The statements were likely to come at any time. They were always prepared to prove a particular point or situation and the "figures" were slanted toward that end. There was no standard format for the statement; they were never in accordance with Generally Accepted Accounting Principles. The BOD has never solicited a standard schedule for reporting numbers to it, but they should insist on one and the staff should provide it.

Bobby felt that his relationship to the BOD was as a conduit to them for financial information. At BOD meetings, he tried to show those board members without a technical knowledge of accounting how to interpret the statements and financial information he generated. Because he felt that there were too many board members without any knowledge of accounting, he had invited a Finance Committee to work with him on financial information for the BOD.

CSCD had recently adopted a policy to have annual audits, in addition to the various audits performed by funding sources. A recent audit disclosed that CSCD had less than 1 percent total disallowance of expenses for the previous three years.

Bobby measured the success of his department by "how fully and timely CSCD was reimbursed for expenses, how timely the financial statements were generated, and if their cash flow allowed them to meet their monthly obligations." Two years prior, cash flow had been a significant problem at CSCD. Due to the nature of its funding, the organization had to spend money in order to obtain money. CSCD did not have the operating capital necessary to meet the monthly obligations. A short-term note for $46,000 was obtained from California First Bank. This was later converted to an optional advance note. While the note had been open for nine months at a time, in November it was open for about 15 days/month. The interest rate fluctuated with the prime rate. Interest expense was not reimbursable.

Bobby considered the time-consuming and repetitive work necessary for the grant reimbursements to be the major problem of his department. Bobby and the bookkeepers spent most of their time preparing and monitoring grant reimbursements. Most of the reimbursement forms required either different information or a different format than those prepared by CSCD. Therefore it was necessary to translate all of the information. Bobby was in the process of proposing to the State Department of Rehabilitation that they accept CSCD's statements in their original forms.

Bobby thought that the accounting department was on the verge of generating timely statements for the organization. He estimated that, by January, the computer service would be turning out monthly statements for each grant, each budget line item, and CSCD as a whole.

Clerical

Julie Witcoff said, "I like to think of the clerical department as the glue that holds the place together." The clerical staff were overworked and often under stress. They frequently received work at the last minute, but always managed to get it out on time.

Julie's duties overlapped between those of office manager and those of administrative assistant. As the office manager, she ordered supplies, supervised the clerical staff, and ensured that communication flowed smoothly throughout the agency. As the administrative assistant, she helped with grant proposals, interfaced with everyone in the agency, and acted as liaison between the community and the agency.

Because the secretary of the BOD could not take notes and participate in the discussions at the meetings concurrently, Julie was volunteered to act as a pseudo-secretary. She attended the board meetings to take notes. She did not participate in any discussions. In addition, Julie acted as liaison between the board members and the agency. She set up BOD meetings, dispensed written materials to directors, phoned directors to remind them of the meetings, and supervised the preparation of the minutes.

In addition to her official duties, Julie also acted as the unofficial "catchall" for the agency. During her interview with this casewriter, Julie was besieged by phone calls and interruptions from employees who wanted her to do everything from explaining where something was, to calling someone to fixed a clogged toilet in the bathroom. Julie explained the situation this way:

I've been doing some of this stuff for so long that everyone expects it. If I didn't do it, it wouldn't get done. Many small things aren't part of my job description—they aren't assigned to anyone, because I've always done them.

Bill and Ray felt that they weren't getting enough backup clerical support. Bill considered it a high priority for him to redefine Julie's position. In order to free more of Julie's time for supervision, Bill wanted to direct some of her activities to the assistant office manager. Julie was in favor of redefining her position, but didn't expect it to happen soon. An earlier attempt had been made to change her job description. Julie's office had previously been downstairs with the clerical staff. She had spent half of her time upstairs with the EDs. The EDs decided they wanted more of her time, so they moved her upstairs into the reception area right outside their office. The EDs appointed an assistant office manager to assume some of Julie's duties downstairs. Julie still spent "too much of her time" downstairs, so Bill made a further change in Julie's job description. Instead of supervising ten people, Julie was to supervise only five. In spite of these efforts, the clerical staff continued to come to Julie for help because "she had always been available." Julie preferred to have her desk downstairs because she "felt isolated" upstairs.

Julie measured the success of her department by how well everyone got along and how productive they were. Because they all had to work so closely together, Julie had the clerical staff participate in interviews with new clerical applicants. Julie said that also helped with morale because the staff liked being involved in the selection process.

Julie felt that morale tended to be lower among the clerical staff because their positions were "underplayed and underpaid—more underpaid than others in the agency that were underpaid. This was due to the way the grants were written." The clerical staff were the only employees who did not have the opportunity to attend workshops or training sessions. Julie realized that it could hurt the operating ability of the agency if any of the clerical staff were away from the office. She requested in-house workshops and guest speakers, but received no support from the EDs.

Julie said that there were a dozen reasons why it was hard to work at CSCD. Tears welled up in her eyes as she talked about her belief in the mission of the organization. (The casewriter was impressed by Julie's dedication.)

Public Affairs

Bill Tainter defined the function of the Public Affairs office as:

to work on public relations issues, to promote the agency in the community, and to develop the BOD—to encourage the participation of those that could have an impact on private funding. In many ways, the Public Affairs office is a fundraiser, but that's not its primary function.

The Public Affairs office consisted of two positions—the Community Resource Development Specialist (CRDS) and the editor of the "Voice."[19] The head of the department was the CRDS.

At the November BOD meeting, the CRDS, Milton Savage, tendered his resignation. He had accepted a position in another part of the state. Milt's absence left a big hole in the Public Affairs department and neither the EDs nor the BOD were quite sure how they would fill it. Bill had sent out job notices nationwide. He was looking for someone who: (1) already had a good understanding of the independent living concept; (2) had some experience in public relations and fundraising; (3) had the ability to write well; (4) was comfortable talking to diverse groups of people; (5) had personal experience with disabilities, preferably his or her own.

Bill Tainter was helping Marti Gasioch, editor of the "Voice," to assume some of the duties of the CRDS until the position could be filled. Bill wanted the future CRDS to concentrate on educating board members in fundraising, recruiting future board members, developing a new Board of Trustees (BOT), and identifying private funding sources in the community.

The Spoke Shop—A New Venture

Rod Tompkins said that an entrepreneurial idea was considered at CSCD because private funding was so hard to obtain. A wheelchair repair business was a "natural because the needs of the disabled population were not adequately met in that area." CSCD's only business subsidiary, the Spoke Shop (SS), opened its doors in July. Ray, Bill, and the BOD had "seriously" considered a wheelchair repair program for three years. Rod asked the EDs to either establish a wheelchair repair business, or quit talking about it. Bill said there would never have been a Spoke Shop without Rod's advocacy.

The start-up money for the Spoke Shop was provided by a $60,000 matching grant from Easter Seals. The SS had to obtain another $60,000 to match the grant. The SS had obtained $55,000 of that, primarily from the Bulova and Parker foundations. Bill and Ray felt that the $120,000 would enable the SS to operate at a loss, if necessary, for 12-18 months.

The function of the Spoke Shop was "to provide fast, high quality, inexpensive repairs and modifications for mobility aids." The shop also sold wheelchairs and wheelchair accessories. A second function was to generate profits to subsidize other CSCD services.

The Spoke Shop occupied a suite on the second floor of CSCD's office building. There was a repairman, a billing clerk, and a manager. Roy Gash, a post-polio victim from the age of five, was hired as the manager of the Spoke Shop. He set up the accounting system and obtained the certifications necessary for the SS to bill Medi-Cal, Medi-Care, and private insurers. After four months of operations, Roy said his activities as manager were still changing and evolving. He dealt directly with the customers. He attempted to find alternative suppliers that could provide quality parts less expensively than the traditional wheelchair parts suppliers. He checked inventory and ordered supplies. He visited community college campuses to post advertisements on bulletin boards and to distribute business cards to people in wheelchairs. To promote the SS, he visited agencies which offered medical and social services to people in wheelchairs. He placed advertisements in the "Voice" and "Mainstream," a San Diego-based magazine for disabled people. At times he worked on wheelchairs. Finally, he monitored the accounting data.

The Spoke Shop's accounting system was computerized through Accounting Corporation of America (ACA). The billing clerk put data for the disbursements, receipts, and sales ledgers into the computer. The sales ledger was also the accounts receivables ledger. Subsidiary records were kept in the office. ACA compiled the data and provided the financial statements. (See Appendix B.) Selected control figures were checked by Roy and then by Bobby Williams. Bobby kept the petty cash in his office as a further control measure. Bobby also prepared the bank reconciliations and any financial information presented to the BOD. The SS operated on a cash-on-delivery basis with its suppliers. There were no liabilities.

Approximately 75 percent of the Spoke Shop's sales (including repairs) were billed to Medi-Cal. The billing and reimbursement procedures were complex. Before the sale was made, it first had to be approved by the local Medi-Cal office. Once approved and the sale made, the state office was billed. The state then had to approve each billing by line items, for example, four spokes @ $.25 each. If the billing was approved, the state could send payment within 30 days. The reimbursement time varied from 30 days to several months. There was no guarantee that the state office would approve a billing. If the state decided not to make immediate payment, the billing was placed in suspension, sometimes to be reviewed by a medical board. Roy wasn't sure why only 10 percent of the Medi-Cal receivables were paid within 30 days, while 90 percent were placed in suspension. He did know that it created a problem. The SS "could not afford" to turn away the Medi-Cal customers. Roy did try to discourage Medi-Cal customers from making large purchases. A policy decision had not been made by the BOD on whether or not to bill customers for sales that the state Medi-Cal office would not approve. The Spoke Shop did not have significant billing problems with other insurers, such as the VA and Blue Cross.

The other problem Roy identified was that of "getting the word out that we're here." Advertisements were placed in publications appealing to disabled people. Flyers were put on the bulletin boards of college campuses. Many of the Spoke Shop's customers had been referred by CSCD staff. Roy also thought some customers heard about the SS by word-of-mouth. He originally asked customers how they knew about the SS, but discontinued the practice. He did not know how many customers heard about the SS from each source.

The criterion Roy used to measure the success of the SS was "mostly the number of customers we have. Eventually, it will be how much money we make."

Roy thought the future of the Spoke Shop was in sales of wheelchairs and accessories. He said the repair side of the SS was really only a break-even business. Bill and Ray wanted to see the SS expand into sales of other types of durable medical equipment, such as crutches, walkers, and commodes. They also wanted to see the SS test durable medical equipment for a fee. Ray Zanella wanted to see the SS "do as well as it can and provide CSCD with as much money as it can, with no limits on either." Bill Tainter stated:

> The Spoke Shop will be a long-term service of CSCD. It will succeed, maybe not the way we want it to, but in some way. Ray and I have various ways to salvage it. We're committed to its success. It was a big risk to start with.

Policy

There was no formal process for establishing policy at CSCD. Though everyone thought that the BOD was in some way responsible for policy, there were different opinions as to how the process actually worked. Directors and staff had individual views:

> *Dr. Bonnie Hough* (a recent director)—"Legally, the BOD [is responsible], actually it's Bill and Ray with the BOD reviewing problems and modifying as necessary."

> *Norma Lorimer* (a recent director)—"The BOD sets policy on an ad hoc basis."

> *Rod Tompkins* (director)—"The process is informal and loose. The BOD is responsible but no one on the board knows how to discharge it in a formal manner. It's spontaneous. A lot of policy is made de facto in daily operations."

> *Dr. Cathy Johns* (chairperson, BOD)—"If it seems to be a policy issue, it's brought to the BOD, usually by the executive directors; unless it is already clearly policy, such as personnel and editorial."

> *Ray Zanella* (Co-ED)—"It is established at two levels: 1) staff does the administration, non-agency wide, non-philosophical [policy-making]. 2) BOD does the broader, agency-wide policy, such as the decision to go with the Spoke Shop."

> *Bill Tainter* (Co-ED)—"Conceptually it's the BOD; practically, it's the executive directors and managers, ideally with input from providers and consumers. It is different from a non-grant funded organization because our

funds are mostly from categorical grants. These are limiting and the BOD can't make many decisions about them. The BOD sets salaries, establishes personnel policy, etc."

Board of Directors

"Well-connected people who give a damn" is how Dr. Bonnie Hough described the 13-member BOD of CSCD. (See Appendix A.) CSCD's members elected 12-15 directors by mail-in ballot each year. The BOD appointed new directors throughout the year to fill vacancies. Prospective directors were first nominated, then screened, before being placed on the ballot.

The nominating/screening process was informal. People were usually nominated by board members or CSCD staff. Some prospective directors responded to nomination notices in the "Voice." The EDs and an ad hoc committee of board members would then interview the nominees, focusing on their backgrounds and attitudes. The committee selected the nominees they thought were the most appropriate and sent their names to the BOD for approval. There were never more nominees selected than there were vacant seats. Once approved, ballots were sent to all CSCD members. About 50 members voted in the last election. The election process varied from one to five months. Norma Lorimer didn't hear from CSCD until six months after her interview, when she was told she had been elected.

The process for appointment of interim directors was also informal. The EDs usually interviewed the prospective directors. Some were appointed at their first or second BOD meeting; others weren't notified for several months.

The function of the BOD was not clearly defined. Some individual views were:

Bill Tainter—"policy making that affects the overall operation of the agency, goal setting, budgeting, and fund development." (See Exhibit 5.)

Julie Witcoff—"to give CSCD approval of its policies and directions, as determined by the EDs."

Dr. Cathy Johns—"to decide policy issues and set policy as a whole, to publicize the agency to the community, and to raise private funding."

Rod Tompkins—"(1) first and foremost to raise money; (2) strategic direction for what services should be provided and how to handle its resources to give maximum benefits to the disabled; (3) to keep it [CSCD] out of trouble . . . Some of the board's direction is what the proper political stance is that the organization should take on in various matters."

EXHIBIT 5   Community Service Center for the Disabled, Inc.

MEMO

To: CSCD Board of Directors
From: Bill Tainter
Date: March 10, 198–
Re: Responsibilities of Board of Directors and Board of Trustees' members

At the February Board meeting, Board members requested a further clarification of the role of Board and Trustee members. The discussion centered on developing a clearer understanding of the similarities and differences of their roles, and a greater delineation of their specific expectations. Each member of either Board should have a clear understanding of the agencies' mission as well as a familiarity with the programs and services.

Board of Directors	Board of Trustees
Setting major policy	Establish specific funding goals
Establishing long-range goals	Develop case statements
Salary setting	Giving based on one's ability
Periodic review of programs	Attract volunteers
Volunteer development	Securing institutional donors
Fund procurement	Call on donors to meet goals
Securing community acceptance and support	
Budget approval	

Source: Company records.

Norma Lorimer—"to support and monitor, in a way, the staff and organization as a whole; to find funding by possibly starting a Board of Trustees (BOT); to be a backup and backdrop and, when problems arise, to be there for its [CSCD's] use."

The directors selected their activities. Rod Tompkins, considered to be the veteran of the BOD, spent about eight hours per month on BOD issues. He estimated that one or two directors spent more time than that, but many of the others spent far less. Some only attended the monthly meetings. Committees were formed on an "as necessary" basis.

Cathy Johns said that there had not been much Board activity until the personnel crisis earlier in the year. She didn't know why, but the BOD then seemed to realize that they needed to be more involved. An example of this was to be found at the November meeting when the BOD had been called on to decide on the editorial policy of the "Voice." A controversial poem attacking the federal administration had been published. Some directors felt it could hurt CSCD's chances of obtaining funds from conservatives in the community. Others felt that CSCD's first responsibility was to the "feelings" of the disabled community. The issue was not resolved at that meeting. Cathy described it as the biggest and most controversial issue the BOD had faced. Jon Barbre, CSCD's Director of Client Services, said, "At what price do we compromise the principles CSCD was founded on in order to obtain funds?"

A long-standing problem of the BOD was that of raising funds in the community. At the beginning of the year, they voted to establish a BOT, whose primary function would be fundraising. Milt Savage had been responsible for coordinating BOT development with the BOD and the community. By November there was only one Trustee, Nat Ward. Nat, an attorney, and about 40 others attended a recruitment party. None of those people heard from CSCD for four months. When they were contacted, Nat was the only one who was still interested. Rod Tompkins said that it took four months for the matter to be fully discussed at the BOD meetings. Rod didn't think the board was totally "fired-up" about raising funds. The BOD seemed to be waiting for the staff to initiate the action.

Nat Ward was made Acting Chairman of the BOT. He was given a list of responsibilities. (See Exhibit 5.) He didn't think "the list made much sense." He was not certain what authority the BOT would have, or how they would acquire it. He thought that the BOD would set the parameters for the BOT, and he wasn't sure what the relationship between the two boards would be. As Rod put it, "Nat is ready, willing, and able, but nobody has given him anything to work with."

Various staff and directors thought that the BOD had some basic problems. The most recent directors felt that there should be a more thorough orientation for new board members. "This should, at least, include the history of CSCD, where to go for information, and the status of current projects." Another suggestion was that the BOD should organize social activities for directors, so they could get to know each other better.

Rod thought that the BOD would benefit from better committee structure, direction, and the use of "Roberts' Rules of Order" at meetings.

Bill Tainter wanted to see more permanent committees on the board. He thought that the BOD would be more effective if the meetings consisted of committee reports. This, he felt, would make the BOD meetings more "action-oriented, rather than just informative."

Future of CSCD

The EDs and BOD considered raising funds in the private sector to be the major problem at CSCD. Ray and Bill, however, were also faced with the recruitment of a new CRDS, employee morale, evaluation problems, and significant cutbacks in government funding. The BOD was additionally faced with developing a BOT, deciding on what image CSCD should present, and trying to understand and work with the different accounting information.

When asked about the probable or desired future of CSCD, the following responses were given:

Ray Zanella, desired future—"That we would have enough money. That we would grow substantially in terms of size, money, resources, branch offices, and services. That we would get into some really dynamic kinds of programs. We have wheelchair repair now, but how about van modifications and equipment design. We could pull it off if we get more money. I would like to get more branch offices so we could be a neighborhood-based organization, sprinkling the counties with centers. I don't want us to be an agency that is totally self-supporting—one that would refuse government money."
Probable future—"CSCD will continue to go on pretty much as it has."

Bill Tainter, desired future—"I'd like to have a very effective BOD that is very committed to independent living and the understanding of it, though controversy among them is okay. I'd like to expand services to encompass more of the disabled community, such as the developmentally disabled (for example, mentally retarded) and the sensory disabled (for example, blind, deaf). I'd like to see CSCD more recognized in the general community, with the majority of people knowing that CSCD exists. I'd like to see a large membership with quarterly meetings, so we could get direct input from them. I want to avoid the temptation to become just a bureaucracy that doesn't listen to consumers. I'd also like to see CSCD get involved in more business enterprises like the Spoke Shop, to provide a power (money) base to reduce reliance on public grants. I'd also like to see some branch offices."
Probable future—"CSCD will continue to be a prominent agency that provides services and advocacy for disabled people. I can see problems ahead. When you have a very stable, highly qualified staff and decreased funding, somebody has to go. I hated it before; it was very uncomfortable. But it could happen again."

Dr. Cathy Johns, desired future—"I'd like to see the Spoke Shop really take off and be financially helpful to the agency. I think it has good potential. I'd like to see us get lots more private funding, not lots more employees. I'd like to see growth as needed."

Probable future—"We'll have some years of continuing struggle due to government cutbacks, but we won't go out of business. There's a problem in the private sector because there's a lot of strain on that money. The Spoke Shop is a start for that."

Rod Tompkins, desired future—"I'd like to see slow, steady, and reliable growth with an ever-increasing source of funds coming from the private sector. I'd like to see more ongoing businesses at CSCD that give it substantial revenues, as well as providing a source of employment and business knowledge. I'd like to see the regionalizing of some services to other areas in the county because geography is an important factor when you're immobile. I would like to see CSCD run more like a business. That is my hope."

Probable future—"There are two possible futures: (1) that CSCD would have a very reduced service mode, due to funding cutbacks—CSCD could lose its heart and spirit and die (except maybe the Spoke Shop); (2) more possibly, it would have explosive growth due to the regionalization into a major metropolitan area and offer a number of services for the disabled. CSCD would be a 'natural.' Government agencies, serving the disabled, would cease to exist. Perhaps some of those would come to work for CSCD as subsidiaries, etc. . . . . It's all been a learning experience for me. It has been my first experience working with such a young board. Had I to do it over again, I'd probably give everybody a copy of *Roberts' Rules of Order*."

In a final conversation with the casewriter, Ray Zanella said, "Lack of business management is something we have a lot of around here."

COMMUNITY SERVICE CENTER FOR THE DISABLED, INC.

Personal Histories

Ray Zanella was raised in San Jose, California. Because he missed a lot of school due to his hemophilia, he always had to struggle to keep up with his school work. Consequently, he described himself as an "overachiever" and "very competitive." Ray received his BS in Electrical Engineering from SJSU. When he realized that he could not earn enough to pay his medical expenses ($25,000 per year), Ray became more involved in the disabled movement. He became interested in organizing people. His graduate studies were in Cybernetic Systems (social planning, people systems).

Bill Tainter, at 13, was one of the last persons to contract polio. Bill finished high school with a home teacher. He received his BA degree in psychology from San Francisco State University. He obtained his MS in psychology from SJSU. Bill had intended to be a school psychologist, but had by that time become involved in the disabled movement. He met Ray Zanella when both were trying to block Governor Reagan's proposed cuts in disability benefits. When Ray asked Bill to join him at CSCD, Bill was developing an ILC in San Jose.

Julie Witcoff, raised in Texas, received her MS in Education at SDSU. She had two teaching credentials, one of which was in Special Education. For her first two years at CSCD, Julie also worked as a substitute teacher. She said that she had always been oriented toward "special" children.

Bobby Williams of New York received his BS in accounting from St. Francis University. When he came to CSCD, Bobby said that though he had had no experience in fund accounting, he had enough knowledge to set up the consolidated books. He wanted to work in a social service organization so he could help people. He also wanted to have the freedom to use his accounting knowledge as a controller.

Roy Gash, raised in Kentucky, contracted polio at the age of five. He went to public schools and received his BA in accounting from Eastern Kentucky University. He was an accountant at Purdue University for five years. While there he acted as liaison between the computer and the staff, did cost studies, and prepared annual financial reports. Roy was the senior accountant when he left Purdue. He then worked as a contract administrator in the School of Engineering at UCLA. After 18 months, he left UCLA to sell wheelchairs. Within another 18 months, Roy had moved to San Diego, where he became involved in wheelchair sports.

Cathy Johns, raised in the Midwest, had been disabled with rheumatoid arthritis from the age of ten. She received her BS in psychology at Southern Illinois University, her MS at SDSU, and her PhD in social psychology at the University of Missouri. She worked as a Resource Specialist for the disabled for the San Diego Community College District. Cathy met Betty Bacon at SDSU and became more active in the disabled movement. Cathy became a board member of CSCD in its third year of operations.

Rod Tompkins, raised in San Diego and Los Angeles, attended private boarding schools as a child. He received his BS in psychology from Stanford University. After serving with Air Force Intelligence, Rod returned to San Diego. He went to work as a manager-trainee at San Diego Federal Savings and Loan. At the time of this case, he was the First Vice-President of the Operations Group. Rod's group was in charge of six departments and was responsible for $13 million and 300 employees. Rod had been on the Easter Seals Advisory Board, a subsidiary of Children's Hospital, for eight years. He had recently been elected President of that Advisory Board and also served on the Executive Board of Children's Hospital. He had been a CSCD BOD chairman for two years. As Ray Zanella put it, "Rod's the kind of guy you want on your BOD."

CSCD BOARD MEMBERS

*Elizabeth Bacon
    Coordinator
    Disabled Student Services
    San Diego State University
*Brian Ball
    Freelance writer/illustrator
 Larry Brydon
    Manager, Allied Gardens Branch
    California First Bank
*Bonnie Hough, M.D.
    Physician
*Pam Hoye
    Freelance writer
*Dr. Tom Humphries
    Associate Dean, Special Education
    Resource Center for the Handicapped
    San Diego Community College District

    *Disabled.
    Source: Company records.

Chairperson/*Catherine Campisi Johns, Ph.D.
    Research Specialist
    San Diego Community College
      District
 Charlie King
    Rice, Hall, James & Associates
*Norma Lorimer
    Retired Administrative Assistant of Arthritis Foundation
*Tom O'Neill
    Certified Public Accountant
*Howard Potash
    Attorney at Law
Vice-Chairman/Rod Tompkins
    First Vice-President, San Diego
    Federal Savings & Loan
*Doris Vawter
    MS Rehabilitation Counselor
    Intern, Sharp's Hospital

COMMUNITY SERVICE CENTER FOR THE DISABLED, INC.

BALANCE SHEET
Year End
(Fourth year of operations)

ASSETS
Current Assets
Cash in Bank: General Fund	5,715.83	
Operating Account	1,433.01	
Petty Cash	250.00	
Prepaid Expenses	2,675.00	
Accounts Receivable	76,619.50	
Total Current Assets		86,693.34

Fixed Assets
Office Furniture & Equipment	21,207.14	
Vehicles	11,564.73	
Total Fixed Assets		32,771.87
TOTAL ASSETS		119,465.21

LIABILITIES
Current Liabilities
Note Payable/Short Term	46,000.00	
Accounts Payable	4,553.00	
Total Liabilities		50,553.00

FUND BALANCE
Retained Fund Balance	68,912.21

SCHEDULE OF REVENUE & EXPENSE ACCOUNTS
Year End
(Fourth year of operations)

REVENUES
  Grant Funding:

Department of Rehabilitation	310,872.64	
Department of Alcohol & Drug Abuse (DADA)	72,305.73	
Community Based Advocate (CBA)	32,872.36	
Job Development & Placement (JDP)	65,034.52	
Revenue Sharing: County	6,686.68	
City	18,846.86	
Community Resource Development (CRDS)	13525.24	
CETA – RETC: 026-001	19,540.00	
026-902	63,858.76	
		603,542.79

Other Income:		
United Way	21,364.00	
Easter Seals	5,000.00	
Memberships	145.00	
Cash Donations	7,860.49	
CSCD Pledges	795.00	
Earned Income	12,940.19	
Advertising–Project Survival	604.26	
Refunds (various)	42.68	
		48,751.62

TOTAL REVENUES   652,294.41

SCHEDULE OF REVENUE & EXPENSE ACCOUNTS
Year End
(Fourth year of operations)

PERSONNEL		
Salaries/Wages—Staff	475,798.89	
FICA	28,593.72	
SUI	5,021.99	
Workmans Compensation Insurance	3,068.91	
Health Insurance Expense	7,088.93	
		519,572.44
OCCUPANCY		
Rent	34,201.20	
Utilities	3,761.12	
Building Maintenance	2,860.25	
Equipment Maintenance	46.00	
General Insurance	854.00	
Licenses & Permits	7.50	
		41,730.07
OFFICE EXPENSES		
Supplies	8,242.62	
Reference Materials	1,535.76	
Printing	8,560.85	
Advertising	308.86	
		18,648.09
COMMUNICATIONS		
Telephone	18,792.84	
Postage	3,369.64	
		22,162.48
TRANSPORTATION		
Staff Travel	14,440.10	
Client Transportation	690.00	
Van Expenses	2,759.51	
Van Insurance	2,419.01	
		20,308.62
OTHER EXPENSES		
Professional & Legal	66.00	
Bank Charges	33.85	
Accounting	8,817.31	
Interest	3,424.76	
Temporary Personnel: Student Intern	873.74	
Registrations & Dues	195.00	
Miscellaneous Other Expenses	123.05	
		13,533.71
TOTAL EXPENSES		635,955.41

SPOKE SHOP FINANCIAL STATEMENTS
Presented to BOD at the November Meeting

BALANCE SHEET
September 30, 198–*

ASSETS

Current Assets:

Cash–Bank–Spoke Shop	$13,610.98	
Petty Cash–Spoke Shop	150.00	
Accounts Receivable	270.00	
Sales Receivable	9,219.91	
Pleg Rec Easter Seal	45,000.00	
Grants Receivable	798.04	
Prepaid Expense–WCR	2,714.77	
Inventory	10,508.75	
Total Current Assets:		$82,272.05

Property and Equipment

Office Furniture and Equipment	$ 1,253.81	
Shop Equipment and Tools	2,889.92	
Vehicle	8,750.00	
Accum. Depr.–Office Furniture	(193.98)	
Accum. Depr.–Vehicle	(1,375.02)	
Accum. Depr.–Tools and Equipment	(351.78)	
Net Property and Equipment		$10,972.95

Other Assets

Total Other Assets

Total Assets	$93,245.00

LIABILITIES AND EQUITY

Current Liabilities
Total Current Liabilities
 Long-Term Debt
 Total Long-Term Debt
Total Liabilities

Equity

Net Income (Loss)	$93,245.00	
Total Equity		$93,245.00
Total Liability and Equity		$93,245.00

---

*Fifth year of operations.

INCOME STATEMENT
January 1, 198– to September 30, 198–*

	1-Month Period		Year to Date	
	Ratio	Amount	Ratio	Amount
Income:				
Donations–Individual		$ 16.00		$ 191.00
Donations–Organization		(9,855.00)		43,043.00
Donations–Easter Seals		55,000.00		55,000.00
Property Donations		11,766.99		11,766.00
Total Donations		$56,927.00		$110,000.00
Grants:				
Grant COD		$ 798.04		$ 798.04
Total Grants		$ 798.04		$ 798.04
Sales:				
Sales–WCR		$ 2,576.05		$ 11,239.71
Repairs–WCR		500.25		1,766.74
Rentals–WCR				103.50
Total Sales		$ 3,076.30		$ 13,109.95
Total Income		$60,801.34		$123,907.99
Cost of Sales:				
Parts Purchased–WCR		$ 3,892.95		$ 16,636.04
Ending Inventory		(9,608.75)		(9,608.75)
Total Cost of Sales		$ (5,715.90)		$ 7,026.29
Gross Profit		$66,517.14		$116,881.70
Expenses:				
Salaries and Wages		$ 2,442.53		$ 11,294.33
FICA		156.38		729.06
SDI		54.08		214.81
W/Comp		22.19		87.87
Rent		559.60		3,373.79
Utilities		55.11		108.53
Maintenance				134.73
General Insurance				1,149.00
Business License and Permits				10.00
Supplies		(194.29)		130.42
Shop Supplies–WCR		730.86		1,250.12
Contract Work				37.00

(continued)

	1-Month Period		Year to Date	
	Ratio	Amount	Ratio	Amount
Printing				572.46
Advertising		50.00		424.52
Telephone		10.87		431.84
Postage		4.90		28.59
Staff Travel		21.65		1,203.92
Vehicle Maintenance and Repair				45.00
Depr. Exp.—Off. Furn.		193.98		193.98
Depr. Exp.—Tools and Equipment		351.78		351.78
Depr. Exp.—Vehicles		1,375.02		1,375.02
Professional and Legal				47.00
Bank Charges				2.25
Accounting		191.38		191.38
Miscellaneous Expenses		249.30		249.30
Total Expenses		$ 6,275.24		$ 23,636.70
Net Operating Income		$60,241.90		$ 93,245.00
Other Income and Expenses				
Total Other Income and Expenses				
Net Income (Loss)		$60,241.90		$ 93,245.00

---

*Fifth year of operation.

SALES RECEIVABLE
September 30, 198–*

Medical	$8,758.26	
Total Medical		$8,758.26
Cash Sales	$ 99.20	
Total Cash Sales		$ 99.20
VA	$ 15.25	
Total VA		$ 15.25
Private Insurance	$ 166.20	
Total Private Insurance		$ 166.20
Rental Equipment		
Total Rental Equipment		
Individual Payment Account	$ 85.00	
	96.00	
Total Individual Payment Account		$ 181.00
Medicare		
Total Medicare		
Total A/R		$9,219.91

---

*Fifth year of operations.

Financial Analysis Report of the Spoke Shop*

Prepared by
Raymond Zanella, Executive Director, and *Robert Williams*, Controller

1. Operating Statement (from inception)

   $13,110 - \quad $7,026 \quad = \quad $6,084 \quad - $23,637 = ($17,553)
   Sales \quad - Cost of Sales = Gross Profit - Expenses = Net Profit

2. Operating Statement (less start-up cost)

   $13,110 - \quad $7,026 \quad = \quad $6,084 \quad - $17,673 = ($11,589)
   Sales \quad - Cost of Sales = Gross Profit - Expenses = Net Profit

3. Average monthly sales and expenses (operation time June 1, 198–)

$3,278	$4,418
Gross Sales	Operating Expenses

4. Trend of sales last two months:

$4,111	$3,032	$8,000 (estimate only)
August	September	October

5. Ratio of cost of sales to sales

   7,026 \quad ÷ \quad 11,240 \quad = \quad 62.5%
   Cost of Sales \quad ÷ \quad Sales Parts = CSCD Cost of Parts

6. Ratio of sales to accounts receivable

   9,210 ÷ 13,110 = 70% of all sales for four months are accounts receivable
   Accounts receivable ÷ sales = % receivable

7. CSCD Spoke Shop doesn't have any liabilities as of September 1, 198–. It has prepaid salary expenses as of September 30, 198– for a one month period, $2,714.

---

*Presented to the BOD at November meeting.

8. Easter Seals match donations analysis

$43,234 + $10,866 + $900 = $55,000
Cash   Equipment   Inventory   Easter Seals Donation

9. Easter Seals receivables

$55,000   - $10,000   = $45,000
Easter Seals Match   Received   Match Receivable

10. Financial Forecast and Conclusions

    a. Cash Flow—Cash flow could be a serious problem in the near future especially if there are dramatic increases in Medi-Cal sales, which is probable. This is largely affected by the apparent reluctance of Easter Seal to provide the match on a timely basis. At the moment, CSCD has an outstanding $45,000 account receivable with Easter Seals. Additionally, there is an additional $10,000 budget deficit still outstanding. Easter Seals has agreed to provide $5,000 if CSCD can raise $5,000.

    b. The Spoke Shop breakeven point will be reached within the next six months if we continue to provide individual sales, repairs, and rentals. However, the Spoke Shop can produce enough profit to subsidize other CSCD services if we can arrange service contracts with large third parties. Examples of these are Muscular Dystrophy Association, United Cerebral Palsy, Veteran's Administration, DR, health maintenance organizations, hospitals (especially rehab centers) and private business who use wheelchairs (S.D. Zoo, airlines, museums). The Executive Directors, External Affairs Director, and Spoke Shop Manager will formulate a plan by early next year.

    c. At this point, the Spoke Shop has not been able to generate reliable data to make valid predictions on the earnings potential or fiscal forecast of the Spoke Shop. By spring 198–, enough financial data will be available to make accurate predictions.

NOTES

1. California Assembly Bill (AB) 2687 authorized a feasibility study to be done on the establishment of regional Comprehensive Service Centers (CSC). If it was decided to fund such Centers, CSCD would receive $45,000 for planning and $250,000/year for three years to administer the services. A CSC would coordinate all of the services offered to disabled people in a given area in an effort to eliminate duplication, gaps, and unnecessary complexity.

2. For the purposes of this case, the term "disabled" will mean: a diagnosable disability which affects a person's mobility, perception, or function. Source: "CSCD Department of Rehabilitation Project Proposal."

3. An Independent Living Center (ILC) or Independent Living Program (ILP) was required by California Law AB 204, section 19801, to "be a private, nonprofit organization controlled by a board of directors. A majority of the board shall be comprised of disabled individuals; be staffed by persons trained to assist disabled persons in achieving social and economic independence. The staff shall include as large a proportion as is practicable of disabled individuals."

4. The State Department of Rehabilitation was the agency that administered state monies and programs for the rehabilitation of individuals.

5. According to the CSCD bylaws, there was only one class of members of CSCD. Members had to be residing in the County of San Diego at the time of their application or renewal for membership and were required to pay dues of at least $5.00 per fiscal year. Members were entitled to vote for nominees for the BOD. In its fifth year, CSCD had approximately 150 members.

6. The U.S. Department of Health, Education, and Welfare estimated that one out of eleven citizens had a substantial physical disability. CSCD estimated that there were approximately 150,000 disabled individuals in San Diego in 1976. Source: "CSCD Department of Rehabilitation Project Proposal."

7. "Constituent controlled and operated" means that disabled individuals controlled the organization by comprising a majority of the BOD and by occupying the key executive positions in the agency.

8. Bill Tainter defined civil rights for disabled people as: "Equal opportunities in economic, social, and legal environments. For example, freedom from discrimination in education, employment, recreation, marriage, and transportation."

9. A grant is a contribution from one legal entity to another. At CSCD, most grants were accompanied by a contract whereby CSCD agreed to perform in a specified manner for a specified sum of money. At CSCD, the terms "grant" and "contract" were used interchangeably.

10. With a reimbursable 90/10 percent match, CSCD would send in a reimbursement request for expenditures. The grantor would then reimburse CSCD for 90 percent of the amount. CSCD would have to cover the other 10 percent. Sometimes, the grantor would not provide any funds until CSCD demonstrated an ability to pay 10 percent (or whatever the match) of the expenditures.

11. While most grants were for general operations, some provided only for certain staff positions or for certain projects of the agency. For example, a staffing grant might provide for the salaries of two financial benefits counselors, and

a project grant might provide for a special training seminar for employees or clients.

12. The fair-share concept was that grantors would pay only that percentage of expenditures that represented their contribution relative to the total budgeted. For example, if the total budget was $100,000 and a grantor provided $10,000 for all the items budgeted, that grantor would pay 10 percent of expenditures for each line item.

13. Administrative services included the accounting, clerical, and public affairs departments.

14. As pursuant to Title VII of the Civil Rights Act of 1964, as amended.

15. The College of Business Administration at SDSU had a business internship program that placed students in local organizations for nine hours/week for one semester. Students received three units of credit and $175 for the semester. The program received $175, bringing the total cost to the employer to $350.

16. Bill and Ray periodically attended conferences and seminars that dealt with disability-related issues. They also represented CSCD at the Coalition of ILPs. Ray represented the Coalition on the DR Advisory Committee, and represented CSCD at the American Coalition of Citizens with Disabilities. Bill was on the San Diego County Advisory Committee for the Handicapped and was the State representative to the Long-Term Care Planning Group.

17. "Barrier-removal" refers to the accessibility requirements of certain buildings in accordance with Section 504 of the Rehabilitation Act of 1973, as amended. CSCD acted as consultant, on a fee-for-service basis, for organizations that were removing physical barriers for disabled people. Fees ranged from $18/hour to $24/hour.

18. Fund accounting is a system which utilizes funds and fund accounts. A fund is a fiscal and accounting entity with a self-balancing set of accounts. Each fund has its own asset and liability accounts, with a Fund Balance account instead of Retained Earnings. The primary purpose of fund accounting is to provide a separate accounting for certain monies to enable the organization to comply with legal requirements. As is common with many fund accounting systems, CSCD operates on a modified accrual basis. That is, revenues are recognized in the period in which they become available and measurable. Expenditures are recognized in the period in which a liability is incurred. For details, see Leon E. Hay, *Accounting for Governmental and Nonprofit Entities*, 6th edition, Irwin Publishing Company.

19. Six times a year, CSCD published a newsletter called the "CSCD Voice." It was commonly called the "Voice." It was sent to CSCD members and donors. There were no statistics regarding those who received the "Voice." It offered articles and advertisements of interest to disabled persons.

Appendix II:
Episcopal Community
Services

Episcopal Community Services (ECS) is a nonprofit social service agency affiliated with the Episcopal Diocese of San Diego. (The San Diego diocese is an administrative unit of the Episcopal Church, covering San Diego and Imperial counties.)

The agency was founded on July 20, 1927, as the Episcopal County and City Mission Society of San Diego in order to provide social welfare programs for the elderly, the poor, the sick, people in institutions including prisoners, "and those in trying circumstances who might otherwise be forgotten." It is traditional for agencies of the Episcopal Church to provide such services without regard to religious affiliation and without motives of conversion to Episcopalianism.

Financial support for the agency came from memberships, contributions, and the operation of a thrift shop called the Clothing Bureau. The total income in the first year was $2,363.66, of which $1,453.84 came from the Clothing Bureau. Contributions and paid membership of 117 people provided the balance. A full-time chaplain was appointed at a salary of $75 a month.

The agency's early activities included pastoral visits and religious services at public institutions like the County Hospital and the Poor Farm; a Radio Vesper Service; the provision of furniture, victrolas and records, and books and magazines for the Hospital and Farm; and chaplaincy to sailors and seamen docking in San Diego harbor.

From 1927 to 1954, the activities of the agency continued at a modest level. In 1953, the Bishop of the Los Angeles Diocese (San Diego and Imperial counties were part of the Los Angeles Diocese until 1973) urged the reorganization and expansion of the agency in order to meet the social and spiritual needs of the rapidly growing city. The financial support making such growth possible would come from the Diocese of Los Angeles and from contributions by members

This case was written by Dorothy Anderson, Research Assistant, under the direction of Dr. Israel Unterman, Professor of Management, College of Business Administration, San Diego State University, San Diego, California. It was prepared as a basis for class discussion, rather than to illustrate either effective or ineffective handling of an administrative situation. Copyright 1983 by Dr. Israel Unterman, San Diego State University.

of the local Episcopal community. In 1954, a new director was hired to serve as administrative head as well as chaplain of the expanding agency. Articles of Incorporation were filed with the State of California in 1955. In 1958, ECS signed a contract with San Diego County beginning its Ex-Offender Rehabilitation program, which provides counseling, assistance, and jobs for men released from correctional institutions.

ECS continued to evolve and extend its programs in the 1960s. By 1966, the annual budget had reached almost $135,000 (see 1966 annual statement). The agency, while continuing its traditional activities of counseling for families and young people, and chaplaincy to those in hospitals and correctional institutions, also carried on programs in nontraditional areas. The Ex-Offender Rehabilitation program continued to grow, serving increasing numbers of men. In the mid-1960s the agency, in cooperation with the SDSU School of Social Work, began a program called Neighborhood Services. This program placed graduate social work students under the direction of a School of Social Work faculty member at a center in southeast San Diego, an economically disadvantaged area of the city. The goals of the program were to assist the residents of the neighborhood and also to provide a training internship for the graduate students.

In 1972, ECS, now in its 45th year, appointed its fourth full-time director, the Rev. Dr. Herbert C. Lazenby. Dr. Lazenby, an ordained priest like all the previous heads of ECS, was also a professional social worker with a Master's degree in Social Work from the University of Washington, a Ph.D. from Northwestern University, and training in Gerontology from the University of Michigan. Before joining ECS he had been the Executive Director of Senior Centers, Inc. of Seattle and president of the clergy of the Episcopal Diocese of Olympia, Washington.

When Dr. Lazenby became director, ECS was active in four areas: family counseling, chaplaincy for those in institutions, ex-offender rehabilitation, and neighborhood services—the program for training social work students and developing new community programs. Dr. Lazenby, a man of immense energy and enthusiasm, and broad professional interests, began to lead ECS in new directions.

In a feature article in 1977 marking the agency's 50th anniversary, Dr. Lazenby reviewed the progress of the preceding four years. Under his leadership the agency had moved into its own new half-million dollar, two-story, 15,000-square-foot building in downtown San Diego. ECS was now providing 18 different programs, including such new activities as a health clinic; a counseling, rehabilitation, and job training program for the deaf; Creative Resources for Women, a program to help displaced homemakers; a Grief Center, a program to train counselors for the bereaved; an alcoholism rehabilitation program; and a welfare rights organization. The different programs were operated at the new downtown headquarters building and at branch sites throughout the county.

By 1977, the ECS yearly budget was almost at a half-million dollars, and the agency had a paid staff of 31 and about 100 volunteers, who each donated

10 hours a week to programs. Many of these programs were financed through government grants and contracts, and this kind of financial support, Dr. Lazenby observed, resulted in his "biggest single frustration. . . . The concerns and issues that come before government agencies shift from year to year, and so you can't guarantee continuity in funding."

Dr. Lazenby was filled with enthusiasm for his work at ECS. He estimated that he spent an average of 75 hours each week at his work and called it the ideal job. In addition to his ECS responsibilities, he served as a board member for a number of social service and health agencies in San Diego. He also continued to be active in professional societies and associations, attending conferences and making speeches. In 1977, he served as president of the Episcopal Society for Ministry on Aging, a national organization involved in problems of the elderly. He was also founder and first president of the American Association of Homes for the Aging.

Over the next five years ECS continued to grow, significantly expanding existing programs and adding important new activities. The agency became an important provider of alcohol abuse programs and convicted drinking driver programs at several locations in the county and also began sponsorship of a Head Start program for disadvantaged children. These activities were funded under government contracts. ECS also began its Emergency Assistance program, providing food, clothes, lodging, and financial help, as well as information and referrals to clients whose immediate needs could not be met by other private or public agencies because of their own rules or procedures. ECS described Emergency Assistance as a program which "attempts to fill the gap between the need and the bureaucratic response."

Dr. Lazenby's leadership of ECS continued to be an inspiration to those who were directly associated with the agency and those in the community who provided support for the agency's programs. In recognition of his services to the community and to ECS, he was given the honorary title of Canon by the bishop of the diocese.

The problems in obtaining continuing government funding for programs that Canon Lazenby had pointed out in the mid-1970s became more serious as the years passed. In 1980, the Ex-Offender program (begun in 1958) was threatend with a cutoff of funding by the Regional Employment and Training Consortium (RETC) because of low efficiency in getting permanent jobs for clients in the program. Funds were restored through persuasion from various criminal justice agencies in the area, and enough changes were made in the program so that it was voted the "most improved" program that year by the RETC staff.

Other difficulties, such as obtaining funds to finance agency operations, brought about a cash flow problem which led ECS to default on its payment of employee withholding taxes to the Internal Revenue Service. A loan of $87,000 from the San Diego Diocese, in the summer of 1980, enabled ECS to cover the unpaid taxes, and efforts were made to ensure that the problem would not recur.

Stringent cost-cutting measures were recommended for several programs by an administrator in the agency, and an ambitious and innovative fund-raising program was planned by the board of directorss

In the spring of 1981, Canon Lazenby suggested to the board that the sale of the downtown headquarters building, built by the agency six years before, would be a good idea. He pointed out that the client population served by ECS was changing and that the demand centers for agency services were no longer downtown, but had moved to outlying neighborhoods. Shifts in population were partly due to redevelopment of the downtown area, which had made the building and land more valuable. At the same time, reduced government services were leading to increased demands on the agency. Proceeds from the building's sale would enable ECS to resolve some of its cash flow difficulties as well as help future development of the agency.

The building, appraised at $1.25 million, was listed for sale in June 1981. Several months later it was announced that the building had been sold to a local developer for $700,000.

In late September 1981, with little advance warning, Canon Lazenby announced his resignation as director of ECS, effective on December 31. In a speech at the 1981 annual meeting in September he reviewed his nine and a half years with the agency. In 1972, when he became director, ECS had a staff of 13 and a budget of $306,000.

> Throughout those years with your support the agency has grown to the leading social service agency in San Diego and the star of all Episcopal agencies in the country. We have dared to risk, to be innovative and creative about showing and doing the Gospel of Jesus Christ. We are constantly asked by others to show them how to do what we can do. Within the community we have been in the forefront of the use of public and private partnerships through contracts. This has been a blessing and a bane as well.

He discussed the trend toward reduced government service and cuts in support for local agencies.

> With a demand for increased services, with fewer dollars, what does the future look like? It is bleak . . . .

He touched on the fund-raising program planned by the board of directors,

> Cash flow needs were evident 10 years ago and they are evident today. The Cudney Plan was a creative way to meet that need. Unfortunately the plan was not implemented . . . .

and the plan for reducing agency expenses,

We have curtailed our staff a great deal in the last six months. While our budget for this year is some $2.3 million it is a minimum budget. The future means that we must reduce that budget which means reducing services . . . .

He ended by expressing his feelings about leaving ECS.

The job of executive director is exciting. Reviewing ten annual meetings is thrilling in the sense of involvement of clergy and laity, of board and staff in decisions that are Christian. This job allows an individual to experience both support and separation, accountability as well as alienation, rewards as well as rejection, the positives as well as the negatives, concern as well as criticism. As I review these seeming opposites it has become apparent to me that there is a greater emphasis on criticism, negatives, rejection, alienation, and separation at this time. Therefore because of the spiritual, emotional, and physical stresses that exist I ask the board of directors at its next meeting to accept my resignation . . . .

The reaction to Canon Lazenby's announcement was one of dismay. A board member who had been associated with ECS for 20 years, said, "I am sorry to have him resign because he has been a great leader." Another long-time supporter, praising his energy and vision, said, "I'm not surprised he's resigning from ECS. With the cuts in federal money coming, it will be a one-horse agency. He couldn't gear his brain down to that kind of operation."

The Interim Period

On Monday, January 4, 1982, Glenn Allison took over the leadership of Episcopal Community Services. The board of directors had hired him to serve as interim executive director following the sudden resignation of the previous head of the agency. Allison, trained as a professional social worker and experienced as a social work administrator, had returned to San Diego some months before after serving as program director for the National Association of Social Workers in Washington, D.C. During an earlier stay in San Diego he had been in charge of psycho-social services at a large hospital and had also taught at the School of Social Work at San Diego State University. Unlike all previous heads of the agency, he was a layman, although he had originally intended to enter the ministry and had studied for three years at a theological seminary.

In an interview shortly after he was hired, Allison said, "I was looking for something to do that would be interesting, so when this came along I accepted it as a challenge."

The interim director was faced with a number of serious problems. The agency was in dire financial straits. It had become apparent to board members during the three-month period following Canon Lazenby's announcement that he was resigning, that ECS was running at a deficit. The exact amount and the reasons for the deficit were unclear, but the accumulated amount was estimated at between $200,000 and $250,000. The sale of the downtown headquarters building had been announced, but the transaction was still in escrow. A number of those associated with the agency had begun to have second thoughts about the wisdom of the sale. If the escrow were to fall through, an attempt might be made to save the building. The conditions of the escrow itself created a problem for ECS. Merchants in the neighboring redevelopment area had become increasingly hostile to certain activities of the social welfare agencies in the immediate neighborhood that were thought to attract an undesirable element into the area, one that would discourage the growth of new business. One condition of the escrow was that the Catholic Workers' soup line operating in the ECS headquarters parking lot be moved to another location.

Plans had to be made to move the headquarters offices and those programs resident in the building to other locations. Some of the programs, such as counseling, could be moved without too much interruption. Others, especially Emergency Assistance, required a downtown presence.

Allison also had to work with the board of directors in dealing with the problems of hiring a permanent executive director for ECS, and in addition, with all those who were associated with the agency (staff, board, and members of the public) who had become increasingly dismayed as news about the agency's financial problems began to reach the public.

The transfer of leadership to Allison was complicated by the absence of the previous executive director who was now living in another city. The former associate director, who had been concerned with the agency's fiscal situation and had prepared drastic cost-cutting recommendations in 1980, had left ECS in April 1981.

One resource Allison had was the strong backing of the board of directors of the agency.

The Board of Directors

ECS is governed by a 36-member board of directors who are responsible for the overall guidance of the agency. The members of the board are elected by the general membership of the organization and represent both clergy and lay members of the Episcopal Diocese of San Diego and the general public. The board also includes a number of ex-officio members, including the bishop of the San Diego diocese.

Board members are elected for three-year terms. They are actively recruited by a nominating committee, with help and suggestions by the agency director and other board members. The nominating committee tries to ensure the broadest possible representation from all of the parishes in the diocese and to maintain a balance of clergy and lay members. In recent years, there has been a strong effort to add more women and minority group members to the board.

Board meetings are held on the fourth Monday of the month at noon and last for about an hour and a half. Many who attend the meeting bring a brown bag lunch. The meetings are conducted by the chairman of the board, who prepares the agenda in cooperation with the executive director. The meetings are informal, but *Roberts' Rules of Order* are followed. Each meeting opens and closes with a prayer.

Board members are expected to take an active interest in the agency, and to take on committee responsibilities as well as attending the monthly board meeting. There are eight board committees: Finance, Resource Development, Nominating, Personnel, Program, Special Events, Long-range Planning, and Executive. Board members are routinely active in at least two committees, depending on personal interests and skills. Committee meetings take about one and a half hours each month, although not all of the committees are active year-round (for example, the Nominating committee).

For the most part, new board members have fulfilled the Nominating committee's expectations, attending board meetings regularly and taking on a fair share of committee duties. Occasionally there has been a disappointment. Currently, consideration is being given to drawing up a formal statement of expectations so that there will be no misunderstandings by new board members about how much is expected of them.

The board recognizes that a formal orientation program is important in introducing the complex activities of the agency to new members. In the past, new members learned about the agency gradually by serving on the various committees. Now there are training sessions for new members conducted by the board chairman and managers of the different programs. New members are also invited the attend program committee meetings which meet at the sites of ECS programs (for example, Health Clinic, Head Start, etc.) and whose meetings concentrate on program activities.

MEMBERS OF THE BOARD

Penny Williams

Penny Williams is a very pleasant attractive woman, married with grown children. She is strongly committed to the ideals and activities of ECS. She first joined the board eight years ago, served two three-year terms, left the board for a year as provided in the by-laws, and is now in the first year of her third term. She was recruited for the board by Canon Lazenby, the previous executive director. She had been extremely active in church work, especially with young people, in her own parish, and had served as president of the women's group at her church. She thinks that she was asked to join the board because of her volunteer work and the hope that she might be able to bring others to volunteer in various ECS activities. She believes that her lack of training in finance has been a handicap in her board service and has had difficulty understanding financial information during board discussions.

She currently serves as secretary of the board and normally devotes about 15 hours a month to board activities (two hours, monthly board meetings; four hours, administrative duties as secretary; two hours, Executive committee; two hours, Personnel committee; and about five hours on special projects such as fund-raising events). Some of this time is required because of the office she holds. but some of her work for ECS is at her option. She thinks that many of the other board officers devote about the same amount of time to ECS, although the chairman (Hugh Moore) and the treasurer (Harold Holsonback) probably devote more time, and regular board members, less.

She believes that the role of the board is to: 1) establish direction for the agency, 2) to keep the agency to its purposes as specified in the by-laws, and 3) where possible to originate policy and programs for the staff to implement. The board is very active in discussing activities suggested by the staff. A staff member might report at a board meeting that a new state or county RFP (request for proposal) will make money available for a certain kind of program. The board will then discuss how ECS might extend its activities into the new area.

Mrs. Williams believes that the "crisis period" at ECS has brought about a more positive relationship between board and staff. There is more communication now. People from the board and staff are getting to know each other and getting to understand each other's "attitudes." As a result of the crisis, board members became more directly involved with the agency. Before the "troubles," some board members just came to meetings, listened to reports and discussions, and approved staff decisions. Now, board members ask more questions and engage in more detailed discussion at the meetings. Many of the board members have increased the amount of time they give to the agency. She believes that this is partly because the organization is church related.

Hugh Moore

Hugh Moore is a tall, forceful man of mature years who runs his own advertising agency. He joined the ECS Board in 1969, and has served regularly since then. He was elected chairman of the board in 1981, having previously served as treasurer and second vice president. He was recruited for the board by the previous head of the San Diego diocese, Bishop Wolterstorff. (Bishop Wolterstorff retired in 1982 and was succeeded by Bishop Morton.) Mr. Moore has continued on the ECS Board because he finds it a satisfying and rewarding way of realizing his own Christian ideals. He had previously been a vestryman and served as secretary-treasurer at his parish church.

Since becoming chairman at the end of 1981, he has devoted 30 to 60 hours a month to board work. This has been a result of the agency's recent problems and the process of making ECS financially sound again. In addition to regular board and committee meetings, he meets frequently with Glenn Allison to discuss special agency problems and plan activities and agendas for the board. Correspondence takes a lot of his time.

He sees his role as board chairman as one of joint cooperation and decision-making with the executive director. He believes that this cooperative form of leadership is a necessary change from the previous situation in which the board played a more passive role and the management of ECS was more in the hands of Canon Lazenby.

He believes that the role of the board is to: 1) establish policy for the agency, and 2) to make sure that the policy and activities of the agency are in accord with its by-laws.

Mr. Moore believes that ECS has become a stronger and more businesslike organization as a result of surviving its problem period. In the past, there was no controller, only accountants who reported to the executive director. Now there is a controller who reports both to the executive director and to the board. The agency now retains legal counsel to review any contracts it enters into. In the past, it depended on a board volunteer for legal advice.

Barbara Bright

Mrs. Bright is a silver-haired and vigorous woman who expresses herself with great authority and clarity. She is a professional social worker, and was active in founding the School of Social Work at SDSU. Fifteen years ago, she founded the agency she still directs, Senior Adult Services, which provides counseling and assistance to the elderly. One of SAS's most important activities is the Meals-On-Wheels program which delivers prepared meals to homebound people who are unable to cook for themselves.

Mrs. Bright first joined the ECS Board sometime in the 1950s and has been continuously associated with the agency since then either as a board member or a committee volunteer. She can't remember who recruited her for the board, but was attracted to ECS because of her interest in social work and her membership in the Episcopal Church. She thinks that her professional social work background and her "expertise as an administrator" has been an asset in her service as an ECS board member. She is also a member of several other social welfare and health agency boards.

She normally devotes an average of 10 to 15 hours a month to ECS, currently serving as one of the vice presidents of the board and as such, a member of the Executive committee. She is also the chairman of the Personnel committee. Her estimate is that these activities take about six to seven hours a month. And then there is "telephone time" in a consultant capacity with various ECS staff members, which takes another four to six hours a month.

Her work as a professional social service agency administrator gives her a unique perspective on ECS board activities. She describes the board meetings as well run, with a planned agenda "and we move right through it." Much of the detail work is done within the various board committees "so we don't waste time" at the board meetings.

She believes that the role of the board is to: 1) set policy for the agency, and 2) monitor how it is carried out.

Mrs. Bright believes that a good working relationship between the board and staff of an organization like ECS (or like her own agency) is vitally important. Not only must the board provide support and assistance for the staff in its activities, but the staff must also help the board to fulfill its responsibilities. As a way of illustrating this she mentioned that it had recently been necessary for her own agency to send a letter to many of the people it serves announcing a necessary but unwelcome change in policy. Rather than placing the burden of writing this difficult letter solely on the president of the board, she wrote a suggested draft of the letter for him.

Harold Holsonback

Harold Holsonback is a tall, dignified man with short, well-cut silver hair. He is a vice president of Security Pacific Bank and manager of one of their large branch offices. He has a deep commitment to community service and has served on the boards of many nonprofit organizations over the past 25 years. He joined the ECS Board about 1975 and has served continuously since then. He was recruited for the board by Canon Lazenby because of his knowledge and experience in business and finance. Mr. Holsonback recalled that at the time he joined the board there were many more clergy members and Canon Lazenby was making an effort to "broaden the base" by adding representatives from the business and professional community. He has continued to be active because he is interested in the agency's activities and finds his board work both rewarding and challenging. Currently, he serves as treasurer of the board.

During the year following the beginning of the crisis period at ECS, Mr. Holsonback devoted a minimum of 15 hours a month (but often more time) to board activities. He recalled that before the problems started, his duties had taken less of his time. His hope for the future is that there won't be so many problems requiring his attention.

He sees the role of the board in much the same way as the other members, that is: 1) to set policy for the agency, and 2) to see that it is carried out.

Mr. Holsonback believes that the agency's financial problems stemmed from a combination of factors. One important cause is a "built-in" problem of programs financed by government contract. The budgetary requirements never allow enough for overhead, for management and control functions. Sometimes even the direct cost reimbursements are too little to pay the actual costs of running the program.

He always felt that ECS's accounting department was chronically weak and urged that it be strengthened. It was always understaffed, with too few people each trying to do several jobs at once. Relying on a computerized accounting system didn't help because the reports that come out of the system are only as good as the information that is put into it. The accounting reports were frequently several months late, which meant that board members could not know the agency's financial position in a timely fashion.

An additional problem was that the financial reports were difficult to understand, even for someone with his background, because they were prepared under the fund accounting system.* Because ECS receives some of its financial support from United Way, it follows the format recommended by the United Way for its accounting statements. This results in an extremely complex report. With the combination of two problems, the result was that the board members did not have any real understanding of the agency's financial situation.

Mr. Holsonback recalls that from the point of view of the board, the financial crisis arose very suddenly. Some board members had been aware that the agency had financial problems, but there was confusion about their exact nature, and none were aware of the magnitude of the problem. Once the board realized the enormity of the crisis—that the IRS had filed three tax liens totaling $202,849 against ECS for failure to remit employee withholding taxes, and that there was no cash to cover the default—they needed time to consider the problem so that they could decide what to do. There were discussions with the IRS. Once the IRS understood that the board itself was not the cause of the problem and was taking action to solve it, Mr. Holsonback recalls that they were very helpful.

The Rev. James E. Carroll

Father Carroll is a tall, vigorous man in clerical dress. He is a businesslike, direct person who (were he not a priest) would fit in well in the administrative

---

*Fund accounting is peculiar to nonprofit organizations who must ensure the observance of limitations and restrictions placed on the use of resources available to the organization. Under this procedure, resources for various purposes are classified for accounting and reporting purposes into categories or "funds" in accordance with the activities or objectives specified. The organization using fund accounting presents separate financial statements for each fund. While the concept of separate funds is not difficult to understand, it can cause problems in presenting financial statements that can be understood by most readers.

ranks of a large corporation. He is the rector of St. Paul's Episcopal Church. St. Paul's is the oldest and largest church in the diocese and is the center of the Episcopal community in San Diego. Father Carroll was elected to the board at the end of 1980 and is now completing the last year of his first term. He was recruited for the board by Canon Lazenby because he had become rector that year, coming to San Diego after 25 years of service in the ministry in other cities.

As a relatively new board member, he had the benefit of an orientation program when he joined. At that time, it was a two-hour program with a slide show and presentation by Canon Lazenby who provided a good introduction to the many diverse activities that make up ECS.

There was a "general understanding," but no formal agreement, about the obligations of board members. Father Carroll thinks that it is very important for board members to have a clear idea about what is expected of them, both in terms of time and money. He recalled that when he joined the board, the Cudney Plan was underway. He did not learn that all board members were expected to participate until after he was elected.

He normally devotes about 10 hours a month to ECS, attending board and committee meetings as well as serving on the Program and Personnel committees. Recently he has been acting as chairman of a subcommittee revising personnel policies for the agency.

He believes that one important role of the board is to monitor the scope of social and community problems that need attention and to decide how to allocate the agency's resources in dealing with these problems. He observed that many of the ECS programs have little to do with the religious orientation of the organization.

Father Carroll believes that the causes of the crisis at ECS, the "unraveling" of the agency, go back many years. ECS grew very quickly from what was essentially a "band-aid" organization to an important and very complex social service agency. (Much of this growth, he believes, was because of Canon Lazenby's vision and leadership. Other agencies that Father Carroll has been associated with did not expand in the same way during the period.) The ECS board members always had difficulties in "understanding the intricacies of the financial statements" because of the fund accounting system. They didn't understand what the true financial situation was. One month, there might be a deficit in one of the programs of $10,000. Canon Lazenby would explain that there was a delay in payment from one of the contractors and that it was not unusual or anything serious. These small deficits piled up very quickly and became a serious problem.

Father Carroll believes that it is wrong to place all of the blame for the agency's problems on Canon Lazenby. Rapid growth and changing economic conditions were factors, and the board was partly at fault for not insisting on clear reports about finances.

The Rev. Canon Richard B. Harms

Father Harms is a pleasant, outgoing man in clerical dress. He is married and the father of a daughter in college. His official title is Canon Missioner of the Episcopal Diocese, which means that he is a member of the bishop's administrative staff. He is in charge of the financial affairs of the diocese and speaks with great knowledge and tact. He has been a board member since 1978 and serves ex-officio as the bishop's representative, rather than as an elected member. Although he joined the board as a function of his office, he has a great concern for the agency's activities because of his view of his role as a clergyman, that of "social ministry."

He normally devotes about 10 hours a month to board activities, attends the monthly board meeting and meetings of the Executive and Finance committees, and is in regular contact by phone with Glenn Allison once or twice a week. During the crisis period, board activities took a lot more time, but have now returned to normal.

In discussing the role of the board, he observed that during the period of difficulties, the Executive committee had taken a "stronger and more aggressive role in setting policy" for the agency. He also spoke in favor of the size of the board (36 elected and several ex-officio members) which allows broad representation from the parishes and different constituencies in the community.

Father Harms believes that as a result of the problems the agency has faced, it must develop "stronger ties" and "a more organic relationship" with the diocese as a whole. This will involve training in the "social service" aspects of the ministry in the member churches. During the agency's period of rapid growth it came to depend too much on paid staff which led to a separation, even isolation, from the diocese. He believes that ECS must develop ways of directly involving more people from the Episcopal community in the agency's programs.

EPISCOPAL COMMUNITY SERVICES
BOARD OF DIRECTORS ROSTER—1982-1983

The Rt. Rev. C. Brinkley Morton	Bishop of Episcopal Diocese of San Diego
Mr. Hugh Moore	Newspaper Advertising Executive
Mr. Edward D. Chapin	Attorney-at-Law
Mrs. Barbara Bright	Social Worker
Mrs. C. Brian Williams	Community Volunteer
Mrs. Charles Dick	Community Volunteer
Mr. Harold E. Holsonback	Banker
The Rev. Juan M. Acosta	Priest
Mr. Ted Adams	Insurance Broker
Mrs. Richard Backman	Community Volunteer

Mr. George W. Banks	Retired School Administrator
Mrs. Rosemary Bensz	Retired Businesswoman, Community Volunteer
Mrs. Lionel Brooks	President, Diocesan Episcopal Churchwomen
Dr. Robert Buffum	Retired M.D.
Mr. Bernard Carroll	Retired Army Colonel, Engineer
The Rev. James E. Carroll	Priest
Mr. Willard T. Cudney	Real Estate and Insurance
Dr. Paul Erickson	Professor, San Diego State University
Mr. Stephen Gassaway	Retired
Mrs. Gerald H. Graves	Community Volunteer
The Rev. Canon Richard B. Harms	Canon Missioner, Episcopal Diocese of San Diego
The Rev. John H. Hauser	Priest
Mrs. Ralph D. Haynes	Community Volunteer
The Rev. David L. Heaney	Priest
Mrs. G. Arleen Hunter	Nurse
The Rev. Tally H. Jarrett, Jr.	Priest
Mrs. Clyde Jones	Community Volunteer
Dr. Melville Klauber	Bio-statistician, San Diego State University
Ms. Linda Kresser	Banker
The Rev. Benjamin V. Lavey	Priest
Mrs. Titus G. LeCalir	Community Volunteer
The Rev. Richard C. Lief	Priest
Mr. James C. Parks	Retired Accountant
Capt. A. Kenneth Romberg, USN Ret.	Retired Naval Officer
Mr. Peter Schlotman	Insurance
Miss Helen Shell	Community Volunteer
Mr. Stuart H. Swett	Chief Deputy City Attorney
Mrs. Robert Traylor	Community Volunteer
The Rev. Kenneth R. Treat	Priest
The Rev. Michael Williams	Priest
Mr. Glenn Allison	Executive Director of Episcopal Community Services

THE FINANCIAL CRISIS

The financial crisis that befell the agency in December 1981 had been developing for well over a year. ECS ended the fiscal year of 1979-80 on June 30, 1980, with a loss of $30,160. They began fiscal 1980-81 with a budget that predicted a deficit for the year of $166,581. Plans were discussed for making up this amount through a combination of cost-cutting and fund raising, but neither was successful. The fund raising plan was never implemented and costs, rather than being cut, exceeded the predicted amounts by about $35,000. The actual loss for the fiscal year ending June 1981 was $213,709.

With expenses outrunning support and the long-standing problem of slow reimbursement on government contracts, cash flow became an insoluble problem. The agency began to default on payments of employee withholding taxes to the IRS. The first missed payment, for $47,862, occurred in January 1981 (for the October to December 1980 period). The defaults continued: in April, $120,443; in July, $34,544; in September, $58,000. Liens were filed by the IRS against the agency's property in July and September 1981 for taxes due for the periods ending in June, totaling $202,849 plus interest and penalties.

The decisions that led to the defaults have never been made clear. Canon Lazenby, in a newspaper interview after his resignation, said that the decision about what bills to leave unpaid was "an internal matter. The decision was made by my associate." The associate referred to was Carol Ackerson, who served as the agency's associate director starting in 1975. She left ECS in April 1981. It was Ackerson who had prepared the plans for reducing agency costs:

> I indicated in both verbal and written reports that drastic programmatic changes had to be made to correct the deteriorating fiscal situation and recommended several actions I felt were necessary. . . .

Her recommendations included eliminating salaries for counselors and instead paying them a percentage of the service fees paid to the agency, and closing an office in an outlying area. But few of them were acted upon, Ackerson said later,

> By the final quarter of 1980, revenues were not sufficient to cover both payroll and taxes. I recommended to Lazenby that payroll be paid and taxes deferred until sufficient revenues were generated.
> It was my understanding that Dr. Lazenby was responsible for making the decision as to what facts about the agency's fiscal situation were to be presented to the finance committee and the board of directors. . . .

Senior members of the staff recall that they were aware of the defaults as they were occurring. Members of the board, however, have said repeatedly that the situation was not made clear to them until December 1981.

Board members were well aware that ECS had severe financial problems. Plans for cutting costs and fund raising had been proposed some time before, but the vital information about the missed tax payments was never conveyed to the board until almost a year after the first default.

The Sale of the Building

In the spring of 1981, Canon Lazenby began discussing the possibility of selling the downtown headquarters building with the board of directors. The six-year-old building had been built at a cost of $500,000, much of this contributed by members of the Episcopal diocese. Lazenby told the board that the agency's client population was leaving the downtown area for other neighborhoods in the city and that it would be appropriate for ECS to relocate. He reminded them that one of the original goals of building a downtown headquarters had been to participate in the humanization and redevelopment of the neighborhood and that this had been accomplished. In addition, economic conditions at that time meant that demands for the agency's services would increase at the same time that government financial support for these activities would be cut. Selling the building would make it possible for ECS to continue providing a high level of service and allow for future development of the agency.

Canon Lazenby's arguments persuaded the board of directors and the building was listed for sale in June 1981 with an appraised value of $1.25 million.

It was a difficult time to sell property. The boom in San Diego real estate that had taken place in the preceding few years had been ended by high interest rates and uncertain economic conditions. Mortgages were extremely difficult to obtain and were available only at very high rates.

The sale of the building to a group of local investors for a price of $700,000 was announced at the end of 1981. The difference between the appraised value and the selling price caused considerable comment, especially in light of the agency's financial problems. Some members of the Episcopal diocese believed that it was a mistake to sell the building at a time when conditions in the real estate market precluded getting its full value. They also raised the point that the decision to sell had been made at a time when the board was not fully aware of the agency's true situation, that is, that the decision to sell had been made "for the wrong reasons."

Board members and officials of the diocese defended the terms of the sale. There had been a relatively large down payment, $250,000, and a five-year note at 12 percent with a lump-sum payment at the end of the period. The sale would net ECS approximately $862,000, including the $250,000 in cash that would enable the agency to satisfy the tax liability owed to the Internal Revenue Service. In addition, a six-month lease-back agreement was arranged in order to allow ECS time for moving its operations in an orderly way.

The Cudney Plan

In the summer of 1980, when cash flow problems had led ECS to default, for the first time, on payment of employee withholding taxes to the IRS, the board of directors began work on a fund-raising plan to improve the organization's financial situation. It was called the Cudney Plan, after Willard Cudney, a board member, and was designed to deal not only with the immediate shortage of cash, but also to create a working capital fund for agency operations.

The creation of a working capital fund was believed to be important because of the agency's dependence on government grants and contracts to fund many of its programs and activities. When the Cudney Plan was developed, ECS was projecting a $2.5 million budget for the fiscal year of 1980–81, with $1.5 million provided by grants and contracts with federal, state, and local governments. Many of these contracts required the expenditure of funds before reimbursement to the agency. At that time, there was often a delay of 60 to 90 days before the funds were received. Thus, a working capital fund was a necessity.

The Cudney Plan proposed to raise $450,000 by selling 450 $1,000, 6½ percent, 10-year promissory notes, each unit secured by a deed of trust on the downtown headquarters building. The sale of the notes was limited to individuals who, prior to the offer, were associated with the Episcopal Church or its activities in some way. The $450,000 was to be used as follows:

1. To extinguish the existing note and trust deed
   on the property: $190,000
2. To repay a line of credit from a local bank: 25,000
3. To repay a loan from the Epsicopal Diocese of San Diego: 86,500
4. To establish a working capital fund: 148,000
                                                       _____

                                                              $449,500

In the event that the full amount was not raised, the available amount would be used in the order listed above. A minimum of $200,000 would have to be obtained before the plan was implemented. A sinking fund was to be used to provide for repayment of the promissory notes.

In 1980, when the plan was proposed, the board of directors believed that the terms were realistic. Although the interest rate offered on the notes was under the market rate (the annual yield on three-month Treasury bills in 1980 was 11.5 percent; average for June to August 1980 was 8.1 percent), the board believed that members of the Episcopal community would be willing to participate, considering the differential in interest to be a kind of charitable contribution to the agency.

Two unforeseen problems contributed to the Cudney Plan's failure. It was necessary for the offering of promissory notes to be approved by the State of California. This approval process took substantially longer than anticipated. During the delay, the economic environment changed radically. Interest rates rose, and money-market funds began to compete vigorously for small investors' participation. By the time ECS received permission from the state to make the offering, the different between the 6½ percent offered and the market rate made it impossible to attract the full $450,000. The board decided not to go ahead with the plan.

REORGANIZATION

In September 1982 Episcopal Community Services began operating at its new office—a spartan, cramped complex of rooms in a neighborhood of small business and professional offices several miles from the downtown center of San Diego. The move to new offices was the most visible symbol of the reorganization at the agency which had been underway since Glenn Allison had taken over as interim director nine months before.

The major problem Allison faced was maintaining the agency's major programs while reducing costs and restructuring the organization into a more businesslike operation.

It was clear to Allison that ECS lacked the means for effective managerial control. During the preceding ten years, the agency had grown tremendously in program activities and budget, but had not built an administrative control staff with systems and procedures to provide for overall agency management.

The position of controller was created and steps were taken to strengthen the accounting functions.

All of the agency's contract-funded programs were required to be self-sustaining; that is, they could only spend what their contract budgets allowed. Program managers were made responsible for the fiscal administration of their own operations. In the past, agency policy had been that the program managers should concentrate on the service aspects of their divisions and not concern themselves with financial matters. They did not get cost reports so that they did not know how much they were spending and all responsibility for contract reimbursements was left to the understaffed and overstretched accounting department.

Under the new system, program managers get cost reports from the accounting department during the first week of the following month and they file their own cost reimbursement reports with contractors by the tenth of the month. The agency often receives payment within a week, so that cash flow problems have been greatly improved.

The move to smaller offices meant that some programs had to be relocated. Counseling programs found space at Episcopal churches in the diocese, and this has resulted in a strengthening of ties with the parishes.

The agency, in cooperation with the diocesan administration, has set up a liaison-volunteer committee to recruit more volunteers for the agency and to educate members of the Episcopal community about the agency's work, which, it is hoped, will result in more private financial support.

In order to reduce expenses, staff reductions had to be made, and all nonessential expenses curtailed.

The Controller

Dale Moritz is an attractive, friendly young woman with shoulder-length brown hair. She has a BA is business administration. She joined ECS in March 1982 as a temporary accountant and was appointed as controller on May 1. Her previous experience had been as an accountant for profit-making businesses. She is responsible for the financial affairs of the agency, and cost control is one of her most pressing problems. "We have become experts at scrounging, here, and making do with what we can find." The agency has cut general administrative costs to the bone, one water cooler for the whole office building and if you want coffee, you have to bring it yourself.

During her first few months at ECS, she had to spend a lot of time clearing out the results of years of inattention. The files were a mess and it was hard to find the documents she needed. In order to create an effective control system, the program managers had to be instructed and guided in learning to administer their own programs.

At first, it was all so confused and disorganized that it was difficult to get a clear picture of where the agency stood financially, but gradually the situation improved. She recalled that in September 1982 the financial situation had been clarified enough that she was able to put together cash flow projections for the coming months. Prospects for September and October were not good because ECS did not begin its big fund-raising campaign until the late October to January period. She met with Glenn Allison and Harold Holsonback and discussed the cash flow projections. They made some very useful suggestions, which helped, but not enough. The next day, the agency learned that they were the beneficiaries of a large and unexpected bequest from a member of the community. It was enough to put ECS into the black.

THE FUTURE OF ECS

Forecasts of the future depend very heavily on perceptions of the present. The success that ECS has had in working out the immediate problems of the crisis period has brought about an attitude of cautious optimism and hope for the future. At the same time, there is a recognition that the agency will succeed only if it continues to evolve and respond to changes in the environment in which it operates.

When board members were asked about their expectations for the future of the agency, their comments centered on two concerns, the needs of the people served by the agency, and the problems of obtaining financial support.

Penny Williams recognized the growing needs of the elderly in our society. There will be more of them, and many of them will be in need because of changes in the economy. She expects that ECS may begin new programs concentrating on the problems of older people.

Hugh Moore observed that the future of ECS depends greatly on support from the local Episcopal diocese. The agency's dependence on contract-supported programs has brought about many problems. He hopes that ECS will be able to develop a higher level of private support from the community.

Barbara Bright also stressed the need to move toward a different support base and predicted that this might lead the agency toward different kinds of programs and activities. There could be a move toward more advocacy and working with other agencies so that the services that ECS now provides would continue, but at less cost to the agency.

Harold Holsonback emphasized the need to respond to constant change in the financial environment. The changes in government support for programs mean more dependence on the private sector, but private contributions are limited by the state of the economy.

Father Carroll sees the next few years as a period of stabilization. The need for the agency's existing major programs is great and they must continue. The time will come when the agency will look toward expansion, but this must always be with the guidance and support of the Episcopal diocese.

Father Harms also spoke of the importance of strong ties with the people of the diocese. Any new programs that ECS develops must involve "more volunteerism" and a better use of the resources available to the agency.

Senior staff members at ECS share the board members' upbeat views of the future. While they all recognize that many problems, especially funding, remain to be solved, so much progress has been made in rebuilding the agency that they feel confident that ECS will continue to serve the community.

Dale Moritz, the newest of the senior staff, summed up her own feelings about the future. "I'm very happy at ECS and glad that I came to work here when I did." Of course the agency still has problems and will have to continue working to solve them. But she has great faith in Glenn Allison's abilities. He is the kind of forceful leader that ECS needs, with the vision to keep the agency moving in the right direction.

Glenn Allison, himself, is more cautious in his optimism. ECS is now a much stronger institution than it was at the beginning of 1982. The most serious financial problems are now under control. Revenues are covering expenses, there are no creditors, and the outstanding loans have been repaid. The agency ended fiscal 1982 in the black because of a bequest, but ECS ended fiscal 1983 in the black, "on our own."

Looking toward the future, he sees how much the success of ECS depends on uncontrollable factors, the economic, political, and ideological climate. Strategic planning is a necessity. The time will come when the agency will want to begin new programs, but these new areas of activity must fit into the overall plan. They must strengthen the agency as a whole, not just make it larger.

Directory of Programs

Alcoholism Programs

Clairmont Neighborhood Recovery Center
East County–ACCORD Neighborhood Recovery Center
South Bay Neighborhood Recovery Center

These three programs are comprehensive, outpatient service agencies focusing on prevention, intervention, and treatment of alcoholism. Services include individual and group counseling for recovering alcoholics and their families, referral services, alcohol education programs, and Antabuse monitoring.

The programs are funded in part by the County of San Diego and by donations and service fees.

Counseling

The Counseling Program provides a range of services to children, adolescents, and adults seeking help in resolving personal problems. Currently, the program has offices at several Episcopal churches in the diocese. It is supported by service fees based on the client's ability to pay.

Grief Center. The Grief Center is a division of the Counseling program which serves clients who have suffered a loss through death or other traumatic cause. Counseling and training programs are offered. Currently, the program sponsors two support groups: Survivors of Suicide and Parents of Murdered Children.

Deaf Community Services

Deaf Community Services provides advocacy, counseling, interpreting and Telephone/TDD relay services, employment and placement counseling, and various support activities to hearing impaired people in San Diego County. The program receives financial support from the California Department of Social Services, RETC, donations, and service fees.

Emergency Assistance

Emergency Assistance provides food, clothing, referrals for temporary housing, and information and help with welfare, unemployment, medical, and alcohol and drug problems. The office is in a downtown San Diego storefront. During 1981–82, the program served 5,497 clients. The program relies heavily on volunteers and is supported by donations.

Ex-Offender Re-Entry Program

The program is designed to help men and women who have been released from correctional institutions make the transition to a more productive "straight" life. The program provides temporary work and income, assistance in adjusting to life outside institutions, and training in basic job skills—especially, how to find a job and keep it. Financial support is provided by RETC, United Way, and donations and service fees.

Otay Community Clinic

The Otay Community Clinic provides health care services to residents of Chula Vista and other communities in the South Bay area. A general medical program offers diagnosis and treatment of medical problems. Ancillary services include hypertension screenings, perinatal and gynecological programs, nutrition counseling, a drug dispensary, and referral services to other health care providers and social service agencies. In 1981–82, 5,873 client visits were recorded.

A great share of the clinic's financial support comes from San Diego County's revenue-sharing program and the California Department of Health Services. The clinic accepts private insurance, Medicare, and Medi-Cal. Fees for patients without financial aid or insurance are set on a sliding scale according to family size and income.

South Bay Head Start

Head Start is a developmental pre-school program for three- to five-year-old children of low income families. The program stresses parent participation. South Bay Head Start is operated at four centers in National City, Imperial Beach, Otay, and Otay Mesa. In 1981–82, 278 children and their families participated.

Head Start offers the following services:

Education—Children attend pre-school classes four days a week and are taken on field trips to such places as fire stations, the zoo, and museums.
Health—All children receive a complete physical assessment, a dental exam, and follow-up services.
Nutrition—Meals and snacks for the children are served every day.
Parent Involvement—Many parents volunteer in the classrooms and serve on planning committees. There are training programs given in child development, parenting skills, health, and other problems.
Social Services—Home visits by family resource workers, crisis intervention, and referrals are provided.
Handicap Services—Diagnostic and follow-up services are offered to children with suspected or diagnosed handicaps.

South Bay Head Start is financed under the federal program started 17 years ago.

Definitions

Bishop. The chief clergyman of one diocese. He is elected by a convention of the diocese which he is to head. His duties include visiting the parishes for various ceremonial occasions, serving as pastor to his clergy, presiding over meetings of the Executive Council and the Diocesan Convention, and looking after administrative matters generally.

Canon. A canon is a clergyman who is a member of the staff of a cathedral (the bishop's church, the center of diocesan authority). These men are called canon because they are listed in the Canonical (official) Register of the cathedral. Honorary canons are just what the term suggests. The bishop, wishing to honor a clergyman, makes him an honorary canon of the cathedral. It is something like an honorary doctorate given by a university or college.

Diocese. An administrative division of the Church under the supervision of a bishop.

Parish. An organized congregation within a diocese that supports its own church.

Rector. The chief clergyman over a self-supporting congregation. A parish may have several clergypersons, but only one rector. The others are assistants on the rector's staff.

Seminary. A general term for all theological colleges.

For more information, see Howard Harper, *The Episcopalian's Dictionary*, The Seabury Press.

EPISCOPAL COMMUNITY SERVICES—BRIEF HISTORY

1927 —July 21—Organization of the Episcopal County and City Mission Society of San Diego, by All Saints Parish, San Diego. 117 members. Full-time chaplain.

1939 —Reorganization, with bishop as president, and local board of directors elected at an annual meeting

1944–1954 —Reduction to half-time chaplain; reduction in income

1954 —The Rev. Ralph D. Bonacker, Director, full-time women's auxiliaries render favored support

1955 —Articles of Incorporation filed

1956 —Youth Consultation Service

1957 —Financial support from Community Chest (now United Way)

1957 —Work Project begins (now Ex-Offender Program)

1958 —Moved from 722 Broadway to 555 - 19th Street

1958 —Name changed to Episcopal Community Services

1960 —The Rev. Arthur G. Elcombe, Director

1963 —Church counseling services offered—extension of chaplaincy

1964 —First governmental grant (County of San Diego)

1966 —Neighborhood Services begins (student unit)
1967 —Adult Rehabilitation Facility approved by California Department of Rehabilitation.
1971 —Work Facility moves to 2459 Market Street, after their building on 19th Street burned.
1972 —Coalition of Ex-Offender Project begins (Metro, Project JOVE, Western Behavioral Sciences Institute, and ECS)
1972 —The Rev. Herbert C. Lazenby, Executive Director
1972 —Neighborhood Services changes to Community Development
1973 —Sweetwater Youth Services begins
1974 —Central Deaf Association became affiliated (now Deaf Community Service)
1974 —Otay Community Clinic became affiliated
1974 —First RETC contract for Ex-Offender Program
1974 —Grief Center programs begun
1975 —The Caged Dove Boutique program for women ex-offenders
1975 —The new building at 601 Market Street occupied
1977 —The first "Evening with the Bishop" Dinner Dance
1978 —South Bay Head Start program begun
1979 —Neighborhood Recovery Center alcohol programs contracted for at the request of the county
1979 —Provided space for Catholic Workers' Soup Kitchen
1982 —Sale of 601 Market Street property; move to 3427 Fifth Avenue
1982 —Glenn S. Allison, Executive Director

EPISCOPAL COMMUNITY SERVICE: Statement of Income and Expenses
(For the Year Ended December 31, 1966)

Income

Administrative Income	$ 1,382.50	
Interest and Endowment Income	932.23	
Contributions—All Sources	5,966.38	
Bishop of Los Angeles	3,000.00	
Memberships	9,615.76	
Counseling Fees and Miscellaneous Revenue	543.98	
United Community Services	21,568.00	
Work Project		
Income from Jobs	47,083.96	
County of San Diego	5,000.00	
California Department of Corrections	2,880.00	
Diocese of Los Angeles	27,000.00	
Project Grant/Executive Council		
of Episcopal Church	10,000.00	
TOTAL INCOME		$134,972.81

Expenses

Salaries and Salary Expenses	$37,955.47	
Office and Building Maintenance	2,166.12	
Administrative Expenses	10,381.63	
Program Expenses		
Rehabilitation Project	59,113.97	
Church Counseling Project	9,000.00	
Youth Consultation Project	10,000.00	
Housing Allowances	4,500.00	
Other Expenses	231.29	
TOTAL EXPENSES		$133,348.48
EXCESS OF REVENUES OVER EXPENSES		1,624.33
		$134,972.81

Deficit Beginning of Year	$ (6,097.06)
Excess of Revenues over Expenses	1,624.33
Deficit End of Year	$ (4,472.73)

EPISCOPAL COMMUNITY SERVICE

Combined Funds Statements of Support, Revenue, and Expenses and Changes in Fund Balances (Years ended June 30, 1981 and 1980)

	1981	1980
Public support and revenue:		
Public support:		
Contributions	$ 123,451	$ 83,079
Allocated by United Way of San Diego		
County (less related fund raising expenses)	89,374	121,572
Episcopal Diocese of San Diego	55,702	42,724
Total public support	268,527	247,375
Fees and grants from governmental agencies	1,289,129	1,174,941
Other revenue:		
Rental income	5,578	46,008
Program service fees	649,195	648,767
Investment income	1,241	432
Miscellaneous income	42,800	20,117
Total other revenue	698,814	715,324
Total public support and revenue	2,256,470	2,137,640
Expenses:		
Program services:		
Ex-offender	299,212	354,881
Counseling	96,545	95,463
Project improvement	78,366	54,316
Community development	68,104	35,424
Otay Community Clinic	201,750	180,440
South Bay Head Start	371,675	318,565
Deaf Community Services	174,321	138,492
Welfare rights organization	(227)	18,577
Alcohol program	876,274	655,876
Emergency assistance	6,900	—
E.P.I.C.	11,767	—
Total program services	2,184,687	1,852,034
Support services:		
Management and general	252,007	279,959
Fund raising	33,485	35,812
Total support services	285,492	315,771
Total expenses	2,470,179	2,167,805
Expenses in excess of public support and revenue	(213,709)	(30,165)
Fund balances beginning of year	132,111	162,276
Fund balances (deficit) end of year	$ (81,598)	$ 132,111

MANAGEMENT ALLOCATION POLICY

The purpose of this plan is to allocate management costs equitably to the various programs.

Process

Each year at the time the budget is developed, the administrative costs for the year are *estimated* and an average monthly figure is computed for management costs. This figure is used throughout the year. At the end of the year adjustments are made to the government grants if the total of the actual costs is less than the amount charged to the grant.

A percentage of the total management costs will be allocated to each program by the following formula: (Program Expenses do not include Contract Management Fee)

$$\frac{\text{Individual Program Expenses}}{\text{Total Agency Expenses}} \times \text{Total Management Costs}$$

New programs started during the year will be charged a percentage based on the following formula:

$$\frac{\text{Total Management Costs}}{\text{Total Agency Program Expenses}} \times 100$$

The above process helps identify costs with revenues, correctly charges administrative time and services provided to programs, and best represents the actual cost of operating any given program. Properly charging programs for management helps insure that ECS is not subsidizing government programs.

ALLOCABLE ADMINISTRATIVE COSTS
July 1, 1982–June 30, 1983

	General Administration
Salaries	$ 92,013*
Employee Benefits	2,700
Payroll Taxes	8,970
Auditing and Professional Fees	12,000
Office Supplies	5,055
Telephone	4,008
Postage	1,240
Occupancy	36,027
Printing	850
Local Travel	1,005
Subscription/Publications	12
Insurance	6,276
Computer—Lease Interest, Maintenance, Depreciation	36,000
Equipment and Furnishings	3,800
Total Allocable Administrative Costs	209,956
Other Interest	2,100
Moving Expenses	3,000
Total Unallocable Administrative Costs	5,100
Total Administrative Budget	$215,056

---

*Includes the following positions and percent of salary charged to administration:

Executive Director	60%
Executive Secretary	60%
Receptionist	100%
Clerical	100%
Accountant	100%
Accounting Clerk	100%
Controller	100%

1982–83 ALLOCATION PLAN

Amount of Management Costs to be Charged to Programs = $189,379

Program	(1) 1982–83 Agency Budget*	(2) Percent of Total Agency Budget	(3) Amount of Management Allocation (column 2 X 209,956)
Administration	$ 215,056	9.8	$ 20,577
Fund Raising	32,706	1.5	3,149
Chaplaincy	12,040	0.5	1,050
Counseling	47,019	2.1	4,409
Community Development	25,386	1.2	2,519
Emergency Assistance	28,114	1.3	2,729
Ex-Offender Re-Entry	292,826	13.3	27,924
Otay Community Clinic	161,569	7.6	15,956
Deaf Community Services	263,525	11.9	24,985
South Bay Head Start	402,481	18.2	38,212
East County ACCORD	307,716	14.0	29,394
Clairemont NRC	257,880	11.7	24,565
South Bay NRC	152,576	6.9	14,487
TOTAL	$2,198,894	100%	$209,956

*Program budgets exclude contract management cost.

Appendix III:
Annual Strategic Plan for the San Diego Economic Development Corporation

INTRODUCTION

The purpose of this document is to update EDC's strategic plan, specifying the programs needed to continue to develop efficiently and effectively San Diego's economic opportunities. This strategic plan was designed for implementation during the 1981-82 fiscal year.

The foundation for the plan is a combination of several years' experience and a comprehensive series of studies, surveys, and investigations concerning San Diego's industrial development needs, problems, and opportunities. Much of the original background for this plan was documented in EDC's 1978-79 marketing plan and "Bootstrap," a study for accelerated industrial growth in greater San Diego prepared by the Economic Research Bureau of the San Diego Chamber of Commerce.

From this background data, experience of the past years, and continued contact with public and private sector leaders, the problems and opportunities confronting the Economic Development Corporation of San Diego County have emerged. EDC's mission remains clear. It must maintain a leadership position in creating new jobs for San Diego County residents by actively pursuing the development of industry which will result in economic growth, diversification, and capital formation.

The area's essential growth in employment during the decade of the eighties requires careful focus on appropriate strategy. The overall strategy will be implemented with a strong array of marketing elements, including advertising, public relations, direct prospect contact, support programs, and collateral materials.

The success of this plan requires the support of all individuals and organizations desiring appropriate economic growth for the San Diego region. Close coordination between the county and municipal governments, the Port District, and private sector interests is essential.

BACKGROUND

Founded in 1965 as a private, nonprofit corporation, San Diego's EDC was chartered to "promote the area's economic growth and diversification by assisting firms to locate here."

Through the late 1960s and early 1970s EDC worked actively with the public and private sectors, the San Diego Chamber of Commerce and other organizations to help create new jobs, manage the development and sale of San Diego city-owned industrial land and assist in locating an average of six new industries per year in San Diego. Started by 100 local firms contributing $1,000 per year and partially supported by City of San Diego funding, EDC operated with an annual budget in the $150,000-200,000 range.

By the mid-1970s, however, San Diego unemployment was over 11 percent due to long term population expansion and stagnation of the growth of San Diego's manufacturing sector. Manufacturing employment in 1976 actually declined from 1975 levels—and averaged an annual increase of less than 1 percent for the 1970-76 period. Population increases were +2.6 percent per year on average for the same period.

In April 1977, the San Diego City Council commissioned the Economic Research Bureau of the San Diego Chamber of Commerce to develop a plan to accelerate the industrial development of the San Diego region. The study was completed in July 1977 and called for a substantially expanded program, a reorganization providing direct public sector participation with more aggressive private sector job goals. During the July 1977 to January 1978 period, the County of San Diego, the City of San Diego, the Unified Port District, the League of Cities, and the San Diego Chamber of Commerce all pledged support to a revitalized EDC. In December 1977 EDC's membership formally approved its reorganization; and EDC embarked on its current program.

Private sector support has increased from 65 members providing $65,000 in the fall of 1977 to over 100 members providing approximately $200,000. 1980 unemployment of 6.7 percent is a recent low; and EDC has assisted directly or indirectly in the annual average creation of over 10,000 jobs since 1977.

MISSION

San Diego's Economic Development Corporation provides a variety of services and interacts with a wide range of local groups in order to maintain a leadership position in creating new jobs for San Diego County residents.

The major focus of this mission is the development of primary sector employment opportunities which will result in economic growth, diversification, and capital formation.

Policies

In carrying out its mission, EDC will:

Impartially serve all communities and competing interests within San Diego County.

Encourage the growth of employment opportunities which are compatible with the community's environmental standards.

Encourage and assist the expansion of local industry.

Promote and assist the relocation or expansion of outside business and industry to San Diego County.

Encourage the creation of jobs most suited to the area's employment needs or potential.

Advocate and facilitate the cooperative efforts of the public and private sectors in the pursuit of San Diego County's economic growth.

Support specific private sector needs which coincide with EDC's primary mission.

Maintain a solid, continuing base of support from the private sector while encouraging public funding from all sectors of the county to maximize its accomplishments.

Coordinate its activities with other public and private agencies whose programs are complementary to EDC's mission.

Advocate and coordinate with the public and private sectors to insure a positive business climate.

Situation Analysis

Expanded employment opportunities are needed in almost every area of the United States, and competition for the expansion and relocation of industry to create job growth is intense. The competition for industry takes two forms. First, the inherent or developed industrial advantages of an area are considered as objectively as possible by relocating or expanding business. Secondly, the nature of the effort to attract and accommodate prospective industry can enhance the first and is an important element unto itself.

Natural Advantages

Several studies have attempted to isolate the most important natural advantages for industrial site selection. A consensus of these studies provides the following site selection criteria in order of priority:

1. Labor (cost, availability, and/or skills)
2. Transportation
3. Proximity to markets
4. Business climate
5. Energy (availability and cost)
6. Proximity to support services
7. Quality of life
8. Lack of unionization
9. Taxes

Metro areas such as Phoenix, Tucson, Sacramento, Dallas, Houston, Miami, Atlanta, Denver, San Jose/Santa Clara, Los Angeles/Orange County, Austin, San Antonio, Salt Lake City, and Colorado Springs are formidable competitors for San Diego. Additionally, while not in the "Sun Belt," the Seattle and Portland areas are strong competition, particularly for the electronics/aerospace industries and Japanese business.

A. *Organized Economic Development Programs*

Most major metro areas have an organized economic development program. These programs typically include prospecting activities, advertising, promotion, public relations, research, and special incentives for relocating or expanding businesses. These metro areas quite often have one or more advantages over San Diego. First, they are recognized metro areas that have demonstrated, in addition to their population, strong markets for retail and wholesale sales. San Diego, although the eighth largest city in the United States, sometimes suffers in market visibility because of Los Angeles. From many perspectives, San Diego is simply a smaller part of the Los Angeles/Southern California megalopolis, a concept which underestimates the area's true market strength and generally strong individuality. Many traditional methods of measuring market strength contribute to this confusion, such as retail sales which are normally computed from wholesale purchases. Approximately 70 percent of all civilian supermarket items are provided to San Diego retailers by Los Angeles buying offices. Often times Tijuana's million+ population is also ignored. Very importantly, most competitive metro areas, including smaller cities in the southeastern states (North Carolina, South Carolina, Georgia, Mississippi, Alabama, Louisiana, and Florida, specifically) have the advantage of an aggressive and committed state economic development effort. In that San Diego is a region with a population larger than 15 states, we are competing as much at the state level as at a local level. Total advertising spending is estimated to be in the $30-$50 million range. At the large end of the scale, North Carolina has a staff of 200. Additional competition comes from Port Districts, utilities (outside California), and other nations.

In reviewing the individual programs of competing economic development agencies it is difficult to objectively assess their effectiveness on a basis of job generation. In that manufacturing jobs are declining in the country as a whole, however, San Diego appears to be outperforming most competition. By most standards of staffing and program, however, the cities of Seattle and Philadelphia and of the South in general consistently stand above most competitors. In recent years New England and selected midwestern states have also expanded their economic development activities. Most have had sustaining, long term, programs. The two city programs have also benefitted indirectly from federal Economic Development Administration (EDA) spending. It is important to note that according to the American Economic Development Council (AEDC) the areas with the strongest, local/regional programs have private, nonprofit economic development efforts. Below the state government level, relatively few areas really have total, integrated marketing efforts. It seems clear that the region that can better define its market and resources, build awareness and interest, provide organized and professional materials, demonstrate community support, and maintain continuous follow-up during the site selection process will maximize its chances of attracting desirable business.

B. Opportunities and Problems

San Diego and EDC are supported and confronted by a variety of positive and potentially negative factors in helping San Diego's economy to expand. In offering the San Diego area as a "product" to corporations considering San Diego for relocation or expansion, these factors must be considered, and, where possible, improved if San Diego is to be successful in fostering the desired level of economic growth.

San Diego's *opportunities* include:

Commitment of the board of directors and membership
Government recognition of employment needs and the significance of strengthening and diversifying the regional economy
Support for EDC's mission from the public and private sector
Growing financial support from both private sector membership funding and City/Port annual appropriations
Flexibility of a private corporation
More reliable and comprehensive data base than most other economic development groups
A proven record of success and growing national recognition
San Diego, as a product, provides a variety of strengths:

National

Government attitude and participation
Labor supply and cost
Quality of living
Desirable climate
Low energy use due to climate
A part of the second largest market and fastest growing population center in the United States
Potential for industrial land sites
Twin Plant opportunities
Better air quality than most other major cities
Increased awareness and desirability

Increasing national prominence in several key industries
Deep water port access

California

Cost of doing business versus Los Angeles, Orange County, and San Francisco Bay area
Cost of housing versus other major California coastal communities

San Diego's *problems* include:

Opposition within some segments of the general population to growth
San Diego, as a product, suffers from weakness in terms of:

Housing costs versus United States as a whole
Ready availability of usable properties
Rapidly increasing electricity costs
Long term concerns over water and energy availability
Industrial land costs
Location on national basis
Business support services for certain industries
Special incentives
Government regulations and restrictions
State levels of taxation
Environmental constraints

OBJECTIVES

EDC's operating plan is designed to contribute significantly to creating jobs in San Diego. EDC's goal, on average, is to assist in the creation of 3,000 *extra* jobs per year from new industry.

Accomplishments

Calendar Year	Relocation-Expansion Decisions	Local Expansion Decisions	Employment Commitments	Average Facility* Investment	Average Annual Payroll
1978	7	8	4,950	$8,742,414	$4,294,615
1979	9	3	2,285	$5,621,857	$2,919,750
1980	10	3	4,020	—	—

*Includes land, buildings, and equipment.

If new industry job generation is matched by local job generation, and compounded by a "multiplier" effect, as many as 15,000 jobs can be created annually that would not have been otherwise generated.

The above table summarizes the results of EDC's involvement with new companies choosing to come to San Diego and local expansion assistance. Of the jobs generated, experience indicates that over 85 percent will be offered to San Diego residents.

ORGANIZATION

The thrust of EDC's mission has required staffing by a small cadre of dedicated professional managers. The confidential nature of corporate relocation work—and the caliber of outside management people involved in the relocation process (chief executives and real estate managers) must be met by San Diego volunteer EDC members and staff of comparable quality and knowledge.

From an organizational standpoint, EDC is currently supported by:

Board of Directors
Mayor's Task Force
Real Estate Committee
Audit Committee
Membership Committee
Marketing Committee
Outside legal, advertising/marketing, and public relations counsel
Professional staff

During 1981–82 increased emphasis was placed on membership involvement in nonconfidential EDC activities. Other volunteer activity addressed the problem of housing cost and availability.

While EDC's professional staff provides certain specialized services, each staff member must be broad based enough to handle all facets of EDC's work on an occasional basis. Major duties include:

Executive Director, Richard Davis
Supervise all operations, with primary focus on marketing/direct contact and consulting with prospects.

Associate Director, Mac Strobl
In addition to industrial consulting, responsible for membership/government relations, industrial land inventory/planning, and budget planning and control.

Assistant Director, Jane Signaigo-Cox
All facets of consulting with prospects and information services. Responsible for supervising research services and in-house promotion work.

Research Analyst, Susan Madaii

All areas of general research; and preparation of specific data for individual projects.

Office Management and Support Services, Sue Dedman and Sarina Hook

All facets of office administration and membership support with operational emphasis on direct mail to prospects, completion of routine research, and response to general inquiries.

OPERATING PROGRAM

A. Background

Prior to 1978, EDC's program was extremely small. Media spending varied from zero to $15,000 per year; and media-generated responses never exceeded 1,000 per year. With a revitalized EDC program in 1978, responses have averaged 4,000+ per year; and prospect activity has increased correspondingly.

The key criteria in measuring our current success and future prospects are:

1. Have we achieved our job goals?
2. Does our current "backlog" of prospect interest indicate that our current program is on target and will lead to future success?
3. Does research verify the usefulness of the various tools of our marketing mix?

The answer to the first is clear cut, in that job goals have been exceeded. Prospect reports confirm the continued success of our marketing and operations programs. Continuing research documents the success of individual program elements.

Although San Diego has suffered from increasing housing, industrial land, and money costs, the vitality of high technology industrial targets has helped San Diego come through an economy that has stopped industrial growth in much of the United States.

San Diego's geographic location and increasing contact with coastal California and Japan has also helped EDC in building an inventory of future prospects. It's been especially fortunate that the growth industries of the 1980s are largely headquartered in our key areas of geographic interest. At the same time, the efficiencies of a national marketing program, albeit modest, have built and maintained visibility with those Midwest, Eastern, and Canadian companies capable of considering California expansion.

Additionally, San Diego's unique location at the junction of the "Sun Belt" and coastal California, proximity to Mexico, and a position as a "window" to the Far East, make the region uniquely attractive to manufacturers and shipping interests, as well as other commercial and industrial entities.

As EDC continues to compete in the marketplace, more industrial land must be made available. Careful and creative planning for future growth, both residential and industrial, will be a prime undertaking for elected officials, community groups, and the business community. EDC will be directly involved in this process, at the local policy level, through the activities of its Industrial Real Estate Committee.

The strength of the program created and executed by EDC has been recognized by a variety of outside groups. Most prominent recognition includes that of the American Marketing Association (1978-79 Industrial Marketer of the Year), American Industrial Development Council (1979 "Individual Prospect Presentation" Award—1st Place), and the San Diego Sales and Marketing Executives International (1980-81 "Special Award for Outstanding Achievements During the Year—Bringing Honor and Benefit to the Community").

Although targets of opportunity have narrowed because of changing external conditions, EDC and San Diego as a whole have nonetheless prospered by taking advantage of the area's unique combination of advantages.

B. Strategy

The primary focus of EDC's strategy is to continue to *remind* current prospects and *inform* new prospects considering corporate expansion or relocation. The objective will be to generate bona fide prospects from defined target markets of opportunity and follow up those leads with direct, one-on-one, staff contact. The major communications targets are corporate decision-makers and site selection influencers.

Expansion or relocation is generally a several year process of review and evaluation of alternative sites. During the process, consultants can play a significant role. Therefore, in addition to communications to top corporate decision-makers, secondary priority will be given to industrial development consultants, site selection specialists, and investment and commercial bankers.

Over the past several years EDC has been most effective in generating interest and response from certain geographic areas and industry categories. Of the 38 major companies that expanded or relocated in San Diego in the last three years, 37 percent were the result of local expansion, 24 percent were from Los Angeles and Orange counties, 3 percent from the San Francisco area, and 3 percent from other areas in California. (California companies represented 67 percent of the expansions and relocations.) Additionally, outside of California, 12 percent of the relocations were from Japan, 12 percent from the Midwest, and 9 percent from the eastern United States. In terms of jobs generated, California and Japan have become increasingly important.

The strategy for 1981/82 focused on the primary targets of opportunity, principally California, Japan, and the rest of the United States. These targets were priorized in order to achieve maximum results and use limited marketing funds most efficiently.

In addition to specified geographic targets, several types of industries have demonstrated a preference in selecting San Diego. Those industries will receive priority attention and include electronics and high technology companies, light manufacturing, service companies, and corporate headquarters.

An essential element of the strategy will be to present to prospective companies throughout the relocation or expansion process a unified, organized, and professional San Diego effort. All communications tools will have a uniform theme to project a consistent, professional image. The benefits and competitive advantages of San Diego will be communicated in an exciting way to generate maximum awareness and impact, clearly indicating to prospects that the community means business. We must continue to "beat our competition" with timely, factual, and thorough assistance.

All the development resources, public and private, of the community will be coordinated to respond to prospects' developing interest. A key element of the marketing strategy will be the "out front" involvement of key public and private sector leadership.

C. Advertising Plan

1. Advertising

a. *Objective*—The site selection process is usually a long one. EDC must remind existing prospects of the area's desirability; and it must also find new ones just entering the process. The primary objective of the advertising will be to create or maintain awareness of San Diego as having many needed and desirable advantages, especially for targeted industries, and produce specific expressions of interest in the form of inquiries.

b. *Media*—There are three magazine categories included in the strategy:

Horizontal business publications reaching corporate executives in major U.S. and international companies. Readership is skewed to top and middle management.

Site location trade publications reaching industrial development and real estate consultants and specialists. Key readership includes corporate real estate executives and facilities planners.

Vertical industry publications, reaching top executives, as well as lower level management and technical staffs, within a specific industry.

The primary media effort will be to reach top corporate decision-makers, in all major industries, with at least minimum required frequency to meet established advertising objectives. Major business publications will be used. Coverage will be weighted to deliver more impressions to California, western United States, and Japan, but will also include coverage of the Midwest, eastern United States, and Western Europe.

A secondary priority will be site location trade publications. These traditional trade publications will be used to reach site selection consultants and professionals. This will provide "bottom-up" support to insure that the top corporate decision-makers receive appropriate support and recommendations.

Additionally, key industry publications will be used to focus on specific industries that have clearly established a "critical mass" or emerging position in San Diego.

Because the media effort requires minimum frequencies in "effective" reach, duplication or overlap of readership will help provide adequate advertising impact. Except for the use of special editions or supplements, minimum frequency is judgmentally considered to be three impressions per year.

Consistent with overall marketing objectives, special advertising and editorial text "supplements" will be vigorously pursued. These advertising supplements encourage local advertising support, which helps provide editorial coverage of San Diego and maximum impact with a minimum EDC investment. Even more importantly, they provide collateral material for continuing sales promotion, direct mail, and personal sales calls.

c. *Creative Plan*—The EDC creative direction evolved from initial research in 1978. "San Diego is Zoned for Success" was the theme and headline for the first campaign. The second year, based on early successes, the theme was modified to "San Diego: Proven Site for Success." Evaluation of readership studies and verbatim comments suggest that EDC's advertisements needed 1) more specific facts; and 2) "dialog" with top corporate executives who make site selection decisions and had a major problem in securing final approval of the Board of Directors. Keeping these thoughts in mind, the "success" theme was retained, but modified to "San Diego: The surest way to get a unanimous decision on a new site."

The 1981/82 creative plan was an extension of the previous year's approach. Appropriate copy points were adjusted to reflect current benefits, problems, and successes. Improvements were made in the use of current graphics, especially the skyline photograph.

2. Media Schedule

The following was the recommended media plan for 1981/82:

Business Publications

Business Week (3x)	1 western edition
	2 full run editions
Fortune (2x)	1 western edition
	1 full run edition
Forbes (1x)	1 full run edition
California Business (6x)	California
PSA In-flight (3x)	Western United States
Subarashii (1x)	Japan
U.S./Japan Business News (1x)	Japan
Nikkei Business (1x)	Japan

Budget: $72,000

Trade Publications

Area Development (3x)
Plants, Sites and Parks (3x)
Site Selection Handbook (3x)
National Real Estate Investor (1x)

Budget: $10,000

Industry Publications

Electronic Business (3x)

Budget: $3,000

Total Projected Media Budget:	$85,000
Total Production Budget:	5,000
Total Budget:	$90,000

D. Public Relations

1, . Public Relations Strategy

Public relations support is a critical element in the overall marketing program. This effort is divided into three categories:

1. Publicity
2. Special target representation (Japan and electronics industry)
3. In-market communications

Publicity—The San Diego economic development story will be developed through nonpaid editorial coverage. News releases regarding new expansion and relocation announcements, improving or already superior services and benefits, and favorable governmental regulations or decisions will be developed. Business, industry, and trade publications will be pursued for feature and editorial coverage. Significant articles that support EDC's efforts will be reprinted and used for marketing support.

Special Target Representation

Japan—In order to fully exploit opportunities in Japan, a Tokyo representative will be engaged. This representative will follow up or make initial contact with Japanese prospects, seek publicity coverage in appropriate business and trade publications, and seek all opportunities to extend and maximize San Diego's interests in Japan.

Electronics Industry—As a continuation of 1980/81 efforts, a PR film specializing in the electronics industry was used for trade show and media work. For specific contacts, assistance was also provided in arranging Los Angeles and Santa Clara based group presentations.

In-Market Communications—Past surveys have indicated strong support for EDC's mission. But, it is recognized that there can be strong differences concerning the meaning or interpretation of "development." Since community support is vital to creating the environment necessary to attract desirable industry, it is important that EDC's efforts be clearly communicated to the various publics. An on-going, "low-level" program to reach all targeted publics will be maintained. *EDC News* will be mailed quarterly to all media, elected and government officials, members, and selected individuals. The newsletter also will be used with key prospects and out-of-market contacts.

A program of luncheon presentations on EDC activities will be continued and community groups actively solicited for speaking engagements. Additionally, visitations to EDC's offices by selected groups will be occasionally scheduled to strengthen communications

2. Program Schedule

The public relations schedule is on-going. To a great extent it is geared to relocation or expansion accouncements or changes in San Diego that have news value.

The presentation in Japan is also on-going. Special emphasis was placed on the EDC trade mission scheduled for November 1981.

The EDC newsletter was distributed quarterly. Membership meetings were held in fall 1981 and spring 1982. The Annual Meeting was held in January 1982.

E. Direct Mail Plan

1. Background/Performance

Direct mail solicitation received maximum emphasis in 1981/82. Operating experience during the last several years has clearly shown the cost effectiveness of direct mail solicitation of targeted prospects. A major direct mail program was conducted in 1979/80. Approximately 2,500 original letters were sent to the president or chief executive officer in industry categories that were EDC targets. The companies were determined by further segmenting them by volume of gross sales and number of employees. The letter was signed by E. L. McNeely, representing the Mayor's Task Force for Economic Development, and included a business reply card.

Approximately 46 percent of the reply cards were returned, of which 125 or 5 percent indicated interest in San Diego as a possible site for expansion or relocation. These prospects were added to EDC's "active file" for follow-up and eventual one-on-one contact.

2. Prospect Solicitation

Based on the success of the initial and subsequent direct mail programs, the same methodology was continued in 1981/82. The only difference was a more defined targeting of prospects and an expanded mailing list. Top area CEO's like E. L. McNeely and Forest Shumway were used to sign the letters for these targeted mailings.

The major prospects included the following target industries: electronic, high technology, health sciences, research and development, selected manufacturing, corporate headquarters, and companies projected by outside research services to be in an expansion mode. These target industry categories will be further segmented by concentrating primarily on California, western Unites States, and Japan, using size of company as limiting criteria.

3. Program Schedule

The direct mail program was scheduled in three phases, as follows:

Phase I   Western U.S. electronic and high technology companies, selected manufacturing, insurance, and financial firms and corporate headquarters.
August 1981

Phase II   Major Japanese prospects and selected overseas companies.
November 1981

Phase III   Midwest and eastern U.S. electronic and high technology companies, selected manufacturing and corporate headquarters.
February 1982

F. Support Programs

1. Trade Missions

Visitations to Japan by EDC staff, area executives, and officials have been extremely successful since 1977. These missions clearly demonstrate San Diego's commitment to industrial and corporate growth, as well as genuine interest in the Japanese market. In addition to a hosted reception, one-on-one sales calls by EDC members of the San Diego delegation are made on selected prospects.

In addition to Japan, other overseas targets are closely evaluated for long-run potential. Canada, the United Kingdom, and West Germany appear to be next in priority, if budget levels allow testing of additional marketing efforts.

2. Executive Tours

California real estate brokers, solid industrial prospects, key consultants, and influential media representatives will be hosted by EDC on a limited basis. Generally, bona fide prospects will pay their own way. The program will counteract resistance to Southern California and give credence to the information disseminated by EDC.

3. Mayor's Task Force

EDC's membership forms the base for an executive "visitation" program that utilizes San Diego executives when they are traveling. EDC provides a "fact kit" for its members, as well as public officials, for use with key prospects.

New Mayor's Task Force members receive a special training program. Task Force members notify EDC when they are traveling to "key target" areas. EDC, in turn, sets up prospect visits. Past experiences have been positive. This "high level prospecting," sometimes with Chief Executive Officers of prospective firms (or embassies of targeted foreign countries, etc.), will not generally substitute for EDC staff visits. But, it does serve to enhance San Diego's impact on prospective firms—and, in some cases, can be the crucial "added advantage."

Mayor's Task Force membership is limited to representatives of EDC member companies who:

—Complete the EDC training program
—Travel extensively on business outside the community to EDC target areas
—Are not directly involved in industrial real estate sales and development

G. Collateral Materials/Sales Promotion

1. Collateral Materials

Essential to EDC's effective response to inquiries is the availability of appropriate collateral and promotional materials. The following materials were used in 1981/82:

a. *The Economic Development Corporation of San Diego County*—This brochure defines the goals and program of EDC for prospective members, community, and prospects.

b. *San Diego Expansion and Relocation Fact Book*—This folder describes in detail the basic facts on costs and benefits of doing business in San Diego.

c. *EDC News*—This is a quarterly newsletter published to keep in continuous contact with current prospects, target industry decision-makers, and local members and officials.

d. *San Diego is Zoned for Business and Industry*—Folder that describes the overall benefits of expanding or relocating in San Diego.

e. *San Diego is Zoned for Electronics*—Folder that describes the specific benefits that electronics firms find in San Diego and lists some of the electronics firms that are located in the area.

f. *San Diego is Zoned for Research and Development*—Folder that describes the specific benefits that R&D and other high technology firms find in San Diego and lists some of the firms that are located in the area.

g. *San Diego is Zoned for Corporate Headquarters*—Folder that describes the benefits that a corporate headquarters can enjoy in San Diego and lists the top companies that are already in the area.

h. *San Diego is Zoned for Twin Plants*—Folder that describes the benefits of production facilities in San Diego and Mexico and lists the companies currently operating twin plants.

i. *San Diego is Zoned for Success*—An indexed folder used when mailing EDC literature and promotional materials and comes in two sizes.

2. Sales Promotion

The advertising supplements planned for 1981/82 provided an excellent opportunity for new promotional literature, plus an opportunity to stage promotional events in key target market cities. These events were hosted by EDC and a major business publication. Key prospects and selected media were invited to the event to receive an update on San Diego from municipal and key corporate leaders.

The ten-minute video tape presentation was used to present an overview of the San Diego region as an expansion or relocation site. Cassettes of the presentation were available for use by companies interested in San Diego County, as well as group showings, where it is not possible to show them the area during the initial contact stage. For Japanese prospects a 17-minute video tape was used. In that San Diego in November hosted the Japan-American Association of Mayors and Chamber of Commerce Presidents, we also coordinated our marketing efforts with the event's prime members/sponsors (Chamber, City, and Port).

H. Direct Prospect Contact

As in the past years, it is direct prospect contact which ultimately results in location decisions favorable to San Diego. Given both San Diego awareness generated by EDC's 1978-81 programs and the dollar limits of the 1981-82 advertising plan, increased emphasis was given to prospect contact.

The promotion of an assistant director in January 1981 recognized the need for this contact; and 1981-82 travel focused more on EDC's prime prospects in California and other key target areas. Participation in appropriate trade shows (electronics industry, IDRC, NACORE, American Chamber of Commerce of Mexico, etc.), executive tours (for example, Japanese External Trade Organization), and other Japanese activity were also expanded.

EXPENSES

Operations: $340,000
    —Salaries (180,000)
    —Payroll Taxes (11,000)
    —Employee Benefits (18,000)
    —Insurance (3,500)
    —Rent (25,600)
    —Office Supplies (12,000)
    —Telephone (8,500)
    —Dues and Subscriptions (6,000)
    —Equipment and Furnishings (12,000)
    —Postage (10,000)
    —Transportation (18,000)
    —EDC Meetings (7,000)
    —Professional Services (18,000)
    —Maintenance and Repair (5,000)
    —Taxes (400)
    —Operations Reserve (5,000)

Advertising: 136,000
    —Media (100,000)
    —Direct Mail (16,000)
    —Public Relations (20,000)

Promotion: 60,000
    —Collateral Materials (37,000)
    —Promotional Materials (12,000)
    —Executive Tours (10,000)
    —"Ambassador" Activities (1,000)

Travel/Entertainment: 60,000
    —Transportation (24,000)
    —Meals and Lodging (12,000)
    —Meetings, Conferences, and Entertainment (24,000)

Research Services and Publications   9,000
                                                                _____
                                                                $605,000

BUDGET

The programs of the Economic Development Corporation, designed to expand the region's employment and industrial base, are reflected in the budget through: a concerted promotional effort; direct contact with potential new industry; and contact and support of expanding businesses currently existing within the San Diego area.

The success of these programs will be measured via the jobs created with EDC assistance, the number of companies assisted in expansion or relocation, the number of companies contacted directly by EDC, the estimated new facility investment and payroll generated by new and expanding companies assisted by EDC, and the number of information inquiries directed to EDC.

Much of EDC's budget is expended on a national and statewide advertising and promotion campaign for San Diego as a community for industrial expansion/ relocation. Direct mail and personal contact with selected industries, executive tours to acquaint selected business leaders with San Diego, periodic newsletters to industrial and corporate prospects, and the publication of collateral material support the program.

Sources and uses of funds:

Preliminary 1981-82 EDC Budget

REVENUE

Membership	$220,000
Interest	2,500
Public Funds:	372,500
—City (262,500)	
—County (55,000)	
—Port (55,000)	
Publication Income	5,000
Miscellaneous	5,000
	$605,000

Economic Development Corporation—Membership List

Action Instruments
Aerojet-General Corporation
American Airlines
Arthur Andersen & Company
AVCO Community Developers, Inc.
Bank of America
Bank of California
Barney & Barney
John Burnham & Company
Business Properties Brokerage Co.
Calbiochem-Behring Corporation
California Electric Works
California First Bank
Central Savings & Loan
Chula Vista, City of
City Investors, Inc.
Coldwell Banker Commercial
   Brokerage Co.
Collins Development Company
Conrock Company
Coopers & Lybrand
Copley Newspapers
Crocker National Bank
Daley Corporation
Daon Corporation
Deems/Lewis & Partners
Deloitte, Haskins & Sells
Dixieline Lumber Company
Dunphy Construction
E. F. Hutton Life Insurance Company
Charles A. Ekstrom Company
Ernst & Whinney
H. G. Fenton Material Company
First American Title Insurance Co.
First Federal Savings & Loan
Robert G. Fisher Co., Inc.
Frazee Industries
M. H. Golden Company
Gray, Cary, Ames & Frye
Grubb & Ellis Commercial Brokerage
Guild Mortgage
HCH & Associates
Ernest W. Hahn, Inc.
R. E. Hazard Contracting Company
Higgs, Fletcher & Mack
Hill/Smyk Associates
Home Federal Savings & Loan Assn.
Frank L. Hope & Associates
Hotel del Coronado
Imperial Savings & Loan Assn.
Intermark
Japan California Bank
Johnson & Higgins
KFMB AM-FM/TV
Kelco, A Div. of Merck & Company
The Koll Co.
Krommenhoek/McKeown & Associates
Kyocera International

Linkabit Corporation
Lomas Santa Fe, Inc.
Luce, Forward, Hamilton & Scripps
John D. Lusk & Son
Mark 8
McGladrey Hendrickson & Co.
McKusick & Associates
National Steel & Shipbuilding Co.
Nielsen Construction Company
Ninteman Construction Company
Oak Industries
Oceanside Economic Dvlpm. Corp.
Pacific Scene
Pacific Southwest Airlines
Pacific Southwest Mortgage
Pacific Telephone Company
Pardee Construction Company
Peat, Marwick, Mitchell & Company
Penasquitos Properties
Peterson, Thelan & Price
Price Waterhouse & Company
A. O. Reed & Company
Rick Engineering
Rohr Industries, Inc.
San Diego, City of
San Diego Construction Industry
   Advancement Fund
San Diego, County of
San Diego County Rock Products Assn.
San Diego Federal Savings & Loan Assn.
San Diego Gas & Electric Company
San Diego Trust & Savings Bank
San Diego Unified Port District
Security Pacific National Bank
Shapell Industries
Sickels & O'Brien
Signal Companies
Solar Turbines International
Spectral Dynamics Corporation
Sumitomo Bank of California
Harry L. Summers, Inc.
Techbilt Construction Company
Title Insurance & Trust Company
Torrey Enterprises, Inc.
Touche Ross & Company
Trammel Crow Associated Companies
Union Bank
United California Bank
University Industries
Van Schaack & Company
R. J. Watkins & Co., Ltd.
Wavetek
Wells Fargo Bank
Western States Investment Corporation
Wheeler Associates, Architects, AIA
Wickes Corporation
Woodford & Bernard Architects, AIA
Arthur Young & Company

Appendix IV:
San Diego Symphony
Survey

This questionnaire has been reprinted with permission from Dinoo J. Vanier and John B. McFall, San Diego Symphony: Marketing Information Study, March 1981.

Hello. May I please speak to _____.

Good morning/afternoon/evening. My name is _____
I'm a student at San Diego State University. We're conducting a public opinion survey on the performing arts and your help in answering questions for this survey will be greatly appreciated.

1.　When you think of performing arts organizations, which one(s) typically come to mind? (CIRCLE ORGANIZATION(S) MENTIONED BY RESPONDENT IN LIST BELOW.) Any others? (PROBE FOR AS MANY MENTIONS AS POSSIBLE.)
　　1. BALLET/SAN DIEGO BALLET
　　2. CHAMBER MUSIC/RECITALS
　　3. LOS ANGELES SYMPHONY
　　4. MUSICALS
　　5. OLD GLOBE/SHAKESPEARE
　　6. OPERA/SAN DIEGO OPERA
　　7. SYMPHONY
　　8. "SAN DIEGO SYMPHONY"　→　SKIP TO *3*
　　9. STAGE PLAYS/OTHER THEATRE
　10. OTHER: (SPECIFY _____)
　11. NONE

2.　Please tell me if each of the following cities has its own symphony orchestra. (READ EACH CITY: CIRCLE ANSWER IN APPROPRIATE COLUMN BELOW.)

City	Yes	No	Don't Know	
New York	1	2	3	
San Francisco	1	2	3	
San Diego	1	[2	3]	→ TERMINATE
Chicago	1	2	3	
Los Angeles	1	2	3	

3.　Which of the following is most essential to the cultural life of our city? (READ LIST)

Rank

　　Ballet
　　Opera
　　San Diego Symphony
　　Los Angeles Symphony
　　Old Globe

Which one of these do you feel is most essential? (INDICATE 1st IN RANK COLUMN.) Which next? (INDICATE 2nd IN RANK COLUMN.)

281

4.   I'm going to read to you the names of some organizations. For each, please tell me if you think this organization would gratefully accept *small* contributions of $10 or less. (MENTION EACH ORGANIZATION: CIRCLE RESPONSE IN APPROPRIATE COLUMN.)

	Yes	*No*	*Don't Know*
San Diego Zoo	1	2	3
Old Globe Theatre	1	2	3
San Diego Symphony	1	2	3
San Diego Opera	1	2	3
Mercy Hospital	1	2	3

5a.   Have you received the 1981 Winter Season brochure from the San Diego Symphony?

    1. YES   [2. NO   3. DON'T RECALL] → SKIP TO *6a*

5b.   Did you have time to take a look at it?

    1. YES   [2. NO   3. DON'T RECALL] → SKIP TO *5i*

5c.   Did you (READ LIST)

    1. Skim it
    2. Read it partly
    3. Read it thoroughly

5d.   Whose letter was printed in the brochure?

    1. ATHERTON
    2. OTHER: (SPECIFY _____)
    3. DON'T KNOW/CAN'T RECALL

5e.   What did the brochure say was "New" about the San Diego Symphony? (CHECK CATEGORIES MENTIONED BY RESPONDENT)

    ____NEW SOUND
    ____NEW LOOK
    ____NEW CONDUCTOR
    ____NEW SOLOISTS
    ____OTHER: (SPECIFY _____)
    ____DON'T KNOW/CAN'T RECALL

5f.   What did the brochure contain that could assist you in getting tickets for the Symphony? (CHECK CATEGORIES MENTIONED BY RESPONDENT)

    ____PRICE INFORMATION
    ____ORDER FORM
    ____CONCERT SCHEDULE
    ____GENERAL INFORMATION
    ____OTHER: (SPECIFY _____)
    ____DON'T KNOW/CAN'T RECALL

5g.   What was "tipping the scale" all about? (CHECK CATEGORIES
MENTIONED BY RESPONDENT.)

____MAKING CONTRIBUTIONS
____OTHER: (SPECIFY _____)
____DON'T KNOW

5h.   Now suppose you were to give this brochure to your friends. Generally
speaking, do you think they would find it to be:

1. Easy to understand	or	2. difficult to understand?
2. Easy to use	or	2. difficult to use?

5i.   Did anyone else in your household read the brochure more than you did?

1. YES   [2. NO   3. DON'T KNOW]   →   SKIP TO 5k

5j.   And who was it? (CHECK CATEGORIES MENTIONED BY
RESPONDENT)

____MY HUSBAND/WIFE
____SON
____GRANDSON/DAUGHTER
____GUEST
____OTHER: (SPECIFY _____)
____DON'T KNOW

5k.   And then what was done with the brochure? Was it: (READ LIST)

1. Kept it so it could be referred to again
2. Thrown away
3. Passed along to someone else outside your household

6a.   Did you see the ad for the San Diego Symphony in Sunday's newspaper?

1. YES   [2. NO   3. DON'T RECALL]   →   SKIP TO 7

6b.   What *specifically* was the ad about? (CHECK CATEGORIES MENTIONED
BY RESPONDENT)

____DAVID ATHERTON
____SYMPHONY SCHEDULE/CONCERTS
____OTHER: (SPECIFY _____)
____DON'T KNOW/CAN'T RECALL

7.   What do you *perceive* to be the overall quality of the San Diego Symphony:
Do you rate it: (READ LIST)

1. EXCELLENT
2. GOOD
3. FAIR
4. POOR

8a.   What do you think is the average price of a San Diego Symphony concert ticket? (IF RESPONDENT ANSWERS "DON'T KNOW," SAY "PLEASE LET ME HAVE YOUR BEST GUESS")

$_____

8b.   What are the chances (from zero to 100%) that you would go to the San Diego Symphony more frequently if the average price of a concert were: (READ EACH PRICE: RECORD ANSWER IN CHANCE % COLUMN. STOP ASKING QUESTION AS SOON AS RESPONDENT SAYS "100%" TO ANY PARTIC- ULAR PRICE.)

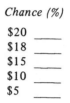

Chance (%)

$20 ____
$18 ____
$15 ____
$10 ____
$5 ____

9a.   During the last 12 months or so have you made a contribution, other than ticket purchase, to the San Diego Symphony?

1. YES   [2. NO   3. DON'T RECALL] → SKIP TO *9c*

9b.   What are some of the reasons why you made this contribution? (CHECK CATEGORIES MENTIONED BY RESPONDENT)

____ SOMEONE ASKED ME
____ GOOD CAUSE
____ TAX DEDUCTIBLE
____ COMMUNITY SUPPORT
____ CONCERNED ABOUT RECENT CRISIS
____ OTHER: (SPECIFY _____)

9c.   Generally speaking, what are some of the reasons why individuals who can afford to contribute to the San Diego Symphony don't do so? (CHECK CATE- GORIES MENTIONED BY RESPONDENT)

____ GIVE TO OTHER ORGANIZATIONS
____ DON'T CARE FOR SYMPHONIES/SYMPHONIC MUSIC
____ DON'T CARE FOR THE SAN DIEGO SYMPHONY
____ GIVE TO THE LOS ANGELES SYMPHONY
____ CONTRIBUTIONS ASKED ARE TOO LARGE
____ THE BIG COMPANIES/WEALTHY PEOPLE ALREADY DO
____ DON'T BELIEVE IN HELPING ORGANIZATIONS WHICH CAN'T
BE SELF-SUPPORTING
____ OTHER: (SPECIFY _____)

10a. Let's suppose you were to go to a San Diego Symphony performance this winter season. Please tell me which words would best describe it *for you.* I'm going to mention some pairs of words. For each pair, please choose one word only. (CIRCLE RESPONDENT'S CHOICE)

Performance

1. Relaxing	2. Tense
1. Professional	2. Amateur
1. Good value for money	2. Poor value
1. Boring	2. Exciting

10b. And how about the *overall experience* of an evening at the San Diego Symphony? Would it be:

1. Fun	2. Dull
1. Cold	2. Warm
1. Worthwhile	2. So-so
1. Just right	2. Just a little uncomfortable
1. Convenient	2. Inconvenient
1. Not *quite* my kind of thing	2. My kind of thing

10c. And how about the *typical person* who you think goes to the San Diego Symphony? Would this typical person be:

1. Younger	2. Older
1. Upper income	2. Middle income
1. Friendly	2. Somewhat stuffy
1. Somewhat educated	2. Well educated
1. Nicely dressed	2. Elegantly dressed
1. Knowledgeable about symphony music	2. Not too knowledgeable about symphony music
1. Status conscious	2. Somewhat unconcerned about status
1. Male	2. Female

11a. Have you ever been to a San Diego Symphony concert during the winter season?

1. YES
2. NO   → SKIP TO *11e*
3. DON'T RECALL → SKIP TO *12*

11b. And was it by way of winter season tickets or single tickets?

1. SEASON   [2. SINGLE   3. DON'T RECALL] → GO TO *11d*

11c. Are you a season ticket holder for the San Diego Symphony for the current season?

1. YES → GO TO *13*
2. NO

11d. What are some of the reasons why you did not buy a season ticket for this season? (CHECK CATEGORIES MENTIONED BY RESPONDENT)

____ TICKETS PRICED TOO HIGH
____ DON'T HAVE ENOUGH TIME
____ DON'T LIKE THE SAN DIEGO SYMPHONY
____ BOUGHT TICKETS FOR LOS ANGELES SYMPHONY
____ BOUGHT SEASON TICKETS FOR OTHER PERFORMING ARTS
____ PREFER BUYING TICKETS FOR INDIVIDUAL CONCERTS
____ DON'T LIKE TO BE "LOCKED-IN" FOR TOO MANY PERFORM—
ANCES/DON'T LIKE FIXED SCHEDULE/INFLEXIBILITY
____ OTHER: (SPECIFY _____)

11e. What are some of the reasons why you have never been to a San Diego Symphony winter concert? (CHECK CATEGORIES MENTIONED BY RESPONDENT)

____ GO TO THE LOS ANGELES SYMPHONY
____ THINK SAN DIEGO SYMPHONY ISN'T GOOD ENOUGH
____ JUST HAVEN'T GOTTEN AROUND TO IT
____ DON'T KNOW ENOUGH ABOUT CLASSICAL MUSIC
____ GO TO OTHER PERFORMING ARTS
____ WHY PAY TO GO WHEN I CAN LISTEN TO THE MUSIC ON
MY STEREO
____ JUST DON'T LIKE SYMPHONY/CLASSICAL MUSIC
____ OTHER: (SPECIFY _____)

12. If you could choose a convenient time and you were invited to go to a San Diego Symphony concert free of charge, what are the chances (zero to 100%) that you would go?

____ %

13. To what extent do you feel the recent financial problems of the San Diego Symphony have hurt your image of this symphony? (READ LIST)

1. NOT AT ALL
2. A LITTLE
3. QUITE A BIT
4. A GREAT DEAL

14. Are you a season ticket holder for the Los Angeles Symphony for the current season?

1. YES ____
2. NO ____

In order that we may classify you among the many people that we talk to, could you please tell me:

15a. What is your current employment status? (READ LIST)

1. Full-time employed
2. Part-time employed
3. Retired
4. Homemaker
5. Student
6. Not employed

15b. In which of the following age groups do you belong? (READ LIST)

1. 18–24
2. 25–34
3. 35–44
4. 45–54
5. 55–64
6. 65 or older

15c. How much formal education have you completed? (READ LIST)

1. Some or no high school
2. Completed high school
3. Some college
4. College graduate

15d. What of the following best describes your annual household income? (READ LIST)

1. Under $10,000
2. Between $10,000 and $20,000
3. Between $20,000 and $30,000
4. Between $30,000 and $50,000
5. Between $50,000 and $100,000
6. Over $100,000

15e. 1. MALE   2. FEMALE

You're part of a very select sample that has been chosen for this research study. To show our appreciation for your participation, we'd like to send you a coupon for two free tickets for a San Diego Symphony concert of your choice. Could you give me:

Your name _____
Address _____

(IF RESPONDENT REFUSES OFFER)
In order that my supervisor can validate this interview, could you please tell me:

Your name _____

THANK YOU VERY MUCH FOR YOUR HELP AND COOPERATION.

Appendix V:
Blood Bank Focus Group
Market Research

An Analysis of the Range of Donor/Nondonor Attitudes
and Experiences Relating to Giving Blood

INTRODUCTION

Background

The need for blood donors in the United States amounts to over 7 million pints a year, or better than 18,000 pints daily. These figures represent transfused blood, actually, rather than "needed blood," which is likely a greater figure. Over 100 million individuals in the United States between the ages of 17 and 65 years are physically eligible to donate blood; however, the incidence of donors in this group is about three percent.

In San Diego County, roughly 300 donors are needed daily, and with new advances in surgical techniques such as open-heart surgery and transplanting of body organs, the need for blood will accelerate well in advance of the rate of population increase. (About 15 open-heart surgeries alone occur weekly in the area.) The projection for 1980 is that 90,000 units will be needed annually.

Whole blood must be transfused within 21 days, precipitating the need for a continuous fresh supply, though it is possible to freeze parts of the blood for longer storage, such as red cells. However, this does not negate the need for a fresh supply, as for example, red cells can serve for only 30 to 50 percent of all

This report has been reprinted with permission from Martin M. Buncher, Intercontinental Marketing Investigations, Qualitative Investigation of Advertising and Promotional Opportunities for a Local Association of Blood Banks Branch—Focus Group Report, 1980.

Moderation, analyses, and report were completed by Intercontinental Marketing Investigations.

transfusions. And because of the difficulty and expense of freezing blood, it is generally limited to the more rare types.

The American Association of Blood Banks (AABB) represents more than 1,700 hospitals and community blood banks nationwide. An exchange of blood and blood credits is made possible by the National Clearinghouse Program of the AABB. However, the Red Cross Blood Centers are not members of the Clearing-house, preventing such exchanges between them and other groups.

The San Diego Blood Bank was organized in 1950. As a self-sustaining, nonprofit organization, it supplies blood to all hospitals in San Diego County. It also belongs to the AABB.

Purpose and Objectives of the Research

The San Diego Blood Bank relies heavily on public service time in the media to deliver its message to the local population. There is one basic message to communicate, "Blood is needed now." However, the general public will not respond sufficiently to this appeal *unless strategies are used to motivate individual response.*

The proper positioning of the Blood Bank's appeals requires an understanding of current awareness levels, attitudes, and behavior of the San Diego County population which in some way relate to the concept of blood donation. Several elements comprise the ultimate marketing strategy for the appeal:

Proper utilization of the media—that is, the right ones at the right time

Effective formulation of the appeal itself, so as to develop maximal impact among the general population

Identification of any need for population segmentation, suggesting corollary strategies of communication which will have an impact on the different segments found to exist (for example, current donors, past donors, non-donors)

Understanding how the act of blood donation, or even the basic concept, may or may not fit into the current lifestyle of the populace, by developing lifestyle profiles

The overall *purpose* of this investigation was to take the first step in developing the ultimate marketing strategy of the Blood Bank appeal. It was logically a very qualitative and exploratory undertaking, whereby we would be able to formulate hypotheses for later testing. The data generated were not intended to give immediate answers, but rather, to help determine what questions we should be asking, and how we should be asking them.

The specific *objectives* of the study were to generate examples of the range of attitudes and behavior which exist among donor and nondonor populations relating to the idea and act of donating blood. Specific areas of informational need included:

Awareness and attitudes regarding the Blood Bank, its purpose and operation

Awareness and reactions to Blood Bank advertising/public service announcements

Identification of specific factors which make blood donation appealing to some individuals, and unappealing to others

Isolation of specific circumstances precipitating original donating experiences, and continuation of the donation behavior

Self-perceptions of donors, how they may be different from nondonors, and vice versa

Method, Timing, and Organizations Involved

The group discussion technique was utilized to generate the qualitative information needed in this exploratory phase. The technique consists of accumulating a small sample of the target population and interviewing them simultaneously. The discussion session is directed by a moderator knowledgeable in the subject area, who uses a loosely structured outline to evoke relevant commentary. Statements are usually probed and interaction of ideas and opinions encouraged. Depending on the situation, a moderator may act as an unbiased mediator, or take a position, to draw out respondent reactions. And at times, the moderator may play "Devils Advocate," taking a viewpoint opposed to the entire group so as to force a defense of their position.

The basic concept of the group discussion session is to comprehensively explore the various ideas or behavioral patterns which may exist relative to any given subject. Almost without exception there is *no* attempt to quantify these feelings or actions, since the group discussion samples do not reliably represent the general population being examined. Also, there are inherent bias factors in the group context, such as the influence of the moderator and the magnification of specific topics. Thus, the approach was consistent with the research purpose, which was to develop hypotheses rather than firm conclusions.

Two group sessions were utilized as the base of information in this report. The first group consisted of *loyal donors*, defined as those who have donated at the San Diego Blood Bank within the past year and are likely to do so again in the coming year.

The second group consisted of *nondonors*, recruited from the general San Diego population at random and qualified as not having donated blood within any reasonable period of time (five-ten years or more), and not having any immediate intention of so doing in the future.

Both groups of 10 to 12 respondents included a mixture of males and females, married and single, between 18 and 65 years of age. Sessions were held at the Blood Bank facilities. The donor session was conducted on March 1, 1978, and the nondonor session on March 22, 1978. Because of anticipated lack of involvement, nondonor participants were promised a $10.00 incentive to attend at the time of recruitment. In fact, it may have been wiser to use this incentive among donors as well, given that substantial over-recruitment was necessary to obtain a sufficient number of participants arriving at the specified date. It has been established that such an incentive does not significantly affect group responses.

LOYAL DONOR REACTIONS

Becoming a Donor

Critical to developing ideas regarding how to attract new donors is the understanding of exactly how current donors got started. Inevitably, each member of the donor group related an experience where there was some personal confrontation with the blood-giving process. Such personal confrontations included situations wherein:

- A friend or relative needed blood
- The Red Cross showed up at work and asked directly
- Working in a hospital forced seeing the real need
- It was a way to pay back the system when a friend or relative "received" blood

In light of the consistency of the comments, it seems safe to hypothesize that *personal involvement* is a prerequisite for initiation of blood donation behavior. It does not appear totally mandatory, however, that the personal involvement relate to some altruistic need. But among the donor group, there is strong evidence that altruism is a key element in personality structure and is crucial in *repeat* donorship.

Remaining a Donor

Comments suggesting "altruism" (the term was never highlighted in the group sessions) were evoked when the moderator probed for reasons why people gave beyond the first time:

"I feel better psychologically."

"I feel freer a few days later."

"It's just the thing to do . . . a community responsibility."

Also prevalent along this line of thought were comments reflecting the idea that there is just one source of blood, that it is not a product which can be manufactured, and that "somebody" has to give it. Many donors identify strongly with that "somebody." And interestingly, they are reluctant to describe the donor personality in great detail. Asked to compare themselves to nondonors, they were reluctant to suggest differences.

"Something happened in our lives to get us started giving. That something just hasn't happened to them (nondonors)."

"We are caring people, but as a group, no more caring than others. We are probably just more informed."

Lack of fear in donating blood also is a prevalent element among donor personalities. The inherent fear in the blood donation situation is obvious and needs no comprehensive examination, though it did receive commentary among the group, who tended to joke about it. It was perhaps significant that these donors almost universally did not recall having any adverse reaction physically during their *first* donating experience. And instances of significant adverse reactions in later cases are described as rare.

In recalling earlier as well as present donating experiences, suggestions of how relaxing and enjoyable the experience is far overshadowed any mention of anxiety.

"It's an easy thing to do."

"I like to see how fast I can make the blood flow."

"We see who can be first off the table."

"I like the slides, though I can't always see them too well. You have to get a good table."

It is likely that members of the group do have a certain degree of reservation, or some level of fear or anxiety associated with giving blood. This fact was suggested in one instance by the nervous laughter surrounding discussion of carrying the medical package into the donation room.

"They have it wrapped up, so you can't see it (the needle) inside."

"You are taking something in that you know you aren't going to take out."

Nonetheless, "fearlessness" and "altruism" have to be considered as the two major psychological factors suggested as supplying the proper mental frame of reference for participating in the donor syndrome.

However, almost overshadowing these internal stimuli as motivation for repeat donations is the *external stimulus, universally acclaimed* by the entire group. This fact, the *scheduled eighth-week phone call* by the Blood Bank to remind the donor that the required waiting period between donations has expired, may very well be the mainstay of the loyalist group. Under heavy probing from the moderator for negative reactions to these phone calls, about all the group would admit to was that the calls usually come "at an inconvenient time." No substantial negative reaction to the method in which the calls were handled, or the fact that they recurred, could be elicited from the group. It is possible that the calls represent an important psychological link with the Blood Bank, which generates a partial "team" attitude that repeat donors seem to want to establish.

"I don't think I would give if they didn't call."

"They call you and you have to make a commitment."

"When they phone, you get the feeling your blood is needed."

"The eighth week phone call comes like clockwork."

In investigating the possibility that there are fraternal feelings and *social interaction* among loyal donors, it seemed that *such was not the case.* Playback from donors suggested that for some, social interaction such as scheduled get-togethers at the clinic would be very desirable. However, in general, donors seem to have little outside contact with each other, and have a group experience limited to the encounter at the bank during donations. Thus, peer group pressure did not appear responsible for donor loyalty, though this is not to suggest that such a factor could not be developed as a stimulus in the future.

Feelings About the San Diego Blood Bank as an Institution

It was difficult to generate negative comments about the atmosphere and medical procedures used by the Blood Bank, as experienced by the donors. The warmth of the environment and staff were much favored over a potentially "sterile" atmosphere one might find in hospital settings.

However, there have apparently been recent policy changes which have generated considerable negative reactions among the loyal donors. A major objection related to the "loss of credit" after a certain period of time expires, so that one's family cannot be covered for an extended number of years. The donors feel very cheated by this action. Even when an "intellectual" rationale for the policy is presented—that is, to encourage continued donations and prevent even loyal donors from "resting on their laurels"—the donors remained hostile about the policy. They indicated that as volunteers they should not be coerced, or cheated of something which they have given freely (their blood for blood credit). Many claimed that such a policy was not needed, and that repeat donors had already established their understanding and appreciation of the need for continual support of the bank. The negative feelings were so strong that on several occasions, as other topics were being discussed, group participants managed to redirect the conversation back to the policy change. It was clear that both confusion and misunderstanding has ruffled the feeling of personal closeness which many donors feel toward the bank, and the experience of giving blood, to the extent that there is mention of "wanting to screw up the system."

Another policy seems to create unfavorable feelings among donors. In the eleventh and twelfth months of the year, it is theoretically possible if a donor gives once every eight weeks on schedule until his five yearly donations are spent, that if the donor's family was mentioned as the donor's credit recipient the first month, that credit can expire. The donor cannot give a sixth time. Some apparently have felt "trapped" in this situation.

> "If we had ulterior motives, such as to store things up, we would go find some place that pays." (Not all were aware of recent legislation eliminating payment for blood donations in California.)

> "We have a very unselfish attitude. We resent the policy."

> "I don't understand why credits expire. The blood was used."

> "If you give it for free, why do they limit you with rules."

Company policies also may be generating negative feelings about donating which may have some negative rub-off on the blood bank.

The perception that Red Cross and San Diego Blood Bank agencies do not work together was a further area where considerable unfavorable feelings arose. There was lack on understanding why such cooperation was not possible, though some respondents generally attributed it to the bureaucratic structures involved, or the "big business" aspect of blood donation programs. Donor outlook on this situation is best depicted by the following comments:

> "Business is not the basis for our giving blood. Credits should be transferable."

> "I don't know if they are different. I don't like to think of them in those terms."

> "I know the Red Cross and the Bank are different, but I can't understand why."

> "The point is that there is a lack of cooperation."

Advertising and Word-of-Mouth Communications

The reaction of donors to advertising seen and heard did not suggest it was having any great impact on their donations, except in isolated instances. The donation cycle was more affected by the phone call system. Reactions to advertising stressing a general "urgent need because of few donors" was rated as a mediocre approach, similar to those used by other charities. A "sharing-is-caring" emotional appeal inferring some altruistic goal fulfillment was rated as "too broad."

The single approach felt to be most effective among donors was that stressing an individual identified as having an immediate need for blood. This appeal gets as close as any to putting the blood-giving experience on a personal level. The insurance aspect—that is, protecting your family's future with blood credit— generated a mixed response. Some group members indicated that "other insurance" took care of blood and suggested that the insurance approach go further and present the question to potential donors, "Where will blood come from if you don't give it?" Again, this question reduces the appeal to a personal level, which is where donors feel the advertising becomes most effective.

The medium most strongly associated with blood bank publicity was radio, followed by television. However, when bumper stickers were probed, all group members showed familiarity with them, but reactions were indifferent for the most part.

> "They are not really impressive. I don't remember seeing them until I became a donor . . . ."

> "I see them all over. They are clever."

> "Yes, they are clever, but not motivational."

> "It's more like an indication of belonging to a club."

One new approach for promoting blood donations was raised by the group which they had not heard suggested—giving a friend a gift of blood for a year, much in the same vein (no pun intended) as one gives to the Heart Fund on behalf of another.

In probing for word-of-mouth communication, the moderator found that there was significant hesitancy among many group members to discuss their donation practice with nondonors. Apparently this feeling results from two factors:

1. The personal or private nature of the experience of many donors, where the reward of giving is an intangible and perhaps spiritually uplifting emotion, certainly cathartic to the individual in terms of relieving stress.

2. Bitter experiences in the past with attempts to induce nondonors to participate. The success rate reported seemed exceedingly low. In fact, there may
be only isolated instances in the donor population of donor families, where
more than one member gives blood regularly.

> "The children leave home."

> "They are just chicken."

> "When I am dealing with somebody else on that personal of a subject, I
> get very impatient. I just don't like wasting my time on somebody who
> I don't think is going to go along with it."

> "It takes a feeling of strong self-motivation. A feeling of need within
> yourself."

> "It's difficult to get people to come down. It's hard to badger them if
> they really don't want to come."

None of the members of the donor discussion session had succeeded in
bringing a new donor to the bank. Thus, it is suggested that unlike the situation
involving many consumer goods and services where word-of-mouth can be the
single most effective motivator towards purchase/participation, there is something about blood donation which defeats word-of-mouth influence, at least by
laymen donors, unrehearsed in motivational sales strategy.

The Reward of Giving to the Donor

If advertising and word-of-mouth or peer group pressure are not mainly
responsible for developing donation habit, one must ask the question of whether
it is purely a function of personality type (altruism and fearlessness), circumstance ("I had to give for a friend") and the phone call, or whether the loyal
donors are in fact getting something more tangible from the experience which as
an end result of giving, in itself becomes a drive. The obvious tangible reward
would be the insurance aspect of the donation—that is, the bank concept of
storing blood credits. However, after discussion of this element, and in consideration of donor explanations, it would appear that the importance of the
tangible benefit is less critical than the intangible (psychological need satisfied).

"In the consumer field, if you buy something, you want to show it off to
somebody and in effect say, 'Aren't I smart because I bought this thing.'" The
product you get for giving blood is a very intangible thing. It is very hard to tell
people what good you can get out of it. You can't show it to anybody."

Another potentially more tangible reward was explored by the moderator,
the "mini-check-up" received when blood donors are screened at the bank prior

to giving. The notion of finding out about blood problems (low iron, high blood pressure, anemia, etc.) was seen as worthwhile information, and also as a potentially good promotional concept by group members. However, it too failed to match in intensity the element of psychological need satisfaction pointed to as the main reward of donating by most respondents.

Level of Knowledge Among Donors

Members of the donor group demonstrated above-average familiarity with facts regarding the need for blood, and how the Blood Bank system operates. However, there were often large gaps in understanding relating to many aspects of blood donation which could be filled, and if filled, alleviate some of the concerns of the donor, and perhaps produce even stronger donation motivation.

From physical annoyances ("Why prick my finger? I hate that worse than the needle. Why not use my ear? It would hurt less.") to lack of understanding policy formulations ("Why can't the Red Cross and the Blood Bank exchange credits?"), there was room for increased education.

Greater feedback on the nature of the tests done on the blood, how it can be used, stored, etc., are found in the various pieces of literature produced by the San Diego Blood Bank and the American Association of Blood Banks. However, much of this information has failed to penetrate. And it may be worthwhile to personally carry the information to donors via an instructor present at the blood bank during the donation time. The waiting areas in the lobby prior to donating, and in the coffee shop following donating, could offer a convenient time and locale to utilize the services of a volunteer instructor, and reinforce the pamphlet information.

Finally, one piece of information, perhaps the most important piece of information, is apparently not universally understood, accepted, or appreciated by all donors. It is the basic message of the blood bank, that fresh blood is continually and seriously needed. Donors voiced the opinion in some cases that "constant advertising of this message, when they don't really need it" is not a good idea. If loyal donors still feel there are times when blood is not needed, then the communicative effort of the AABB and the SDBB is still in some respects not much past the starting line.

NONDONOR REACTIONS

Not Becoming a Donor

Throughout the discussion session, there were two characteristics of the nondonor group which seemed to predominate, and shade all other attitudes and behavior relating to the concept of blood donation. Nondonors were uninformed and uninvolved.

It was determined that a few of the nondonor group had in fact given blood at some point in their lives; however, usually seven, ten, or more years had passed. And there was no "repeat donorship" pattern generated following that initial experience.

The major donation syndrome element missing from this group was the "personal confrontation" situation so prevalent among current loyal donors. Usually it was some personal confrontation which, in some cases, had precipitated that long-ago donation. However, there was no follow-up or subsequent contact with individuals representing donor organizations. And communication with donor laymen was limited and ineffective, where it had occurred at all.

"I gave to get a three day pass extended in the service."

"I have never been directly confronted."

"I gave for somebody who needed it."

"I gave because I needed the money."

It was revealed that two members of the group, both married, had husbands who in fact were reported to fit the loyal donor description. The resulting attitude among the wives present in the discussion was that they did not have to give since their husbands were doing the job.

The lack of information pervaded all areas relating to donation, except that the San Diego Blood Bank existed. Many group members seemed to know of the bank's existence. However, there were few strong impressions about such basic SDBB and donation aspects such as:

- what the facilities were like
- what effect giving blood has on the individual
- how much blood is taken
- how much is needed
- how long it takes
- what the experience of going through the process is like
- the relationship of the SDBB to the Red Cross and the AABB

One immediate outgrowth of this lack of information was, in some cases, fear of donating. However, in other instances it was obvious that fear was present first, as an original association with the idea of blood-letting, "the needle," etc. But the fact that *not all* the resistance or lack of involvement related to fear suggests the possibility of having to overcome less formidable factors of resistance in precipitating donor behavior among many current nondonors.

First reactions to the research project calls, prior to the point where the recruiter presented the full intention of the call, evoked such comments as:

"I thought about the $10.00."

"I thought I might learn something."

"I thought, do I have to donate?"

"I remembered about thinking of giving blood before, but I have child care problems. I wanted information on any child care facilities (at the bank)."

The Potential of Personal Confrontation

Indication of the potential effectiveness of soliciting nondonors by phone was suggested by comments revealing that, "coming to the group might help alleviate the fear." One respondent admitted strong guilt feelings, but also "complete fear." The meeting at the facility was thus a way to "take it slow"— that is, come to the center, find out what was going on, but still not be expected/ required to donate.

This type of response suggests that a *two-stage approach* to developing donation appeal might be effective, and overcome some of the strong fear reactions among some nondonors at the first mention of the idea of blood-letting. The first stage would involve the "personal confrontation," yet not demand the immediate blood-letting commitment. The second stage, following the delivery of information and "sales pitch," could thus set the path for the donation. However, this second phase, to be maximally effective, should be closely tied in time sequence to the commitment to give, reducing the opportunity for momentum toward the act to diminish.

The concept of personal confrontation means "personal" in terms of making the donation appeal on a "one-to-one" basis. The potential donor would be confronted in person by the donor recruiter. The rationale for the appeal of the donation would be based further on another "one-to-one" frame of reference, wherein the potential donor would have some idea that the donated blood is *going to an individual* in need, most likely within a short (three-week or less) period of time.

Nondonors had in a number of instances been exposed to organizational sponsorship of donor recruitment programs at the office or church. Yet through lack of information, involvement, or because of fear, such programs had failed to have the intended impact. Nonetheless, these attempts were viewed in a positive light by many group members: "They are a good idea, because when you are connected with an organization and they request something of you, you tend to pay more attention (and get more information)."

Perceived Benefits of Giving Blood

To understand better what benefits nondonors might perceive (once such elements as lack of information, involvement, or fear were eliminated as resistance factors) the moderator asked group members to focus on what the positive side of the donation might be. It immediately seemed apparent that while there was some degree of familiarity with the concept of blood credit, and that it was the most often mentioned positive factor, it alone could never be expected to be the mainstay of *original* donation rationale. Lack of information, fear, and lack of involvement easily counteracted whatever positive impact the insurance aspect of giving might have had.

"If I could get by the first time, I might become a donor."

"You know you could get your blood back if needed, for you or your family."

"How long do the credits last?"

"If you give to the bloodmobile, you don't get anything back. You have to go to the blood bank headquarters."

"You get two pints credit for every one given."

"I am not certain if medical insurance covers blood."

Once the Blood Insurance Programs provided by the San Diego Blood Bank were explained to the nondonor groups, they were described by some as the "strongest point for being an annual giver." However, not all had a high emotional response to the idea, for two reasons:

1. Some felt insurance covered it.

2. Some felt that it was more than likely that their healthy families would not need blood.

Another tangible benefit of blood donation, that of getting a "mini-medical examination," was viewed as "a nice thing," but again fell far short of being effective in developing appeal, because of current apathy and fear. Nonetheless, it seems safe to hypothesize that elimination of overriding negative factors will provide the opportunity for tangible benefits to play more of a role in the development of donor appeal. However, the implication is that the development of appeal must be at least in *part defensive*, suggesting that, "No, it isn't anything to be afraid of"; *part informative*, suggesting exactly what happens and how; and then *aggressive*, suggesting tangible, if not psychological, rationales for donating.

It seems important to point out here that we have been dividing donation benefits into "tangible versus psychological" categories. It is not intended to present psychological need fulfillment as an intangible. To many, as evidenced by donors, it is quite a specific and strong feeling which can be isolated, experienced in and of itself, and recognized as having an immediate, positive effect on the donor. They would not consider the need fulfillment any less tangible than the insurance program. However, in those cases, more prevalent among nondonors, where the "self-fulfillment" concept might be presented, it would most likely be viewed in many cases as "too intangible a reward" to supply adequate rationale for donating.

Perceived Community and Individual Need for Blood

It seems safe to suggest that nondonors, in many cases, do not have any thoughts about a critical community need for blood. When the point is presented, it is explained away by such statements as:

"Other people are giving."

"If I needed it, it would be handled through work."

"Insurance covers it."

One donor-oriented individual in the group debated briefly with a "hardcore" nondonor. The discussion went something like this:

Hard-Core: "I know that if I get sick and go to the hospital the the blood would be there. I have no guilt about this (taking blood without giving) because to me, guilt implies a willful act of harm."
Donor-Oriented: "But blood always isn't going to be there unless somebody puts it there."
Hard-Core: "You always have relatives or friends . . . there is always somebody to count on."
Donor-Oriented: "Some people don't have relatives . . . (or friends to count on)..."

Accordingly, it appears that "hard-core" nondonors remain uninvolved and disinterested by taking an "impersonal attitude," detaching themselves from the basic fact of what the source of blood is, and stating the probability that most likely they will never have the need anyway, but if they do, there is a "rescuer" who has already provided blood, or will be ready to. To them, an apathy about the subject is not equivalent to "guilt." The absence of action is differentiated from willful malevolent action, a viewpoint quite different from that held by donors. Asked to give some rating to the importance of the concept of blood donations, nondonors clearly demonstrated the feeling that it was not seen as a priority community need:

"It's about in the middle."

"I would put it below voting."

"It's about equal to any other type of charity work."

"There is no glory in giving."

But one or two members felt it was slightly higher in importance than other types of charity work because it was really "giving something of yourself."

Impressions of What It Would Be Like to Give

The physical experience as perceived by nondonors is often inaccurate. Factors such as the length of time, how much blood is drawn, etc., as already mentioned, are misjudged. Fear of the needle is high (they do not know about the finger prick which seems to bother donors more than the needle, in some cases). No spontaneous positive associations are mentioned, such as the potentially nice atmosphere and feeling surrounding the experience, interaction with donors, finding out about blood problems, etc.

"There is no pre-testing to see if your blood is usable."

"There is a lot of waiting around."

"The whole thing would take too long."

"It takes a long time for the blood to drain out . . . they can't pump it out."

Comparing the San Diego Blood Bank to the Red Cross

The group trend was to recognize that the SDBB was somehow different from the Red Cross, though details of how were cloudy or general.

"The bank is local, the Red Cross is national."

"The Red Cross has more money. The bank has to run on what it can get."

"The Red Cross does more . . . other things."

"The head of the Red Cross makes more than the President . . . that's really bad."

Self-Perceptions of Nondonors Versus Donors

While donors mostly tended to view themselves as basically similar to nondonors—that is, they did not feel alienated by the donation concept—such was not the case for nondonors. There was more of a trend in this latter group to have a self-perception of being different.

"Donors are more civic-minded."

"They are generous."

"They are volunteer types."

"They aren't afraid."

The few who felt somewhat more like donors based donating versus not donating on "circumstances," a reaction prevalent among the donor group. To them, reasons for distinguishing donors from nondonors related to absence of peer group pressure, not belonging to organizations where exposure to blood donation programs would have precipitated giving, or simple lack of time to come and donate.

Nondonor Perceptions of Alternative Marketing Strategies

The nondonor group was confronted directly with the question of how, if in any way, they could be influenced by donation appeals. Not surprisingly, advertising was perceived as the *least effective* method, personal confrontation as the *most effective*.

"If I met somebody who talked me into it."

"If a church asks the members of its parish."

"Advertising, a bumper sticker, the radio ... they are not enough. They don't give you enough information ... they don't get you over the fear of the unknown."

"My boss could make me."

"If I got public information at other events ... somebody got to me on a one-to-one basis."

Of the different advertising appeals presented, focusing independently on either critical need, altruism, or insurance, the altruistic theme was substantially weaker as judged by nondonors. It was considered to be "too general." It also failed to provoke guilt feelings, or overcome apathetic attitudes. The critical need approach was rated as more likely to be good when it was directed at a specific situation rather than a generalized one, such as when a public service announcement states that a child is undergoing surgery and needs blood, or that there has been a larger catastrophe (explosion) with many hurt and in need of fresh blood. The insurance strategy held appeal only to those uncertain about whether or not they would have to pay for blood if needed.

Charitable Activities of Nondonors

In fact, the charitable activity level among the nondonor group seemed to be as high in other respects as the donor group. Membership and participation in such groups as the Optimists, PTA, Candystripers, Red Cross, Handicapped Children was common. However, the absence of Blood Bank involvement was keynoted by the fact that more than half did not know their own blood type.

SUMMARY OF HYPOTHESES REGARDING ADVERTISING AND PROMOTIONAL OPPORTUNITIES

The Problem Factors

Even in this small exploratory investigation it seems safe to conclude that marketing to both current donors and nondonors will substantially increase overall levels of blood donations.

Among current donors, problems of lack of information and misunderstanding can be eliminated. Also some utilization of donors as a resource in developing appeal among nondonors seems appropriate, though perhaps difficult.

Among nondonors, *lack of information* is a primary problem to overcome as well. It often is the basis for fear, though not in every case. Eliminating *lack of involvement* is likely to be as productive a strategy as eliminating lack of information, since often there is no related problem of inherent fear of blood-letting.

In both donor and nondonor markets, personal confrontation may be *prerequisite* to increasing donation levels. Advertising and promotions may arouse interest, but do not in themselves seem to be sufficient to evoke the donation act. The occurrence of personal confrontation, whether by chance or otherwise, seems to be a major differentiator of donors and nondonors, exclusive of all other contributing influences, as evidenced by donor/nondonor historical portrayals.

Advertising strategy must then contend primarily with three factors: providing information, overcoming fears, and stimulating involvement.

There is no rank ordering of these three elements in terms of their importance to the general population. Information is probably more important to donors.

Yet it is hard to state whether overcoming fear or stimulating involvement is of greater importance in reaching nondonors. Based on the fact that fear is the most difficult factor to overcome, stimulating involvement could perhaps be more productive of a focal point. Yet there is a hint that in the right approach (two-phase), overcoming fear might not be as difficult.

Using Advertising

Advertising strategy must strive for reducing the appeal to a personal/individual level, even though mass media are utilized to communicate the donation message. There is a strong indication that generalized appeals can be rationalized away very quickly and that the emotional grip needed to capture and maintain interest comes only when the potential donor finds himself drawn into a "crisis story" where people are named or numbered, and details of the need situation described. Thus, the message may be less of an *appeal*, and more of a *story*.

Efforts to promote repeat donations must be quite different from those aimed at inducing initial donations. Media advertising seems more appropriate in the "repeat donation" situation, when personal confrontation has already occurred to stimulate initial involvement. Initial donation drives will probably have to include the personal touch as a major element to achieve highly effective results. Media utilization to get this personal touch seems highly difficult.

Several themes have been suggested, and in fact have been utilized at one time or another by the San Diego Blood Bank. However, quantitative information would be required to fully evaluate them among both donor and nondonor populations. The major point brought to light in the group sessions is that in fact any given theme may have appeal for some segment of the eligible donor population. The *insurance program* can become important; the *altruistic approach* may work; the *critical need position* seems to have strong impact as applied in specific situations.

However, the results also suggest that advertising pressures must be varied. Constant cries for blood donations seem to generate withdrawal even among loyal donors. Thus, a pattern of media utilization at some times, and more subtle and perhaps direct approaches would be applied at others. Such a media/ promotional schedule could be based on patterns of need, as tracked over the previous years of experience by the SDBB. At times when supplies are lowest, the media could be utilized to generate a short-term but large supply of blood. The personalized, smaller-scaled promotions could be used as the keynote of the long-term growth strategy for the repeat donor pool.

For specific themes, the data from these exploratory groups suggest that "slice of life"-oriented public service announcements may be rather effective, delivering "relief" from the continued "urgent cry" for blood, while still maintaining interest and involvement. These "slice of life" presentations could focus on some of the physical benefits of blood donation, such as the insurance programs, the "mini-medical check-ups," social activities, etc. However, they could also draw on emotional appeals, in one direction by showing how individuals have benefited from receiving blood in specific cases, in another direction by showing that the experience of giving (actually what takes place at the bank) can be pleasurable and rewarding in many aspects, more than compensating for the infringement of the needle. These efforts should be oriented to eliminate feelings of "alienation" among current nondonors, suggesting that they are no different from people who give regularly.

Market Segmentation

Certainly, quantification of the different types of potential donors would be valuable information to have. However, in lieu of those data, we can still view the eligible donor population as comprised of the following eight major segments (without relative proportions mentioned):

1. Current Occasional Donors
   (less than eight pints yearly)
2. Current Loyal Donors
   (eight pints yearly)
3. Low Potential Past Donors
   (didn't like the donation experience; gave only because it was necessary to receive a specific physical benefit for self or other)
4. High Potential Past Donors
   (have not repeated donations because of chance environmental factors)
5. Low Potential Nondonors
   (no altruistic feeling; high fear of blood-letting; low evaluation of importance of concept)
6. High Potential Nondonors
   (never gave because never personally influenced by advertising/confrontation)
7. High Potential Nondonors
   (fears which can be overcome by information/confrontation to take advantage of altruistic drive)
8. High Potential Nondonors
   (altruistic, without fear; only needs information and understanding, not confrontation)

It is readily apparent in examining these major segments that a one-sided approach is not going to work. There are several types of High Potential Nondonors and Past Donors, each of whom can be motivated to donate in a different manner, depending on psychological need and physical circumstance. In the development of specific strategies and material, the creative goals set forth should take into consideration exactly which segment of the High Potential Donor population is bring sought out, to insure that interest will be aroused and needs met by the positive donation attributes communicated.

The ultimate goal of advertising and promotional strategy has been suggested by donor reactions. It is to communicate credibly to the eligible donor population a very simple idea:

"It feels good to give."

This concept has both physical and psychological connotations which imply that enough information has been disseminated, enough anxieties eliminated, and enough positive benefit perceived so that donating blood is something which should be desired and is in fact attainable by most people.

San Diego Blood Bank Facility

It is suggested by donor reactions that the Blood Bank is not suffering from critical image problems among either donor or nondonor groups. However, some recent policy changes, plus a general lack of understanding of the AABB structure, does lead to some weaknesses which could probably be quickly rectified with the effective communication of proper information. It is noted that this information has been utilized in at least some of the media, but may not have reached a sufficient portion of the eligible donor population.

Donors of the SDBB seem to want to become more organized as a group in some instances. It is likely that mixing more social activities into the donor experience could facilitate repeat donor behavior, and even widen the donor pool by first bringing nondonors into the picture on a social basis. It seems that current donors do need some help if they are to be counted on as a significant influence on new donor recruitment.

At the SDBB facility itself, the informal approach which has been taken seems to be proper in terms of orientation. There was universal dislike of any environmental concept suggesting the antiseptic, rigid, or formal atmosphere of hospitals and clinics.

More information on blood test results would be appreciated, and could be utilized by current donors in word-of-mouth communications to others.

More facts concerning SDBB policy are needed, particularly as they relate to dealing in the structure of the AABB and the Red Cross. A formal channel of communication should be opened, or if already in existence, reinforced, so that loyal donors can find answers to bothersome questions. The more personal this line of communication, the more effective and efficient it is likely to be.

In summation, the above material is presented as food for thought, to be utilized for developing creative strategies and formulating specific questions to ask about the eligible donor population. Nothing conclusive has been established, though certainly some directions have been hinted at, and new perceptions uncovered. Future research efforts might do well to concentrate on individual market segments, quantifying them in terms of proportion, or focusing on their specific attitudes and behavior to stimulate the feeling of benefiting by donation.

Index

competition: among NFPs, 24, 53; for volunteers, 119-120
Comprehensive Employment Training Act (CETA), 160
Comprehensive Service Centers, 185
Conference Board, 15
consultants, 142, 181
contractors, 64
corporate foundations, 81-84, 122
cost-benefit analysis, 32
counseling programs, 247
coupons, promotional, 69
CSCD, see Community Services for the Disabled, Inc.
Cudney, Willard, 242

data bases, 47
Davis, Richard, 263
Deaf Community Services, 247
Dedman, Sue, 263
demonstration programs, 69
development committees, 78-79
development officers, 79-82
direct mail, 267, 270, 275
directors, boards of, see boards of directors
Directors of Volunteers in Agencies, 123
disciplinary actions, see punishment systems
discounts, promotional, 69
donors, blood, see Blood Bank Focus Group market research
Dyer, Ed, 9, 10, 11, 13, 15, 16, 17

East County-ACCORD Neighborhood Recovery Center, 247
Easter Seals, 190, 205
economic development programs, 161, 260-261. See also San Diego Economic Development Corporation
education, see schools; training
electronic mail, 47

Emergency Assistance, 247
Employee Stock Ownership Plan (ESOP), 39
employment creation and development, see San Diego Economic Development Corporation
endowment funds, 100-101, 102
environmental systems, 24
Episcopal Community Services, 12, 31, 227-255; board of directors, 232-239; Cudney Plan, 242-243; financial crisis, 240-243; future of, 245-246; history of, 227-232, 249-250; programs, 247-248; real estate, 241-242; reorganization, 244
executive(s), private sector, see chief executive officers
executive directors, 9, 16, 145-158, 182; communications with, 48; of Community Services for the Disabled, Inc., 199-200; of Episcopal Community Services, 228-232; fund raising and, 78, 157; management styles of, 148-153; management training and education of, 146-148, 152, 157, 176; personality characteristics of, 153-154; punishment systems for, 141-142; requirements of, 157-158; reward systems for, 134-137; trustees' relationship with, 33; trustees' selection and assessment of, 153-156; value systems of, 22-23, 27-28, 157, 177-178; volunteer management and, 114, 115
Ex-Offender Re-Entry Program, 248

federal grants, see public funding
financial compensation, see bonuses; salaries
financial reporting, see fund accounting
flat organization, 36, 37, 40, 41, 43

About the Authors
and Contributors

ISRAEL UNTERMAN was raised in New York, where he pursued a highly successful business career in financial services. He founded and directed five successful companies and served as a minority owner of several additional firms. At the age of 44, he retired from the business world to attend Harvard Business School. At the age of 48, he earned his doctorate (DBA) at Harvard in Business Administration and embarked on a second career as an educator and consultant.

After several years at Harvard and INCAE in Central America, he settled in San Diego. From there he continues his private consulting practice, teaching, and writing. His consulting clients currently include a broad array of governmental, not-for-profit, and business organizations.

He has served as chairman of ten not-for-profits and a board member of over 50 NFPs. Additionally, he has supervised case studies, or assisted projects with 100 other not-for-profits and public agencies. He has had over 100 articles published on strategic management and negotiation.

RICHARD HART DAVIS was raised in the Chicago area. He has an AB in Politics from Princeton and an MBA in Marketing and Finance from the Harvard Business School. He is a vice president with responsibility for equity lending operations and corporate banking for a major financial institution in San Diego.

Included in his successful management career have been four years as the CEO and executive director of a major regional not-for-profit. He has served as a member or chairman of over 25 not-for-profit boards, ranging from sectarian, educational, and political groups to performing arts, social agencies, and governmental task forces. Private sector board responsibilities include both manufacturing and service industries.

He and Unterman are also co-authors of a *Harvard Business Review* article on "The Strategy Gap in Not-for-Profits."

James W. Ledwith received a BSBA degree in accounting from Babson College in 1966 and an MBA degree from the Wharton Graduate Division of the University of Pennsylvania in 1968. He holds a CPA certificate in Massachusetts and New York and is a member of the American Institute of Certified Public Accountants. In 1968, he joined the audit staff of Deloitte, Haskins & Sells in Boston. While in Boston, Mr. Ledwith served a wide variety of industrial clients as well as clients in the finance, health care, public utility, and publishing industries.

In 1979, Mr. Ledwith transferred to the firm's Executive Office, where he participated as a partner in the development of the firm's policies on financial accounting and reporting pronouncements of the Financial Accounting Standards Board. In September 1982, Mr. Ledwith transferred to the San Diego office as an audit partner.

Patricia O'Neill is currently the Director of Development for the Pittsburgh Opera. For the five years prior to joining the Pittsburgh Opera, she served as the Director of Development for the San Diego Opera, overseeing a tripling in its annual operating budget.

Judy Rauner received her MS degree in Human Resources Management from Pepperdine University. She is author of the widely used book *Helping People Volunteer* and of dozens of magazine articles; she is co-author of *Gaining Momentum for Board Action*. For over 25 years, she has worked in a variety of nonprofit organizations, in both paid and volunteer positions as consultant, trainer, administrator, and board member.